you all grow up and leave me

you all grow up and leave me

A Memoir of Teenage Obsession

piper weiss

WILLIAM MORROW

An Imprint of HarperCollins*Publishers*

HarperCollins books may be purchased for educational, business, or sales promotional use. For information, please email the Special Markets Department at SPsales@harpercollins.com.

FIRST EDITION

Designed by Bonni Leon-Berman

Library of Congress Cataloging-in-Publication Data has been applied for.

ISBN 978-0-06-245657-1 (hardcover)
ISBN 978-0-06-287041-4 (international edition)

18 19 20 21 22   LSC   10 9 8 7 6 5 4 3 2 1

The use of the
word love to
suggest "nothing"
is as old as the
English language.

—MALCOLM D. WHITMAN,
Tennis: Origins and Mysteries

preface

THIS BOOK is based on interviews, police reports, documents written by Gary Wilensky, hundreds of print articles and television transcripts, as well as my own memory, which occupies the same organ responsible for emotional responses and invention. Capitalization is used to denote direct quotations from Gary Wilensky's own writing.

The timeline of events in Gary Wilensky's life is based on reporting. Undocumented moments, chronologies, and conversations from the distant past are pulled from my imperfect memory and intended to reflect an honest but individual interpretation of events.

Several names have been altered to protect those private figures who made their way into this book. For privacy, Bianca, Sarah, and the boys from other prep schools are composite characters based on multiple students I knew growing up.

In addition, an early police report referred to Gary Wilensky's final two victims as Mother and Daughter. Their names were made public in subsequent articles published after the incident. Out of respect for the Daughter's privacy, the victims are referred to herein as the Mother and the Daughter.

Gary Wilensky is Gary Wilensky's real name.

you all grow up and leave me

prologue: new york city, 1988

LOOK. THERE IS A man filming a movie across the street from the bus stop. He lounges on the hood of a parked car in a spandex bodysuit. His face is covered by a handheld camcorder. When he lowers it, you see he's wearing a black ski mask.

Peek through the window of his camera. He is filming two boys, eleven and twelve, waiting for the bus.

Each morning they stand right here on Fifty-First and First Avenue until the first of two public buses takes them to school. The block is at an incline overlooking the United Nations building, where flags flap like dusty rugs shaken out in a backyard. The bus moans toward the stop and gasps open. The boys, with their shirt buttons and book-bag zippers, step through the doors. Follow them. Watch when one of their small hands reaches for the cord above the window. Listen for the ping and see the sign light up in red above the driver's head. Next stop is where they get off.

Notice when they sit down on the bench to wait for their second bus, the man in the mask is already there, standing across the street with his camera pointed in their direction.

There he is again, at the first bus stop, the following morning. Now he hangs from scaffolding like a monkey off a tree and uses his free hand to snap photographs of the boys.

And there he is the following day, kneeling with his camera

aimed up at their faces. He has moved to their side of the street, closer than he was before. Notice his mask is made of leather and fastened with laces at the back of his head.

One morning, as one of the boys leans against a brick building waiting for the bus, the masked man comes over and leans right beside him. When the boy shifts position, the man does the same, mimicking the boy's movements.

You think they must know each other. You think this is performance art. You think he wants money, but he is harmless. You wonder if he does this all day. You wonder if you'll read about him in the papers. You think you'll say something if the man gets any closer to the boys, but the next day he does, and you don't.

On this particular morning, the masked man approaches one of the boys seated inside the bus kiosk and sits down beside him. When the bus arrives, the boy stands up and so does the man. He raises his fist as if he might hit the boy but punches the wall instead. This all seems so choreographed and intentional, it must be an act, you think. But years later, you'll see the boy on TV telling the talk-show host how frightened he was. "It seems as though he was mad," the boy will say. "Like we didn't do something we were supposed to."

The next time the boys arrive at the bus stop, they are joined by an older brother for protection. He spots the masked man and alerts the police. The following morning, when the masked man begins filming, an undercover officer is watching in a parked car nearby.

When the masked man spots him, he gets into his car and drives off. Follow the siren lights down the block. See the man pull over.

Now he is pressed against a car door. He is without his mask, but his back is to you as he's placed in handcuffs so you can't see his face.

You watch an officer open the trunk of the man's car. Inside, there are stacks of videotapes, hundreds of hours of footage the man shot of his three subjects—the two boys at their bus stops, and a third child, a little girl. Every day she walked to school, unaware that a masked man was filming her, following close behind. You wonder if someone will tell her now, or if she's better off not knowing.

1992

girl

I DIDN'T MEAN TO HIT HER. It was an accident. We were practicing serves. I dropped a yellow ball on the green clay court. It bounced twice before I caught it and tossed it upward. One arm reached for the inflatable canvas ceiling overhead; the other swept a Wilson racket clockwise from three o'clock to six to nine. The girl's face was at ten. A bone-crack shot through the tennis bubble. Balls dropped on other courts. Necks turned, eyes followed.

The girl heaved forward and cupped her hand over her nose. Lines of blood ran between the cracks in her fingers, then down one arm and off the cliff of her elbow. When she hurried off the court, she left behind a dime-sized black stain on the clay and two gape-mouthed girls who stared at me but didn't say anything.

It wasn't my fault. You're not supposed to stand so close when someone is serving. You shouldn't talk to other girls when it's someone else's turn. You're supposed to pay attention to the person with the ball.

The girl I hit is sixteen and popular. I know because I've seen her name on flyers for prep school parties. When she steps onto the tennis bus, she pauses to smile for invisible cameras before taking her seat. Her hair is black like my mother's, but around her crown where it shines the most, it's the color of lightbulbs. Her tan is Sephardic and sealed with winter break at the Boca

Raton Resort and Club, or the Breakers in Palm Beach. She has that popular-girl stance: arched upper back, one foot outturned for support—like she's pregnant on her chest, like her whole body is buckling under the weight of her breasts, like they're the heaviest and most important things anyone has ever carried.

A week later, the girl I hit isn't back on the tennis bus. All through the lesson, I checked behind me before I swung my racket to show the other two girls how careful I'd become. On the next court, the girl's younger brother slapped balls into the net and then turned to glare at me.

"My sister had to get an operation," he tells me after our lesson is over and we're on the small yellow school bus headed home.

He is in the vinyl seat in front of me, sitting backward with his knees burrowed into the cushion so he can face me head-on. His hair is black and shiny like his sister's, only his is cut into a bowl over his forehead. When his fingers brush it back, his forehead pops out like a belly from an unbuckled pair of pants. He is my age with sandbag cheeks and a knapsack he straps to both shoulders. There is nothing popular about him.

"It was an accident," I repeat, though I hadn't actually said it out loud before. "Is she going to be okay?"

"Yeah," he says. "But the swelling might not be down in time for my bar mitzvah, so . . ."

I take a hulking bite of the Whatchamacallit candy bar I'd been saving for the ride home, and he throws me a disgusted look.

"My mom's pretty upset," he says before turning around to face forward in his seat.

The mention of his mother makes bits of candy bar rise up in my throat. Although I've never met her, I can picture her: small, tan, and Jewish—nearly identical to my own mother. Her voice is raspy and rises in a room filled with other mothers. Her smell is deliberate. Chanel No. 5 from Bloomingdale's. Black leather handbag from Gucci. Black wool slacks from Loehmann's (*Sixty dollars! Would you believe it?*). Blow-dry from the salon on the corner of Eighty-Fourth Street. A woman with a high tolerance for heat who uses her bare hands to remove tinfoil from a hot oven, who wakes up in the middle of the night to check again that she turned off the oven, who can't hold down sleep. A woman with an exploding Filofax of numbers who picks up the phone when she's upset and won't put it down until something has changed. A woman who's most upset when precious things that belong to her are broken.

"You're too rough," my mother might say if she finds out I broke the girl's nose. "You broke everything," she cried once, collecting glass shards in her hands. I can't help it if I like to touch things, if my hands are slippery, if my arms swing a little too wide. I can't predict how delicate something is until it comes apart or how close I am to anything lurking on the periphery. I am clumsy, klutzy, accident-prone—though my mother calls it "careless," which I hate. It makes me think of bad people with bad intentions.

This is why I hide things. There is a pig figurine with a chipped ear tucked behind a picture frame on the living room shelf. And a coffee mug without a handle in the back of the kitchen cabinet. There are other broken, hidden things, too.

Tonight feels like the night they will all be discovered. I have a sudden impulse to bolt from this bus and sprint the fifty blocks home before the phone rings and my mother learns that I broke the perfect girl's perfect face. Before she considers what else I might have destroyed.

But the bus doors are sealed. We are parked in traffic on the 59th Street Bridge. It was already getting dark when we boarded, but now it's that flat blackness that forces you to see your reflection in the window before you can see through it. Frizzy crown of hair. Crooked nose. The twinkling of flares. Siren blurps.

"An accident," someone inside the bus announces, and the kids without Walkmen mutter in agreement. There are follow-up questions—*What kind of accident? Are we trapped? Are we in danger?*—but they are all too embarrassing to ask.

When the driver turns off the engine, there is a sudden still-ness, an airless, weightless calm that could easily be followed by screaming. *Yes, danger.* I'm hot, breathing fast—the urge to run home has been replaced by the fear that I'll never be home again. If there is a term for my terror logic, I haven't learned it yet. I try opening the window, but it's jammed. The roof hatch is reserved for emergencies and adults who decide on such things. And I am only a teenager, one of many, locked in a tin can on a bridge hovering over the East River.

I've grown up with this river. It borders my school and the apartment where I used to live. Years ago, on the promenade with my mother, I saw a man in a black rubber suit and mask rise up from the water. A police officer, she explained, searching for someone who'd gone missing. The thought of waiting to be found underwater, the condition of being nowhere until you are identified as somewhere, made me think this next: All that keeps you from disappearing is another person who sees you. What happens when they look away?

If I ever make it off this bus, I will tell my mother I'm never going back on it again, that it's unsafe and the kids don't like me, that there's no supervision, that it's a death trap, that I don't even like tennis, that I want to try something else—a new sport, anything she wants as long as I don't have to ride this bus.

"But you're so good at tennis," she'll say. What she'll mean is no.

I NEVER chose to play tennis. It was chosen for me, long before I even knew it was a choice, when it was still just an answer to a family questionnaire that another girl in my class might conduct. *Mercedes or BMW? The Hamptons or Millbrook? Jewish or Christian? Tennis or skiing?* We do tennis.

Tennis in Florida on the holidays, in the Catskills in April, and on Fire Island in the summers, where the game is grunted out in visors stamped with logos of other vacation spots.

My mother's racket is a Prince Classic. The rest of the family has Wilsons. Mine is a Pro Staff Sledge Hammer with fluorescent yellow strings, a yellow vibration dampener, and hot pink Ultrasuede tape wrapped around the grip. It's heavier than my sister's, but lighter than my father's.

Every summer, my sister and I spend two weeks at tennis camp, and before we leave, we shop for new tennis skirts and matching bloomers that look like underwear but are not underwear.

When a classmate invited me to her country club for a tennis match, my mother pinned the waist of a skirt that was still too big for me. Then she told me about the rules of country clubs, how you have to be proper, wear all white, and put your napkin on your lap. She told me how Jews were not always allowed inside of these country clubs, but now they are. She told me that I was a guest, a word I learned long ago has conditions: When you have a guest, you let them decide what games to play and how to play them. When you are a guest, you must be well behaved and say *please* and *thank you*. You must not break anything. Those are the rules.

In tennis, there are other rules. Don't hit the ball outside fault lines. Serve at a diagonal from the baseline. Call out *love* when the score is zero, *deuce* when it's tied, and *ace* when you swing at a serve and miss.

During the school year, I take lessons to build on what I've learned each summer and flip through *People* magazine for an article on Jennifer Capriati, who was thirteen when she went pro in 1990. "Downright dangerous"—that's how the reporter described her on the court. And that is how you have to be if you're a teenage girl with a racket. If you're good, you're taken seriously. You take yourself seriously.

You don't just play the game, you memorize it. You know who is ranked regionally and nationally and which colleges recruit tennis players. You know the players you can beat in the small high school circuit and who will make emotional pudding out of your game.

Every time I lose a match, it hammers down on a general truth: I'm not a winner.

When I used to ask, "*What's* the point of trying if I'm not going to be the best?" the answer was "You don't know that." Now that I'm about to be fourteen, the answer is college. Colleges want to see long-term commitment to an activity. They want varsity team members and girls who play tennis.

It doesn't matter if you don't like the game anymore, if

you've come this far, you keep playing until it means something. All my lessons are a gateway to the varsity tennis team, which is a gateway to college acceptance. When the time comes to mail a piece of paper to the top twenty schools in the country (plus a few safeties), I will write the word *tennis* above one black line, and some other words above other lines to suggest I'm a multifaceted person.

This all puts me back on the tennis bus on the way to another lesson. The girl I hit is back this week, and when I smile at her, she laughs, looking away as if she's sharing a private joke with someone I can't see. The whole ride to the courts feels like an emergency, the same as it did the week before, only worse.

When we arrive at the parking lot, a car pulls up next to us and two girls around my age get out of the backseat. I watch them walk to the entrance of the tennis club, trailed by their driver—a gangly older man carrying a double racket bag.

In the locker room, I approach the girls on a fact-finding mission. They are taught by their own private coach. Just the two of them. And yes, he drives them to and from the courts in a car, not a bus. A car—where the windows open and the doors unlock. A car is safer, familiar, more contained, free from panic triggers and the popular girl and other untold things that frighten me. I rip out a sheet of lined paper from my history binder and write down the coach's name.

"Gary Wilensky," I tell my mother when I get home. "I want to play with him in the fall."

And so my mom makes a call and paces in the kitchen and makes another call and there is good news.

"I got you Gary," she says.

GARY WILENSKY

Private Coach of Tournament Juniors Including Eastern and Nationally Ranked
  Players

Director of Gary's Girls and Guys Adult and Junior Tennis Programs, NYC

LESSON RATES
  Semiprivate One Hour $86

Professional Organizations and Certifications

United States Professional Tennis Association, Master
  Professional (Highest Certification Awarded)

Professional Tennis Registry

United States Tennis Association—Clinician and Panelist

Eastern Tennis Association—Clinician

New York Junior Tennis League—Head Clinician of
  Teacher Training Program

Prince Manufacturing—Professional Advisory Teaching
  Staff

USTA Tennis Teachers Conference (in conjunction with
  the US Open)—Clinician and Panelist

USTA/Volvo National League Program—Tester and
  Verifier

USTA Area Training Scout for Juniors

Eastern Junior Tennis Academy—Coach for Junior
  Excellence Clinics

Mayor's Cup All-Scholastic, New York City—Executive
　Committee

Teaching Experience
　Brearley School—Girls' Varsity Tennis Coach
　Tripp Lake Camp—Tennis Director
　Point O'Pines Camp—Tennis Director
　Tennis Director and Head Professional At:
　Concord Resort Hotel
　Grossinger's Hotel
　Fallsview Hotel
　Central Park Tennis Courts
　Midtown Tennis Club, NYC
　Ocean Club, Paradise Island—Advisor
　Tennis United, NYC
　Holiday Hills Tennis Camp
　Pepsi-Cola National Tennis Program

man

ON A SEPTEMBER DAY IN FLUSHING Meadows, Queens, Gary Wilensky runs into an old friend.

The US Open has always been an unofficial reunion for the local tennis scene. But now, in 1992, the crowds have grown along with notable celebrity appearances.

Everyone is on the lookout for Barbra Streisand, who was spotted the day before, in a floppy white hat and round John Lennon glasses, mooning in the stands over Andre Agassi. In the morning papers, she was pictured in the locker room, sandwiched between Michael Bolton and Agassi, who—in his gold chains and Nike animal prints—glinted with his own Hollywood decadence.

Celebrity gossip. Paparazzi at the Open. Agassi's "Just Do It" campaign on billboards and all over TV. Tennis has a renewed sex appeal with a narrative to match. Agassi, the stud; Pete Sampras, the handsome young underdog. The epic rivalry of Steffi Graf and Monica Seles. And the prodigy, Jennifer Capriati—who, a few months earlier, replaced Mary Lou Retton as every little girl's Olympic hero, ringing in the nineties in her Stars and Stripes windbreaker at the Barcelona games, raising her gold medal as high as her hair-sprayed wall of bangs. In a year, eighteen-year-old Seles will be stabbed on the court by a deranged Graf fan, and in two years Capriati will become a cautionary tale, but in this moment, both represent tennis's emerging new star: the teenage girl.

All of this is good for Gary Wilensky. Group lessons twice a week. Private coaching. Tournament prep. Over the years, his clientele has morphed from mainly adults to mainly adolescent and teenage girls. For a certain type of Manhattan parent, tennis has always been the athletic arm of social etiquette, a necessary part of the budding socialite's curriculum. For others, it has more recently become the female equivalent of high school football—a sport that legitimizes underage players as professionals at the highest level, attracts college recruiters to midrange players, and if nothing else, earns adult admiration in summer communities. All of this translates to $600 a head, per semester, for Gary Wilensky's junior program, his semi-private weekly clinic comprised mainly of Manhattan private school kids.

Fifteen years earlier, he drummed up business with ads in the back of *New York* magazine, right next to the lonely hearts listings.

TIME FOR TENNIS! GARY WILENSKY GETS MORE PEOPLE INVOLVED IN TENNIS THAN ANYONE ELSE IN NEW YORK.

Now, in 1992, it's all word of mouth; the clients come to him. He runs his own program, renting out court time around the city and fielding calls from wealthy parents, some of them famous, most of them rich, all of them eager to get their child into one of his clinics.

Unlike other coaches, Gary has no professional tennis experience and isn't known for his skill as a player. Others are more artful, esteemed, technical, or physically demanding of their students. Gary is fun. He's an entertainer, a clown with a sack full of gags, doling out carnival prizes on the courts, and showing up for lessons in the occasional costume.

Manhattan kids aren't used to being treated as kids—and Gary knows this. He knows that distracting them from their anxieties, rather than tapping into them, is the secret to making even the most resistant young students fans of the sport. And those who love the game get better at it, which is what their parents pay for.

His reputation as a Pied Piper for prep school players was only bolstered this year when he was hired as the varsity coach for Brearley, one of the city's elite all-girls schools. On top of that, he's got a private coaching gig training a gifted high school senior, the Daughter, who has risen in the tournament ranks since she started with him the year before. Within the year, her name will be linked to his in news stories around the country, but for now she is best known in tournament circles for her tennis ability.

"Gary?" A female voice rises above the hot-dog steam in the concession area. A woman whose long reddish-brown curls tangle with a wild bedroom quality materializes before him. "Gary, is that you?"

The sex therapist. Erica Goodstone used to work around the corner from Midtown Tennis, where Gary taught in the late seventies and early eighties. On Friday nights she attended his tennis mixers—a weekly singles event where a game of mixed doubles held the promise of something more. He'd toss a few balls, set up some matches, provide a table of "refreshments" for post-game mingling, and pack the courts on an otherwise quiet night.

Early on, Erica noticed Gary's cleverness in arranging matches. He had a natural ability to read people, easily detecting their strengths and weaknesses. As a therapist, she admired that.

They became friends. Not great friends or intimate partners, but that level of friendship reserved for two single adults who enjoy each other's company enough to dismiss the notion that one party might want something different from the other. At least this was true for Erica, who had only platonic feelings for Gary.

Once they drove to the Concord Resort Hotel in the Catskills, where Gary was performing playing tennis on roller skates at an exhibition.

Another time they went to a movie, Peter Weir's *The Last Wave*, about a murder trial tied to apocalyptic premonitions. When they came out of the theater, Gary's car had been involved in a hit-and-run. It was bent out of shape, totaled. It looked like a wave had crashed over it. Erica expected him to be upset, but instead he laughed.

His is a two-frequency laugh, one that syncs up with outside laughter and one that abrades it, an undercackle that suggests a secondary motive. A joke about his joke and how easy it is to manipulate someone else's response.

Now, over the pop of tennis balls and intermittent roars, Erica and Gary exchange updates. *The practice is expanding. Business is good. You'll never believe who I just saw. And have you heard from —?*

They have plenty of mutual friends from the local tennis scene. One, Gary claims, has spoken ill of Erica.

"She says you're the most selfish person she's ever met," he tells her, although Gary Wilensky has a tendency to lie. It's a game in his repertoire. There are others.

The last time Erica saw Gary was in the late eighties at another US Open. (Graf and Sabatini, or was it Becker and Lendl?) They'd sat in the stands and discussed his dating life.

He was seeing someone and it was going well, great even. What excited him wasn't the relationship itself, but what it produced. A new game: bondage, restraints—not for him, but for his partner. Gary was in control and delighted by it. Considering her line of work, Erica wasn't fazed by any of this, though she noted his desire for dominance. In her practice she found that heterosexual men more commonly preferred the subservient role, a relief from the gender expectations foisted upon them from the outside world.

"Are you still dating the same person?" Erica asks Gary now, a different Gary than he was before.

He is more guarded this year, older-looking. His hair is grayer, his skin rawer since he's shaved off his mustache.

Gary Wilensky shakes his head. "I'm just coaching girls now."

girl: school

AN EMERGENCY ASSEMBLY IS CALLED. THE head of the upper school stands before us in a Laura Ashley floral print dress with princess sleeves. Her hair is in two tight wet braids. In her hand is a stitched potholder, which she unravels into a puddle of thread at her feet.

This is the upper school, she says. "We are coming undone like this potholder." Glassy-eyed, she looks around the gymnasium at all of us girls sitting cross-legged in our kilts beneath the artificial light.

Seven months before, a New York City teenager shot two of his classmates with a .38 caliber pistol in the hallway of their Brooklyn high school. But that has nothing to do with this potholder. At my school, a redbrick mansion on Manhattan's Upper East Side, the list of concerns are as follows: chewing gum, Diet Cokes being carried into classrooms, wearing kilts shorter than six inches above the knee. The point of this assembly is to change our behavior. It's not too late to be better.

I go to one of the top private schools in the country. K-12. All girls. Notable alumni: the daughters of two US presidents, a first lady, an Oscar-winning actress, and a queen. Frequent college placement: Harvard, Yale, Princeton, Dartmouth, and Brown.

Every girl wears a uniform: seersucker tunics for lower and middle school girls, bell-shaped skirts for seventh graders, and plaid kilts for grades eight through twelve. Along with the kilt—which is periodically measured for length—students are to wear a collared shirt (Polo Ralph Lauren is popular, but Lacoste will do); solid-colored tights are permitted in the colder months. Shoes are penny loafers or oxfords (though Dr. Martens have slipped in under the radar). Hair is pushed back with a velvet headband, knotted in a scrunchie, or flipped dramatically to one side. Dangling from wrists are Tiffany belt-buckle bracelets or silver charms or leather and gold bands etched with the names of family-owned horses. Bodies are mostly slim, waifish, sustained on Diet Coke, carrot sticks, saltines filched from the cafeteria and valued for their easy accountability: 84 calories in a pack of two.

I wear combat boots with a rolled-up kilt and a turtleneck. In the front pockets of my Danish bag, an imported canvas satchel you're supposed to cover in pen-drawn hearts and safety pins, are two over-the-counter diet pills (to eat less in front of people, not to lose weight—I'm already too small), along with some loose Sour Patch Kids, a chewed-on pen, and a note someone passed to me in class that reads: "What happened?"

Ten years ago, my mother brushed my hair into two bushy brown pigtails and reminded me to make eye contact when a grown-up asked me questions. I shook a lady's hand, looked into her eyes, answered her questions, and a few months later, walked into a classroom filled with other girls—the tallest and blondest I had ever seen.

We spent our first year at school all together in two big open rooms. On some days, my name was called and I was taken into a smaller, private room to answer questions about shapes and where they belong. "No, try again," the teacher would say.

Friendships were formed based on Cabbage Patch Kids collections. One girl had five all lined up on her bed underneath a canopy. Another had two, along with a Teddy Ruxpin and a miniature Mercedes she was allowed to drive only in the Hamptons. Another had small, butter-soft stuffed animals we'd shove under our shirts and then, grunting, squeeze out, with our legs splayed open inside the bathtub.

One girl had her doll shipped from another country. "It has all the body parts," she explained. The girl's skin was almost see-through and she wore old-fashioned lace-collared shirts to school. Her mother towered over the other mothers and dressed in long wool skirts and lace blouses that buttoned up the back of her neck. Most curious of all was the mother's hair, which she wore elaborately pinned in a puff on top of her head like a Victorian paper doll. They lived in a limestone building across the street from the Metropolitan Museum of Art, with marble hallways and no pets and a playroom with an indoor jungle gym.

When the girl fell asleep during a sleepover, I wandered the marble halls of her home, lined with busts on white columns. I kept my hands flat at my side, just as I do in a museum where everything is breakable. I passed a big open area with a fireplace and old-fashioned satin couches, a long dining hall with dozens of chairs, and a cracked door to a room with a light on. When I looked inside, I saw something I wasn't supposed to see: the girl's mother sitting before a mirror in only her bra, pulling all the pins out of her hair. Strawberry-colored ribbons dropped down the length of her pale white back.

There were birthday parties at Mortimer's, at museums, with a man named Jeremy—a clown who everyone used for their parties. At one birthday, a chimpanzee in a striped suit was brought into a restaurant as a surprise. We circled around him and watched him do tricks. Then he walked up to me, took both my hands in his, and pulled me inside the circle with him. We were the same height and we smiled at each other like we shared a funny secret. Later he was taken away in a cage.

At school we learned about Pilgrims and the *Mayflower*. We drew letters in cursive and sang about the gifts he gave Emmanuel. I told all my classmates I was Jewish, and when they asked what that meant, I said it meant we have different gods. A report card said I wasn't good at using scissors. Another said I needed to listen more.

"They're going to kick you out if you don't change," my mother warned me in third grade. By then I had a problem no one could name. Every day I had visions of her dying—hit by a truck, electrocuted, stabbed, gunned down. Tears streamed down through classes, from eight to three, as if the worst had already happened. I made my mother wear a name tag when she left the house with my name and address on it so that if her body were found, someone would know to contact me. This helped, but not enough. After school, I was sent to a woman's office. She asked me questions while I moved beads along a bent wire. What makes you frightened? What makes you sad? Then she spoke with my mother alone.

In middle school, we wore white gloves and learned to play Christmas carols on bells. We wore white gloves and learned to ballroom dance. We formed friendships based on hair color, wristbands, sticker collections, and our mother's friendships with each other. In class we read about a Greek god named

Zeus, another named Apollo, and a woman with snakes in her hair who turned anyone who looked at her to stone. There was a party at the Plaza, a party at the Drake, a party at someone's apartment with boys. Once there were many gods, we learned; now there's just one.

In eighth grade, there was a mass exodus to boarding school. The students who remained were some of the smartest in our class. We took Latin and algebra. We read *Romeo and Juliet.* We drew on our legs, bent our ponytails into messy buns, followed the hourly progression of a bursting white pimple on one girl's temple, and cupped the soft underside of another girl's new breast in the locker room. By then our friendships had become divided between those who cared more about school and those who cared more about boys. It wasn't just caring about actual boys, but the absence of them—the perpetual feeling that something else was out there and we were in here missing it.

On the first day of ninth grade, there were new students. When each girl stood up in homeroom to introduce herself, the room filled with applause. By then, it had been ten years with the same fifty girls. We were sick of each other and ourselves. Our new classmates came through a program for exceptional students who can't afford private school.

The idea that tuition was prohibitive had never before occurred to me. I hadn't really considered the costs. I believed that not getting into this school had everything to do with intelligence and nothing to do with wealth.

Now the new girls are my friends, but I don't ask them about their lives before they were here. They're here now. That's what matters. Besides, there are some things you just don't talk about in school.

Here's what we do talk about—grades. "What'd you get?" It's not enough to know your own grade on a test, you need a larger context for the grade: Nobody got an A, or so-and-so got a C. The worse other students do, the better your grade becomes.

When we get our tests back, it's a game of poker. The teacher deals the hand facedown, and as each person picks it up, we watch for reactions—glassy eyes (B−), contentment (B+), a bursting expression (A), shame-folding (C), hand-cupping (unclear). Someone is always cupping her hand around her grade or her answers. It's as much a sign of confidence as a way to create boundaries from someone like me, who has none. I dart my eyes under folded papers hunting for letters.

I peel up my skirt to see the answers written on my thigh. I sneak into the empty classroom with the stack of ungraded tests and change my answers to whatever the smartest girl has written. I forge signatures and alter grades on report cards. I Wite-Out my failures and steal my wins because I am craftier than I am smart. But I'm also afraid. I dream at night I have buried a body and all the dogs are sniffing for it.

In science class, the teacher interrupts his lecture to scold me for receiving a note someone passed. He is a small man on the younger side of the teacher age spectrum, with a delicate face and a twitchy body. Supposedly he'd been struck by lightning, which accounts for his white hair and for the fact that he doesn't have complete control over his motor skills. His shoulders hoist back when he talks; his arms flail above his head when he gets excited; a piece of chalk snaps between his fingers.

He has difficulty looking students in the eye, I think, out of fear that his thoughts might be heard. The year has just begun and it is already clear whom he favors—the girl with see-through skin, whose mother's hair I saw though the crack in the door. Now she is tall, with a whispery voice and long golden-red hair like her mother's. When she speaks in class, he flares up with an allergic crush. Anything she says is *very good*.

Everyone knows he has his pets and they are an undeniable type—long-limbed girls with billowing horsetail hair who are soft-spoken and not particularly passionate about science. When I found out he was my teacher this year, a junior told me to flirt with him for a better grade. It is believed to be that easy if you are a sexual creature in his eyes, and I am very much not.

I walk my frizzy nest of hair, my bumpy nose, and my flat chest to the slow math class. I write poetry, but I struggle in English. I act in plays but am cast as the clown. I pick my nose, but only when nobody is looking.

If I am considered cool, it's only because of my older sister. She graduated two years ago and left behind a cool legacy. It began in seventh grade when she starred as a pot dealer in a "Just Say No to Drugs" commercial. Later she acted in school plays, bleached her hair with sun-kissed highlights, and dated boys with poetic names: Hugo, Shep, Christo. She flipped her hair to one side, sunk her feet into Tretorns, glossed her lips in Carmex, spritzed her neck with Calyx, popped a roll of Cryst-O-Mints into her straw bag, and chewed on one side of her mouth, pouting her lips like Molly Ringwald. I watched younger students scan her body for clues. She made maturity seem so easy.

My sister didn't have to be kind to me, but she was. Armed with the senior year privilege to leave school during the day, she'd drop outside food—muffins or cheese fries—in my locker, and when I'd find it, all my classmates would gather around, asking for bites. She taught me about social currency, the value of being perceived as someone with special privileges. She was clever that way.

When she graduated, she assigned other cool girls in the grade beneath her to look after me, and they took it as an honor. They called me cute, their favorite freshman, they asked about my sister. "How's your sister doing at Vassar?" "Is she still acting?" "You'll never believe this, but I saw your sister's commercial the other day!" I relish the attention, even if I haven't earned it.

But my sister's influence goes only so far. Most of our classes are mixed—with the smartest girls and the rest of us in the same classes. But this year, math and French are divided into three sections based on ability. On the first day of ninth grade, we all walked around homeroom asking the typical straight-A students which classes they were in to gain our bearings. My sister had always been in the top French class, so I assumed I would be, too. Then someone saw my schedule and said, "Oh, yeah, you're in the dumb class." *Dumb*. The word itself is embarrassing—framed in bloated letters and weighed down by that sagging U.

Now, there is an internal ranking among us that can only

be overturned with straight As or a phone call from a parent. When my mother found out about French, she called the head of the upper school to have me placed in the medium class. "This had to be a mistake." I listened to one side of the conversation from my bedroom.

"Uh-huh . . . She is . . . I can assure you . . ."

I hate being left out of conversations about me. Somewhere inside them lies the truth about who I am, but I'm not allowed to hear it.

The next day I was moved to the medium French class, but there was no escaping the slow math class.

When I arrived at school today, my homeroom teacher pulled me out of the room for a scenic walk in the hallway to inform me that I received a D on the first math test of the year.

She put her arm around my shoulder and squeezed it. "Would you like to go to public school?" she asked.

This wasn't a question but a threat. I know nothing about public school aside from what has been drilled into my brain from an early age: Bad things happen there.

"We don't get those grades here," the teacher said and broke into a smile that meant *Are we clear?*

Because everyone saw our walk around the hallway, girls keep asking me all day long, "What happened?" That was what was written on the note passed to me in science class. Underneath it was a drawing of a sad face with tears. I didn't write back, not that I blame anyone for asking.

There is a magnetic quality to witnessing someone else get in trouble, and someone is always in trouble. We want to know the rules, what constitutes bad behavior. We want to feel the relief of being in the clear. And then there is the practical side of it all. You're up against everyone in your class when the time comes to apply to college. The less competition, the better. That's all there is to it.

"Your scores in ninth grade can totally ruin your chances of getting in anywhere," the see-through-skin girl says at lunch, tilting her head in a lecturing way, so that her ponytail dips into her fruit salad. "Everything counts starting now."

girl: home

THERE ARE MEN IN THE KITCHEN breaking down a wall. I never saw the old lady who lived on the other side of it. Now she is dead, and we own her apartment, too.

Our apartment is already too big. Three bedrooms, an eat-in kitchen, a TV in every room so we don't have to watch the same thing, a dining room with a long wooden table, covered by a tablecloth we're not allowed to eat on, and stuffed underneath it, department-store shopping bags containing the original store receipts in case my mother decides to return anything.

The living room is where we sit with guests during the Jewish holidays. There is a plate of nuts in a crystal bowl on the coffee table. My sister's head shot is framed in silver on the piano. It was taken six years ago, when she was twelve and acting in commercials. Next to it is another photograph from that same day when I was told to join her on a stool between two silver lamps with blazing hot moons inside of them. When I sat down on my sister's lap, she locked her arms around me and leaned in. Sweaty cotton pressed against my skin. Moonbeams pressed against our eyes. Cheek skin pressed against cheek skin. "And smile," said the man with the camera. So we did. Then my sister pulled her head back and loosened her arms. I missed her already.

My mother is always giving her friends tours of the apartment. She points to the floor and says *wainscoting*. She points to the ceiling and says *crown molding*. She points to a light and says *sconce*. She doesn't say this out loud, but a mandate has been set for all the bedrooms: The curtains must be trimmed with the same fabric as the duvet covers.

This holds true in the master bedroom, where the duvet is white with pink floral bouquets. The bed is king-sized and rests in a sleigh-shaped mahogany bed frame. The TV is in the armoire. Old report cards are in the bottom drawer of the built-in desk. My father's soft pack of Vantage cigarettes is in his night table. (I smoked two.) My mother's bottle of Valium, for when she flies, is in a cosmetic bag underneath their bathroom sink. (I swallowed three.)

In the library my father opens a stack of mail with a gold dagger. Beneath him is a gold trash can stuffed with crinkled paper. When he's finished, he lies on the couch flipping through channels, pausing when ticker tape runs across the screen. I don't care what he watches, as long as I get to sit with his feet on my lap and pull off his wool socks from the toe. Each one is matted to his feet with sweat, and when I yank them off, my father lets out a big, long sigh.

Across from the front door is a gold-framed mirror. When you enter, you see yourself, and behind you, on the opposite wall, a large oil painting of a homeless woman lying on a bench next to a shopping cart. It was by a painter named Serge who borrowed our beach house. When it arrived, my mother carefully unwrapped the brown paper and leaned it against the wall. "Where should I put it?" she asked. It moved around the apartment for a few weeks, before a nail was hammered into the hallway wallpaper.

If you were to count the number of couches throughout the apartment, we'd have enough to sleep ten homeless people. That's including the love seats and two sofas that open up into queen-sized beds. Eleven if someone uses the bed in my sister's room, since she's away at college anyway. It seems such a waste. So many people without beds. So many beds without people.

The first winter after we moved here, I bought a hot chocolate and a doughnut for the homeless man who sings outside the bank across the street. I planned to give him a bag of old blankets, too. That was two years ago. Now he nods at me when I walk by. I try to remember to cross the street so he doesn't have to.

When you walk into our building, two doormen in blue suits and matching blue bellhop hats open the heavy glass doors. A third sits behind a desk with a phone that rings but has no dial. My parents went to a board meeting to vote on whether they should wear white gloves. *It just looks nicer* was the final decision.

Once my mother came home to find one of the doormen had let himself into our apartment. He was in her bedroom, opening drawers. When she found him, he began to cry. He had a wife and kids, he said. He didn't make enough. "Please don't call the police." My mother didn't call the police, but the spare key was removed from the lobby along with the doorman. Now she keeps a lockbox in her closet. The key is in a drawer in the hallway under a pile of silk scarves. If you use it to open the lockbox, you'll find another key that opens another lockbox on Seventy-Ninth Street. My mother has told me this in case she and my father die at the exact same time.

"Everything we have goes to you and your sister," she says.

"I don't want anything," I tell her, not because it's the truth, but because I hate it when she reminds me that she'll die someday.

Two years ago we moved to Park Avenue. Before that, we lived in a smaller apartment on a smaller block across the street from my school. My parents slept on a pullout bed that fit inside a closet. My sister and I shared a bedroom severed in two by a white plaster wall my mother had installed. On my sister's side was an A-ha poster—the first concert she ever attended. Her clock radio was set to 100.3, Z100, and our shared telephone had a built-in answering machine, which we'd use to record raps. I'd beatbox while she'd read from a notebook: "We're not here, but don't you weep. Leave a message right after the beep."

On my side of the room was a window, fifteen flights above the street, that faced the windows of other buildings. At night, my sister and I would watch ourselves in the reflection as we danced to all of Billy Joel's *The Stranger*. The whole album, a litany of grown-up complaints we pretended to understand. Divorce. Heart attacks. Rent money. Difficult women.

And here were our matching Formica beds, pressed against either side of the wall.

"Once this was all one room," Mom would say as if it were a fairy tale. "Now it's two."

When the lights were off and the blankets were over us, I'd talk to my sister through the wall's cracking corner.

"What do you want to dream about tonight?" I'd ask to keep her awake, but she'd always be asleep.

When we were five and ten, we played Thirteen and Eighteen— a game where we pretended we were both teenagers, still five years apart but more mature, more into dance competitions and spraining our ankles and being carried offstage by imaginary boyfriends, who were also our twin brothers.

Then we'd transform my bed into the display case for a boutique called Pizzazz. We sold oily stickers, puffy pencil cases, and an assortment of scented erasers.

When my sister and I grew tired of that, we'd turn the puffy pencil cases into Barbie beds. "I'm so tired, I'm going to sleep," my sister's Barbie would say, resting her head on an eraser pillow.

In a dream, ghosts in nightgowns stood in a circle around my bed. In another dream, they picked up my bed and carried it into the jungle.

In our old apartment, the living room carpet was thick and red. A pink doll-shaped squeaky toy named Baby lived between the fibers. She belonged to our old dog, Tinkerbell. The dog spent her last night alive under the piano in the living room, tucked into a comforter. All through the night my mom photographed Tinkerbell so she would be remembered. When the pictures were developed, Tinkerbell's eyes glowed red. So my mom took a Sharpie and colored round black circles over the redness. A real dog with black cartoon eyes. "Much better," my mother said, and I believed her.

A few years earlier, when I was five, I ran away. I took the stairs down fifteen flights, and when I got to the bottom, I asked the doorman to call my mom on the house phone. "I ran away," I said. "Come back upstairs now," my mother told me. What I knew: Don't take the elevator alone. Something terrible had happened in an elevator once to a girl or a woman, because of a man in a long overcoat. And candy.

So I took the stairs back up, flight after flight, pausing on each landing to catch my breath. The stairwell was gray, dingy, and ice cold, with each floor number painted on the door in emergency yellow.

When I didn't come up right away, my mother grew frantic, believing I had really run away or was lost or stolen. "Mommy, I'm here," I said when I had climbed all the stairs and pushed open the door to our apartment. "It's okay, she's here," she said and hung up the phone. Then she crouched down so she could look me in the eyes, and spoke slowly so I wouldn't forget: "Don't ever leave my sight."

When I was six, I got lost. I was in the park across the street on a playdate. Another girl, another mother in charge. I left the monkey bars to get a drink from the water fountain. When I turned around, I couldn't find the girl or her mother. *Don't ever leave my sight.* Then I couldn't remember what they looked like. *Don't talk to strangers.* Then I couldn't see through my eyes because they were all blurry. In one direction was more park, in the other the street. *Don't cross the street by yourself.*

I walked to the street corner. *Don't get hit by a bus. Don't get in a car with a person you don't know. Watch out for cars.* "DON'T WALK," said the light. The sun was going down. *Don't stay out after dark.* Everywhere were men in overcoats. *If someone you don't know offers you something, run.* I found an old lady. She told me to take her old lady arm. *Don't bother the nice lady.* "WALK," said the light. She led me across the street, and when I pointed to my building, she took me to it. Home.

We went inside the elevator. I stood in one corner; she stood in the other. On a silver panel above the elevator door, a light moved from one number to the next: 11, 12, 14. Our apartment,

15E, was at the end of the hall. *Don't tell anyone where you live.* The door was closed and looked like every other door. *Ding-dong.* I took one big breath and held it. *Ding-dong. Ding-dong.* The dog barked, her dog tags jangled. *Ding-dong.*

I banged on the door with two balled fists. I screamed, "Mommy! I'm here! I'm here!" The old lady crouched down so I could see her face, but I wouldn't look. *Look someone in eye when they're talking to you.* She asked if I knew my phone number. *Don't talk to strangers!*

I kept beating on the door and screaming, this time, not words but one long sound so high and sharp it ripped the back of my throat. Then a lock unsnapped, and another, too. And the dog was licking my legs and the door had become my mother's skirt—navy blue with purple tears falling every which way.

In my parents' old bedroom, my mother recorded movies onto blank VHS tapes. *The Dark Crystal. The Flamingo Kid.* And a movie with Dudley Moore about Santa Claus that my sister almost starred in.

"They went with a girl with red hair," a woman had explained to our answering machine when my sister was eleven and I was six. When my sister heard the news, she cried and cried as my mother held her. I wished I had a reason to cry, too.

My sister always wanted to be an actress, so I wanted to be an actress. She was twelve and I was seven when I accompanied her to an audition. In the waiting room, my mother opened a black case and pulled out the photograph of my sister's face. Around the room were other mothers with other faces in their hands. One mother whisked blush on her daughter's cheeks. Another sat with a pile of sweaters on her lap while her daughter

scanned the room and reconsidered her outfit. My sister's name
was called and she went into a room. When she came back out,
a lady asked my mother if I could go into the room as well.

From there I started going into rooms more often. The waiting areas were all the same, with the same kids and their parents
sitting in foldout chairs. The redheaded twins, the blond boy
with the big lips, the girl with the golden ringlets whose mother
was always whisking blush on her cheeks.

In one room, a woman asked if I could cry on command.
When I said I couldn't, she asked, "What makes you frightened,
what makes you sad?" My sister had already warned me about
this challenge. Her tactic was to imagine our grandfather dying,
and eventually tears would come out, but that didn't work for
me. Instead, I came up with my own method. I thought of the
time I got lost, when for a moment, with the door locked in front
of me, I had no mother and no home. My whole life depended
on her opening that door. My whole face swelled up with tears.

At home, in the old apartment, a message on the answering
machine said I got the part, but then my mother read the script.
It was a TV movie about a man who loves a little girl. That
sounded okay, I told her, because some men are nice and some
little girls are wise and, I imagined, sometimes they could be
friends. But her mind was made up: I was too young to play
a part like that. In her bedroom, as the red record light flick-
ered on the VCR, it was my turn to cry. I didn't care about the
movie, I just wanted her to hold me.

When I was eight, all the suitcases came down from the top
shelf of the hallway closet in the middle of the night. We were
to pack our bags for Florida, our father told us, but we weren't

to bother Mommy. When I went to find her, she was in her bedroom in her nightgown facing the window. Her shoulders were moving up and down and she was whimpering little birdie calls. When she turned around her eyes were swollen. "My daddy died," she said, as if she were the littlest girl in the room.

Once, after a bath, I was wrapped in a towel with a hood and carried to my crib.

Once I reached up from my crib to touch one of my sister's braids.

Once I lay in bed imagining what I would look like when I was older.

Once I whispered into the crack in the wall, "Are you asleep?"

In our old apartment, the dining room was originally a patio, but my parents covered it in windows to seal it up. Once my sister opened one of the windows and dragged on a Marlboro Light. Then she handed it to me just to try. She was sixteen, I was eleven.

When we were seventeen and twelve, my mother announced the wall between our beds was coming down, and it was yanked out like a big white tooth.

A few months later, we packed up our room to move to Park Avenue. My sister's boxes were divided: Half would go with us to the new apartment, half would go with her to college. When all of the rooms were emptied out, we took turns saying "Goodbye, apartment," and after we shut the door, our world changed.

Now it's all heels on hardwood floors and *Missus Weiss* and *Park Avenue* and the guest bathroom and the maid's room and *Your father is tired* and *Quiet, adults are talking* and men in the house with drills and hidden keys and Ralph Lauren on the

beds, the walls, the windows, in the curl of perfumed smoke rising from the wick of a candle and the elevator man, the cleaning
lady, the cleaning lady's lace-collared uniform hanging in the
maid's room and board meetings and *Missus Weiss, can we help
you with that?* and *Would you like us to bring up your dry cleaning, Mister Weiss?* and invitations with silver indented letters
magnetized to the fridge and coming home to darkness and the
sound of the new dog rattling the door she's locked behind and
the new dog's leather leash and smoking alone out the bathroom
window, smoking alone in the stairwell and the armoire and the
foyer and Pierre Deux on Madison Avenue and Demarchelier
between Madison and Park and *Do you know who that was?* and
Can we get a taxi? and *Give him a single* and *Give her my regards*
and the secret thing my mother whispered, palms flat on the
gleaming, white kitchen island: *We're rich.*

man: home

EACH MONTH GARY WILENSKY WRITES "SEVEN hundred and fifty and no/100 dollars" on a check printed with a picture of a log cabin in the mountains—rent money for his Manhattan studio apartment.

There are twenty-nine floors below him and five above him. In the seventies, Donnie Brasco took up residence in the building during his undercover infiltration of the New York mafia. In the eighties, two men tied together by a bedsheet passed Gary's window on the way down.

The windows in his apartment face east in the direction of the river. He has a galley kitchen, hardwood floors, and an alcove that separates the sitting area from the sleeping area. In less than a year, officers will raid his home, climbing over stacks of vintage tennis magazines, to haul out evidence: boxes of VHS tapes—including homemade videos starring Gary Wilensky in compromising positions—and a stack of books—*Peterson's Summer Opportunities for Kids and Teenagers; November of the Soul: The Enigma of Suicide; The Joy of Sexual Fantasy*. For now, however, he isn't known to have visitors.

The Ruppert Yorkville Towers is composed of four buildings that stretch between East Ninetieth and East Ninety-Second Street on Third Avenue and up into the sky. The redbrick towers were erected in 1975 as part of a city housing plan to provide moderate- and middle-income residents, who would otherwise be forced out of the neighborhood by rising costs, an affordable place to live.

Just two blocks west of the towers is Park Avenue, with its scrubbed prewar apartments. Beyond that is Madison Avenue, home to three girls-only private schools, and the Daughter's public school. Past that is Fifth Avenue, the museums, Central Park—an urban garden maze that divides the East and West Sides of Manhattan—and some of the wealthiest homeowners in New York.

To the east of Gary's building, within walking distance, is the mayor's house, the East River, and two more girls' schools— one where he teaches, the other where he picks up one of his students in his junior program. ("Pippa," he mistakenly scribbles on the invoice.)

For Gary, the apartment is a deal; for others in the neighborhood, the building is the dividing line between the "good" neighborhood and the "bad" one. When you're rich, the less fortunate are what frightens you the most. But Gary is used to living modestly under the shadow of other people's fortunes. As a teenager in the Long Island hamlet of Roslyn, not far from the Gold Coast mansions that inspired Fitzgerald's Gatsby, he lived in a small apartment complex with his father, a divorced garment manufacturer. The town wasn't then as wealthy as it would become, but the Victorian homes were still more elegant and fuller than where he lived.

There are things you can't control and others you can.

A basketball, for instance. It didn't matter that Gary was five-eight his junior year, he still brought the varsity team to victory. And tennis. Ping-Pong, even. Give Gary Wilensky a ball and he'll never give it back. He became his own man on the courts.

Gary's grades were low compared to those of his Ivy League–bound friends, but he wasn't working toward his future; he was living it. He was older than the kids in his class, and dressed the part—snappy ties, tailored pants jangling with car keys. Gary had wheels before any of his friends, zipping through town on double dates. And those who doubted his maturity might have second thoughts when they saw him on the dance floor.

He knew all the steps and wasn't flustered by the nearness of a young woman's body, wasn't afraid to pull her close to his chest, to rock her back and forth, to suspend her at an angle above the floor so that she couldn't catch herself should he choose to let her go.

He was different from the other Jewish boys in Roslyn, who were all bound for top-floor jobs in Manhattan. For Gary, opportunities were closer to the ground.

He started as an instructor at Midtown Tennis on Eighth Avenue. The courts were narrow and space was tight, but in the late sixties and early seventies, it was just about the only game in town. On any given day, there was Kurt Vonnegut Jr. trading shots with Mike Wallace, or Morley Safer in the locker room.

One regular, an ad executive who moonlighted doing PR for Catskills resorts, scouted Gary to run tennis programs at two of his hotels: Grossinger's and the Concord, a couple of hours north of the city. The Catskills were still elite summer destinations in the seventies. Elizabeth Taylor and Richard Burton made the rounds, and once Bill Cosby flew in for a doubles match. If the Borscht Belt comedy scene was dwindling, the showmanship remained. The resorts advertised former pro-circuit players as instructors, flew in marquee champions for matches, and built A-frame roofs over their courts for twenty-four-hour all-weather play. Soon Gary started having ideas of his own: tennis as a party, a show, a brand.

Back in the city, Gary became Midtown's tennis director, hosting leagues and late-night tennis mixers with the kind of clientele who were connected to the press, who knew so-and-so at this newspaper or that magazine.

If he had a pet project, it wasn't long before he was talking it up in the papers.

The *Times* covered his singles mixers and the short-lived tennis shop he opened on Lexington Avenue, which sold collectors' items and gear for pros. *Newsday* did a write-up on his tennis-tip hotline. But in 1979, while he was director of the Central Park tennis courts, he received national attention for his signature gimmick: tying on a pair of roller skates and challenging sneaker-wearing players to a match for sixteen dollars a pop. *People* magazine's headline read, "The big wheels in tennis are Borg, McEnroe and Connors. Now meet Little Wheel Gary Wilensky," and featured a half-page photograph of Gary standing at the net in tennis shorts and roller skates. Though the first line of the article must have burned a little. "An aging tennis pro has got to hustle . . ." At the time, he was forty-one and his business was just beginning to take off.

By the next decade, Gary was selected, along with a handful of other coaches around the country, as a United States Tennis Association Master Professional—a title he'd later tack to the résumés on the back of his invoices.

Prince, the athletic company, had hired him to promote and

coach customers who purchased their special edition $1,000 rackets. "For the very serious player, that's not really so much," he told a UPI reporter.

By then he'd given up working for clubs as a tennis director—there was more money to be made renting out courts as an independent instructor. Though his dismissal from Midtown—where, according to one staffer, Gary tried turning fellow pros against his boss in order to take her job—likely contributed to the decision.

Between referrals from his adult students—some of whom enrolled their children in his junior program—and the growing roster of Manhattan girls he'd recruited working at camps up north, his client list grew.

By 1992, Gary Wilensky had narrowed his focus to younger players, firmly affixing himself as an Upper East Side institution. Now he does well for himself, pulling in a solid six figures. And occasionally he gives back, teaching underprivileged kids about the basics of tennis—a move that served him when he was called before a judge, four years back.

Still, he lives modestly. Ramshackle car. Rent-controlled apartment. Low overhead, minimal expenses, no family to support.

He spends his money like an adolescent with a new allowance—collecting vintage tennis memorabilia and costumes and ordering takeout food. Mostly he splurges on his students—doling out gag gifts, movie tickets, candy, and pizza dinners. Over time, his students have come to expect this. He's their Santa Claus, their Grandpa Gary. That's what the girls call him, though he's only fifty-six.

Fuddruckers, a chain of family-friendly burger joints, opened an outpost on the ground floor of his building. Planted out front is a yellow-and-blue mushroom, tall as any ten-year-old. It might as well be a dog whistle for kids. Gary hears it. Every now and then, he takes one or two students there for burgers and shakes. Afterward, he'll drop them off at home and drive back along Third Avenue—the night lit by a patchwork of storefronts still glowing from the inside.

At home, he peels back sticky labels printed with his phone number and the promise of a "new tip every day!"

Gary launched his tennis-tip hotline years ago, and it's still going strong. He records a new message on his answering machine every day. Usually he welcomes callers and offers pointers on the game, sprinkling his message with some patented Gary humor.

"Rhythm is very, very important," he once said in a recording on his hotline. "In tennis you have to synchronize the toss and the backswing. You must get the body to relax . . . Gynecologists may disagree, but rhythm works."

When his hotline was first covered in the papers—the *New York Times*, *Newsday*—he was mostly coaching adults and noodling around with new ways to drum up business. That was almost fifteen years ago. Now his target audience is kids.

When he presses his number onto index cards addressed to his students—Park Avenue, East Seventy-Second, East Eighty-First—he might think of the scrubbed prewar brickwork on their buildings and the glass doors that open for them when they run from his car, tennis rackets bumping at their sides.

He might picture the rest of what they call home: the clean, elegant foyers lit softly by Tiffany lamps leading to long oval dining tables blooming with centerpieces; the bedrooms with tucked-in sheets, ironed and folded underneath two propped pillows, crisply encased in white linen, waiting for hands, heads, and cheeks to press them down. And maybe on a desk beside the bed or pushpinned to a bulletin board overhead is the index card with his number on it. The phone, a portal from their home to his.

He stacks the index cards before dropping them in a mailbox.

In the morning, the Third Avenue bus rolls up outside his apartment building, releasing a gigantic sigh when its doors open. This is not the flashing, screeching, pummeling under-ground subway system that speeds from borough to borough, but a kinder, gentler MTA for the very old and the adolescents who have graduated from school bus to soft public transit.

Block letters request passengers reserve the seats closest to the driver for the elderly or the disabled.

Starting at seven A.M., students in kilts and blazers crowd into the M98. The bus crawls up Third Avenue, stopping along the Upper East Side where the private schools are clustered. Dalton, Nightingale-Bamford, Spence, Brearley.

They load inside, pushing each other's JanSports, flash-ing soft pink bus passes, hunchbacked from their textbooks, shuffle-stepping to the seats in the back, as far away from the adults as possible.

Somewhere among them is Gary Wilensky, perhaps slouched in one of the backseats, or gripping a silver bar overhead, scan-ning the new arrivals as they collect around him.

By the time the bus reaches Ninetieth Street near Gary's building, most of the kids have cleared out. An empty Snapple bottle might roll around on the rubber floor, or a hardened pink splotch of Bubblicious might stick to the edge of a blue seat. And beside it, a candy-colored strip of paper no bigger than an index finger, printed with a phone number. No name, no explanation, just seven numbers in a row—prank-call bait for anybody of a certain age with a certain sensibility.

He has written his number on colored paper and cut it into strips. They are scattered onto seats, waiting to be discovered. A clue in a scavenger hunt. The case of the mysterious phone number.

When he is gone, multiple bus riders will report finding these colored strips of paper, which trace back to Gary Wilensky's home phone. By then we will only assume what his intentions were. We will only imagine him lying in bed when the answering machine picks up, listening to the feathery sounds of their breathing.

girl: first lesson

ACROSS THE STREET FROM SCHOOL, BEHIND a Jaguar, is a weathered tan four-door sedan. Gary Wilensky leans against it.

"Congratulations. You made it onto Gary's tennis team," he says, his lips pursed as best they can around his massive rack of teeth. It's his facial signal, I can already tell, for sarcasm.

He opens the front passenger-side door, and extends his hand, fancy chauffeur-style.

There is a Styrofoam Whopper box on the backseat or there isn't, but it's that kind of car. The smell inside reminds me of putting my nose up to a plastic Silly Putty egg, of twisting the handle of a quarter-slot machine outside the grocery store and waiting for a toy to land.

"So where'd you play before?" We are driving now, turning left onto Eighty-Sixth Street. I watch two seniors in their kilts walk toward the bus stop. Through the car window, I can imagine not knowing them so intimately—the brown-haired one who wears a braided anklet and dates a Collegiate boy and her best friend, head of the literary magazine, who always clips her hair in a barrette, because if she wore it down it would be too puffy. From the car window, it's like watching them on TV. They are extras, just girls from a private school. Not even seniors, but simply teenagers. And I am a grown-up in the grown-up seat of the car.

"I was in the program at East River Tennis Club," I say.

"How'd you like it?"

I like sitting shotgun talking this way—it reminds me of watching my parents from the backseat, their elbow points touching on the armrest between them.

"It was okay, but the buses took forever and I didn't get home till super late." I'm trying to sound normal about the whole bus situation.

"That's the thing with that program—they overextend themselves," he says.

"Totally," I say, nodding to convince us both I understand what he's talking about.

"They take on too many students because they want to make the money, but you lose the quality that way," he continues.

More nodding. His words have already slipped from my short-term memory. I am preoccupied with the urge to tell him how trapped I felt on those bus rides, and the equally strong pull to keep my weird anxieties to myself. I bet he'd understand, or at least encourage my complaints. He has that gabby female quality that suggests he bonds through mutual disdain.

Gary reminds me of a Jewish aunt or one of my mother's more ethnic, older gal-friends—that wild energy of a middle-aged single woman in a caftan with a Bloody Mary buzz. It's that his voice isn't very low, or that he's knobby and thin, or it's his jerky, fluttering hand movements, the recklessly open-mouthed grin of someone who has settled into his own eccentricity as if it was a cushioned papasan chair.

"How many students do you have?" I ask.

"Not many. I coach the team over at Brearley, so I don't need to take on too much. Just the people I like."

He winks at me. Now he is a man again. Another relative—an uncle, tall and coarse-skinned, one who might lift me up when he greets me, and wink should he catch me sneaking a sip of my mother's wine. It's the kind of wink that makes you grateful. He knows your secret, but he won't tell.

We are at a stoplight. I kick my bag under my feet and spot an unopened bag of Big League Chew.

"You want to open that?" he asks.

I do.

"That's my favorite gum," he says. "You know why? Nobody tells you how much of it to eat. I like to take a big handful and just—" He pretends to be a donkey chewing, or maybe he just looks like one.

We pull up in front of the next private school. Two girls climb in the backseat—a brunette and a rusty-haired one, both attractive but not intimidatingly so. They don't have the breast-first swagger of a popular girl, and they smile, not in recognition of their own captivating beauty, but in the way that adults smile when they greet people. Like it's how their faces have been trained to react. As they say goodbye to a group of girls standing outside their school, I note that they're both normal in height—not too tall, not too short, like me.

I am shorter than most people my age, and am reminded of that fact often and by everyone. It is a characteristic that defines me. I am someone who didn't reach the right height, and this strikes people as funny. People lower their elbows onto my head to pretend I'm an armrest. There is a rumor among certain private school boys that I give blow jobs standing up. The rumor had to be explained to me as a jab at my height, but still, I am flattered that there is a rumor about me at all.

I wonder if these girls have heard the rumor, though I doubt it. They don't seem to be the kind of people who use the word *blow job* without whispering.

"Piper, this is Emma and Tara," Gary says after they pile into the backseat. When I turn around to nod hello, I see them thigh to thigh, passing a bag of gummy worms back and forth, and I wish I was in the backseat with them—a kid again.

"How long have you been playing with Gary?" I ask. It's an awkward question I immediately regret. I should have waited to ask it when Gary wasn't present. The rusty-haired girl, Tara, whom I recognize from Fire Island, answers first.

"Well, I've been with Gary, what would you say, since the beginning of fall?" she says. I wonder if she recognizes me, too. Our houses are on the same wood-paneled block, though we've never spoken before.

"Yup, since September. And Emma, you've been with me even longer." Gary eyes Emma through the rearview mirror.

"Yeah, I started when I was nine," she says in a quiet voice.

"She's one of my golden oldies," says Gary.

"Gary, put on the radio," Emma says, and he does.

"What channel do you want to hear?"

Z100, obviously. Mr. Big's "To Be With You" comes on and we all start reciting the lyrics.

"You don't like this song? I'll change the channel." He jokes. He wouldn't dare.

This is the kind of car where you can roll down the windows and loudly sing along to an overplayed pop song you would never even admit to liking if other people were present. It's a safe space where you don't have to try to impress or act mature. You are mature because you are in a car with an adult who's not really in charge. He likes candy, upper-body car-dance moves, rowdy sing-alongs, the breeze from a revved-up engine on Park Avenue, and the dare of a yellow light.

Red light. Gary taps on the case of a mixtape. "This is a good one," he says, but he doesn't play it. One of his older students made it for him. Her handwriting is small and bubbly, confident as any upperclassman.

I used to make mixtapes with my sister. We'd pretend to be DJs and introduce songs recorded off the radio. Then she stopped making them with me and started receiving them from boys. I memorized their track order and the names of who made each mix. I listened for secret messages in the lyrics. Love codes.

More music on the way to our lesson. Toad the Wet Sprocket. Guns N' Roses. P.M. Dawn. Blind Melon's "No Rain." The opening notes bounce through the car, which bounces over the rails of the 59th Street Bridge. I chuck more Big League in my mouth and chew harder.

The tennis bubble beneath the bridge looks poppable, and I blow one so big I can see the sign for Queens Boulevard through the pink scrim.

When we get out of the car, nobody says anything about my height. Gary walks in front of me and casts a slanted, narrow shadow.

Now we are girls changing in a locker room. We know how to pull our sports bras over our heads and under our shirts. We know when to turn away from each other, and when to peek over and see the bones in each other's backs. The arched bones of a miniature model dinosaur buried deep underneath cotton straps, underneath thin layers of skin dappled with pores that bleed teenage oil.

Inside the tennis bubble, Gary doesn't make us do suicides. We jump right into a game. He sets up pickup baskets on either side of the court and stands on the service line pelting us a forehand, a backhand, urging us to knock each basket down, in exchange for points. Winner gets a Ring Pop.

Then we accelerate. The balls start spreading out, coming at us faster, farther away, closer to the net, farther left or farther right. He fakes us out, making it look like he's going to hit the ball deep and then tapping it so lightly we have to dive to return it.

At the end of our lesson, we are giddy, sucking on Ring Pops as we exit the bubble. Gary rips open the Velcro flap of canvas, then unzips a plastic door. The court's tiny clay particles make their way down the back of my throat. Clay clouds tuft around my sneakers. My ears pop from the change in pressure as we each shoulder through the revolving door and return to the club's main lounge. The roar of fans that keep the tennis bubble puffed above our heads is replaced with low ceilings and the ooze of light jazz. Men in tennis wristbands and women in white skirts are folded into leather armchairs. Their happy-hour glasses of drowned cherries sweat through cardboard coasters. Behind two glass doors is an empty outdoor swimming pool— the color of Gary's windbreaker.

"Who wants shotgun?" Gary asks, a little too loudly. He is walking backward through the whisper-filled taupe and brown lounge, its conceit of maturity. He is a cannonball splash of neon—a childish disruption. I'm almost embarrassed until I see the lady at the front desk smiling, raising her hand for a high five. He slaps it and leads us out the front doors into the throbbing purple evening, where the wind inflates Gary's jacket like a wild turquoise balloon.

girl: self-defense

TWICE A WEEK, I WALK TO school with Bianca. We are two girls in a three-girl clique. The third girl is Sarah, who is tall and elegant, and who fits into her mother's silk jumpsuits. We are all fourteen. We know every lyric to the Pharcyde's "Passin' Me By." We smoke. We sit on stoops drinking Zimas purchased from a bodega with my sister's old ID, and wait for Bianca's pager to vibrate.

We ride taxis late at night, funneling through the Helmsley Building on Park between Forty-Fifth and Forty-Sixth into downtown territory until we reach a run-down Irish pub on Twenty-Ninth Street that doesn't card. Sometimes we try to slip past the door guy at Continental on St. Marks Place or Nightingale's between Twelfth and Thirteenth or Flamingo East on Second. Once we went to the SoHo loft of a boarding school boy who paged Bianca "58008." That spells *boobs* upside down.

More often, though, we walk up and down Park Avenue from Ninety-First to Seventy-Second Street searching for boys from other prep schools. When Bianca's pager lights up, we find a pay phone on Lexington and she figures out where everyone has gone—usually somewhere in the Seventies between Park and Lex or on the steps of the Met Museum.

Recently, a crowd of prep school kids gathered on Seventy-Second Street, hugging one another and bumming cigarettes. We met a boy who lived across the street from our school. His hair was short and blond, and he had a pinched face like Pee-wee Herman's, only more serious. He spoke quietly from behind his hand when we asked where he went to school and who he knew that we knew, too. Then everyone ran into the street to hail cabs, because we heard that someone just got mugged. In the cab Bianca said, "I think he liked you."

So now we leave for school a half hour early and wait in a nearby diner in case he walks by on the way to his bus stop.

When Bianca picks me up outside my building, she is wearing a peacoat and standing on her tippy-toes with one arm out in first position. Ever since last month, when she signed up for the dance elective, she's developed this new affectation of practicing ballet, so that her long, lean limbs swing in front of my eyes when I'm trying not to think about them. Another distracting thing about Bianca is her hair, which is textured with golden streaks, cut to her breast, and smooth as the silk camisoles in my mother's closet. If I had her hair, I'd be closer to beautiful. And her eyelashes, too. They are exceptionally long, but when anyone points this out, she sighs and says, "I know, it sucks."

She never brags, even when something good happens. Everything is a "disaster"; she is always "the most" embarrassed, "the biggest" fuckup, or the "ugliest person alive." The opposite is true, but sometimes I'm fooled into thinking we're the same. I try to remember that when she says she failed the history test, she means she got a B. When she says a boy doesn't like her, she means he hasn't called yet, but he will. When she says a boy likes me, she means she's not interested in him.

"We're wearing the same thing," she says when she sees me in my peacoat, which is big and bulky and purchased from

an army-navy store. Hers is from the women's coat section of
Bloomingdale's.

Last year I didn't notice these slight differences, but now
I'm aware of every small thing that makes her better than me.
"She just has that sparkle," my mom said when I told her that
Bianca was elected to student government. A sparkle is a thing
you can't get; either you have it or you don't. It's like fairy dust,
which is what my mom says my sister has with boys. "She just
sprinkles it on them, and they fall in love."

It's a twenty-five-minute walk from Park Avenue to East End
Avenue. We used to stop for cream-filled doughnuts on Lexington and chocolate cat tongues on Second Avenue, making up
celebrity fantasies grounded in logistical facts along the way.
Meeting Leonardo DiCaprio at his regular spot, Club USA;
meeting Robert Sean Leonard outside his show at Lincoln
Center; meeting the guy from *The Heights*, because someone
we know had met him before. New York City girls meet celebrities all the time. There was the girl in my sister's class who
was friends with the Spin Doctors, another who claimed she
met Matt Dillon in a bar. In our version, the encounter usually
begins with a description of our outfits, and ends with a chosen
celebrity picking one of us up at school so everyone can see.

Lately, though, our walks have changed. Now we get iced
coffees and talk about real boys who call Bianca on the phone at
night. Then we talk about our mothers.

Today Bianca is in a fight with hers. Something about a late-
night phone call and her mother getting on the line to say something embarrassing to a boy.

"Seriously, my mother is crazy," one of us always says.

Crazy is what we call our mothers, and we know what we mean. We mean we can't always predict their responses. We mean that sometimes their voices get low and their teeth clench, so that when we look in their eyes we can see that they hate us.

Our mothers are friends, part of an inner circle of moms from our school who on occasion take over our living room, clank glasses, speak in hushed voices, and after their glasses are refilled, erupt in laughter. Down the hallway, in my bedroom, I'll listen for the whispered sound of my name.

Bianca and I are halfway to school and our rolled-up skirts are riding up our waists. We wear sheer black tights on our legs. Foundation on our skin. Sunflowers perfume our necks.

All down Second and Third Avenues, we are followed by hissing sounds. Tongues against teeth. *Psst, psst.* A stout man with bullet eyes watches as we pass him. "Sexy," I think he says, but I can't be sure.

"Eyes, eyes!" I shout, making hooks with my fingers and gouging out the eyes of a person who doesn't exist. This is a joke reference to something we learned in our self-defense class.

This semester a special trainer comes in once a week during PE to teach us to respond to threats of violence, which are everywhere, we're told. We see the headlines in newspaper kiosks on the street. "Nightmare in Central Park." "Ripped Apart a Child with His Hands." "East Side Teen Arrested in Park Rape-Slaying." We hear the local news stories: the Central Park Jogger, the Preppy Killer, Etan Patz, Joel Steinberg, muggings, shootings, stabbings, child abuse, kidnapping, rape, date rape. People on the subways with syringes filled with

AIDS. *Watch out,* we're warned. *They watch you walking in your uniforms; they know where you come from.*

Some girls have drivers pick them up from school because their parents are afraid they'll be snatched away. I'm not one of those girls, but still, my mother warns me, *There are people out there who want what you have.* She is a link on a chain of calls between mothers about the latest prep school kid mugged or attacked on the Upper East Side. They all blur into her stern warning, her index finger shaken in the air. "You travel in groups," she says. "You don't walk through Central Park at night. You take taxis when it gets dark." She has the doormen put me in cabs and write down the taxi number. "You can never be too careful," she says and I wonder what kind of violence she imagines in her mind.

WHEN YOU learn about stranger danger as a child, you learn that other people want you, but nobody ever explains why. Now, when you are a teenager, it becomes clearer. The teacher's ruler to our kilt hems, the assessments of our clothing as "too short" and "too tight." I recognize this paranoia and what it's about. The fear of showing off what you have, the certainty that others will steal from you if they see it—that's wealth, but ours is a different kind.

Our currency is our bodies. We have what others want, what they feel they deserve. At school, we trade stories of being groped by strangers, and boast of what we'll do the next time it happens: kick him in the balls—that is always our revenge plan.

But when a Rollerblader glided downstream along Lexington Avenue, stopping short to cup my chest, all I did was laugh. Not a real laugh, but a noise Band-Aid reserved for moments of shock—to normalize a situation, to shake off any bubbling emotions, to show I'm not afraid, but not mad either. In fact I was both, but fear outweighed the anger and paralyzed any confrontational impulse I might have. When the fear subsided and the Rollerblader was long gone, I was mad again, this time at myself for being such a coward.

There are two kinds of perpetrators: those strangers on the street and those you already know. All of them are men. Strangers lurk in public spaces or follow you down side streets, while those you know could be anywhere.

A girl in my school dated Robert Chambers, the teenager who strangled another girl he knew in the park. My mother set up my cousin on a blind date with our neighbor, a man who murdered a woman a few years later. A doorman was supposedly running a cocaine operation in the basement of our old building.

"You never know who anyone is," my mother said when she told me about the doorman. I remembered the gold flash of his eagle-shaped belt buckle underneath his uniform, as if it were a clue.

The first thing we learn in self-defense is to use our house keys as a weapon to poke out the eyes of an attacker. "And if you don't have your keys handy, you can use your two index fingers," our instructor says, curling her fingers into talons. Then we line up one by one, run to the red line, and scream, "Eyes, eyes!" or "Nose, nose!" bumping an imaginary nose bone straight into imaginary brain matter with our two palms.

We learn to squirm out of someone's hold when he is dragging us by our hair, flipping our bodies like fish, then finishing him off with a knee between the legs. We partner up and practice on each other, miming each movement without actually making contact, all the time screaming the names of body parts, as if the words alone could set us free.

But I have a secret: The steak knife I stole from the kitchen butcher block is buried in the zipper pocket of my book bag. When I'm alone on the street, I slide my hand into the pocket and grip the plastic handle. *Downright dangerous*, I think to myself.

At the diner across the street from school, Bianca and I slide into a window booth. Two coffees. Plain English muffin for Bianca. Toasted corn muffin for me. We each light a cigarette. She smokes Marlboro Lights. I'm experimenting with Capris, the super-thin kind that are only the circumference of a cocktail straw.

Bianca takes a drag and I fixate on her tongue—a strawberry budding in her mouth—where it has been, what it has known. I'm bothered by the way it brags in her mouth, all red and glistening.

Another one of our differences: I don't know what it feels like to be kissed, and Bianca does. I was there for one of her first times with the popular boy on his rooftop.

There were three boys, all from the same co-ed private school in Riverdale. Two of them went to our Hebrew school, which is how Bianca landed us the invitation to sit on the roof of a building and sip wine coolers we brought, while the boys swigged on forty-ounces and bummed our cigarettes.

We played the name game.

"Do you know Eddie Falcone?"

"Yup, he's in my class. Do you know Alix Cunningham?"

"She's in the grade above us, so we know her, but we don't hang out."

"She's really cool."

One boy hit the other boy's side and they both collapsed in laughter at a private joke about Alix Cunningham and something beautiful she must have done.

Alix's name appears on some of the flyers for prep school nightclub parties, which means she's popular not just in her school, but throughout the network of prep schools. The flyers are for parties at rented-out nightclub venues, and they usually feature a rotating roster of about twenty-five names—similar to the charity gala invitations our parents receive, only these invitations have neon writing and black backgrounds. The names of the hosts are written in a larger font. The hosts corral the committee of VIP names that fill up the rest of the card in smaller writing. There is a ten- or twenty-dollar entry fee for most of these parties, but if you're on the flyer, of course, it's free. You are part of the attraction, like a celebrity guest.

"Wanna see the other side of this roof?" the popular boy asked Bianca. He reminded me of Montgomery Clift, an old Hollywood actor whose biography my mother keeps by her bed. Both of their noses had the slightest hook at the tip. Only, Clift had dark, slicked-back hair and wore a blazer and tie. This boy wore baggy jeans with a hooded pullover and had blond hair that parted in the middle. When he ran his hand through it, which he did often, two golden streaks formed curtains around his green eyes.

He put his arm around Bianca's shoulders and walked her around a corner behind a vent so they were out of view. The two other boys laughed at more private jokes while Sarah and I pretended to look at the skyline.

"Is that the Chrysler Building?" I asked, not looking directly at either of the boys, but hoping they would answer.

"What? I don't fucking know."

Sarah rolled her eyes to let me know they were stupid, not me. Still, I wished I could have taken back the noises I made. I hate calling attention to myself when I have the shakes. I get them in the presence of boys. I have to ball my fists to keep my hands still, but the wire that runs through my body still vibrates as if it has been plucked.

When Bianca emerged from behind a vent, the boy was holding her by the wrist and she was chewing on the side of her mouth to keep from smiling. That night I noticed, even in the darkness, how red her tongue was. The color of a lipstick-kiss stain, the mark of a woman, lolling about inside her.

"I think I see him," says Bianca, looking through the diner window for the boy who might like me. "Oh, wait, forget it."

Outside, a tree shakes itself off. An old woman with a walker inches across the street.

"We need a plan if we see him," she says, arranging Sweet'N Low packets into a pyramid on the table. "I don't know—should we wave at him? Maybe we should wave at him to come inside?"

"Let's pretend we're busy talking and see if he notices us," I say, because I'm good at impersonating someone having a conversation. There's a lot of wrist flicking and shrugging involved, but the words don't matter.

"So I'm talking and you're talking, and yes, that's amazing, but no, I'm shaking my head no."

We crack up. We hope the boy walks by right now and sees us cracking up, engaged in our own lives instead of his.

"Anything else for you two girls?" the waiter, Anthony, asks, but he knows the answer.

"Anthony hates us," Bianca says when he walks away.

Our half-smoked cigarettes burn in the ashtray. A kitchen bell dings twice. The cash register opens. There are muffin crumbs all over my kilt.

"He isn't coming," I say, calling it. It's almost eight; he would have left by now. He took another route to the bus stop or he left early. We need to get here earlier. And now another day is about to start without any boys. There is nothing to think about during class. No change. Nothing different.

After school, I walk the dog all the way back to East End Avenue and cross the street on the block where the boy lives. I have done this before, standing outside his apartment in the evening willing him to come outside, but Bianca doesn't know that.

Back and forth, back and forth, along a block paved with hexagons. The dog sniffs each PLEASE CURB YOUR DOG sign staked in tree soil. Behind us, all the lights are out in the mayor's mansion. I watch for shapes behind the wrought-iron leaves of the boy's door. Come out, come out, come out.

I don't even know if I'd say anything to him. I probably

wouldn't. But if I could see him, then maybe he'd see me and want to talk, and ask for my number so we could talk more, and I could go home and tell Bianca and tell my mother, and then maybe she would think I had fairy dust, too.

When the sun sags low, the dog and I give up and walk west, past York, First, then Second Avenues. *Psst, psst.* I keep my head down and wind the leash around my fist.

Now it's Third Avenue, then Lexington, with more buildings with wrought-iron doors, and behind them, men with white gloves gripping their handles from the inside. On Park, the sky is almost navy and light pools under every awning. I look up when I hear someone tapping glass and squint to see through the building's door. There, behind the glass, is a man's white-gloved hand, folded in the shape of a gun, pointing at me.

girl: good

WE EAT DINNER ON THE KITCHEN island. The three of us—my mother, my father, and I—are a revised unit now that my sister has moved upstate for college.

Dad burps a ketchup bottle. Mom nukes a roasted chicken in the microwave and tongs the steaming limbs of the bird onto our plates. She reminds my father, before he takes a bite of a leg, to chew with his mouth closed.

He waves her off and proceeds to chew any way he pleases. Behind my parents' mutual agitation is a romance. They match each other in stubbornness, a trait stemming from their equally matched ambition and confidence. I used to think they were related. It was strange to discover they weren't. Both were raised in Queens by immigrant parents who stowed away in boats to get here. Mom was middle class, Dad was poor, but neither knew any different. Public schools, state colleges, night school, studying, working, watching, always narrowing in on the goal of Manhattan, cracking the code of a certain privilege they'd seen only from a distance. Hardworking Jews, yes, but still white. The barriers were there, but not in the same way they are for others. The law firm my father had started with a near-empty bank account had flourished. My mother's constant monitoring of the real estate market had paid off. And now we live here. *Play to Win*. If my mother could needlepoint this motto on a pillow, my father would rest his head against it.

"Did you get your science test back?" Mom asks me.

"Not yet." That is a lie. I got a C−. My plan is to continue this lie until she forgets to ask again.

"So guess who just called?" she says, taking a chipmunk bite of meat off the bone.

"Who?" Dad and I harmonize.

She recoils at the holes in our faces stuffed with meat.

"You and your father, chew first, then talk . . . What was I saying?" She pushes back the thin curtain of bangs from her forehead. Her forehead glistens with sweat and Clinique bronzer. "Oh, Gary called."

"Who's Gary?" Dad asks. He's eating corn on the cob now and has a constellation of kernels stuck to his mustache.

"Her tennis coach!" There are two things my dad does that exasperate my mother. One is the way he eats, the way we both eat, as if our entire faces were mouth holes. The other is when he can't remember names—she's an encyclopedia of who's who, especially when it has to do with her girls. Right now he is pulling a double.

"Why were you talking to Gary?" I ask. I have been playing with him for only a few weeks, but I've never heard him call my mom before with progress reports.

"He called because he thinks you could benefit from playing a second day of the week," she says, and then turns to my father. "Don't make a face," she scolds. "It's not going to cost anything. He's offering to coach her an extra day a week for free."

"Why would he do that?" asks Dad.

"Why would he do . . . Because she's good! She's good! He called her a promising player—that's what he said—and thinks she might be able to get on the tennis team in the spring."

"Mom, there's no way." Tennis is the hardest team to get on at school. It's a small group of juniors and seniors; only rarely does a freshman makes the cut.

"If you practice, you could. Gary said so. Listen, you'd still play with him during the week, but he'd also coach you on Saturdays—just you and Emma. And afterward, he'll take you out to lunch. How does that sound?"

"He thinks I'm that good?"

"She's good, huh?" says Dad, resting his chicken bone on his plate, to pump his fist and expel a pride-laugh.

I garble out a chicken-stuffed laugh, too.

"She's good," my mother says, reaching across the kitchen island to squeeze my arm. "She's really good."

Here I am, a winner.

2015

archivists, exes, dead people

THE LONG ISLAND I KNOW IS all synagogues and reception halls—a flat suburban sprawl of Jewish celebration and mourning. So many times in the backseat of my parents' car, black tights on tan leather, holding my sister's hand as my father drove the long bean of the LIE—my mother on the passenger side, a perfumery of nerves. An argument outside the car, a combustible silence once inside. *Shit, we're late.* In those moments, she didn't have to say it; I could read her mind.

Now, years later, alone in a different car, the same broccoli trees lining the expressway, the same stop-and-start traffic, the whiff of dead relatives buried along the sidelines, all echo the same mantra: *Shit, we're late.*

The exit for Roslyn is on the right, and I am wrong in thinking I have been here before. Two miles off the highway the trees are looser; their branches shimmy and hang low. A sandstone and granite clock tower etched with the words *She fell asleep* mark the very top of the town followed by a slip of eateries and shops, housed in Colonial- and Victorian-era architecture.

The village center gleams with spotless redbrick sidewalks and freshly painted historic storefronts—a microscopic Hamptons minus the Ralph Laurens and Citarellas. Instead, we have YOLO, the yogurt shop; Yuzu, the sushi restaurant; Transitions, a boutique where the clothes are high-priced and relaxed-fit. From a distance, they all look like quaint country markets.

"Read the fucking sign." A man in his fifties, with a sweater around his shoulders, points to the STOP FOR PEDESTRIANS placard.

It's been a week since I visited Gary Wilensky's old apartment building in Manhattan. The once-subsidized housing development has been converted to a condominium. The Fuddruckers is a gym. The doormen are now called concierges. I talked to one man who had worked in the building when Gary Wilensky was alive. He said he knows everyone who's come in and out since he began. "Are you sure he lived here?" he asked.

I've come to Roslyn, where Gary spent his teenage years, to visit the town library, keeper of the yearbooks. I meet with an archivist in a wood-paneled room at the top of a staircase. Light from two half-moon windows illuminates dust particles. Portraits of local figures and historical maps hang on the walls. An academic calm separates this attic archive room from the library's metallic, childproofed main area downstairs. The whispers up here feel more reverent than enforced. This is a room full of history, the traces of dead things, which must be preserved by hushed voices and delicate fingertips.

I tell the archivist I'm looking for a man who lived here in the fifties. I write *Gary Wilensky* on a paper square, and beneath his name, *Roslyn High School, Class of 1956*.

From a corner shelf, she pulls out what looks to be a photo album—a small rectangular book with a puffy blue cover embossed in gold lettering. It's his senior yearbook. I've seen excerpts from it in old magazines and newspapers. I'd expected it to be bigger for some reason.

I want the archivist to go away so I can be alone with the book. She sits down beside me and looks through a binder with vintage newspaper clippings. I could shake out his photograph as if I were shaking a piggy bank with one coin trapped inside, but this is not a room for children. So I flip through the pages delicately, lingering on the formalities—the dedication to a teacher, the introductory farewell to the senior class.

Each senior's photo is tilted faux haphazardly and pinned to an illustration of a bulletin board. The class is not large. I spot two names I recognize, two of Gary's friends who were quoted in articles about him twenty-odd years ago. Both are described in the yearbook as "dark and handsome"; one is "Ivy League," the other, "smart as a whip."

"Smart as a whip" is Neal Pilson, now a retired network president. On the phone, he recalled driving in Gary's car on a double date and playing basketball together in the schoolyard. He remembered Gary as short but mature, older than the rest of their group of friends. Popular among his classmates, celebrated for his basketball and dancing skills, but never the leader of a group. "He had a surface confidence, but we all understood he was uncertain," Pilson said.

Some of the pages of the yearbook stick together, but when I get to W, the book flattens out, pressed by a copy machine, I imagine.

Someone was here before me, a reporter on deadline in 1993 assigned to dig up information on Gary Wilensky before moving on to the next story. Woody Allen. Michael Jackson. Monica Seles.

I imagine when he whipped into the library, the archivist must have rustled about, propelled by the mere presence of a man who knows what he wants and hasn't any time to waste. If he asked questions, they were few and all the right ones.

Under the table, I lift one swampy heel out of a black pump. I wore pumps and a long schoolteacher skirt so I would look serious, like a grown-up, even though I am a grown-up. Thirty-seven is definitely a grown-up. Thirty-seven is the age of news anchors, congressmen, political speechwriters, parents of middle school children, crime reporters. *Be a grown-up. Be the reporter.*

Here is the picture that brought us both to Roslyn: Gary at eighteen, just a few years older than I was when I knew him. His hair is slicked back with a werewolf's hairline creeping down his forehead. He wears a thin tie with tiny daggers on it. His chin is slightly lowered to downplay his devil's jawline. His expression is gentlemanly, in control—as if he's nodding at the cameraman to go ahead and take the picture, he's ready. He is almost handsome.

Next to the picture is a biography penned by classmates. The first word used to describe him: *argumentative*. Other words follow: *poet, witty character, terrific dancer, tennis and Ping-Pong champ*, and the name of a classmate he used to dance with.

She is fair-haired and lovely in a prim 1950s teenage way, described in the yearbook as a dazzling blonde whose passions are dancing and *Gary Gary Gary*. Together they were named Best Dancers. In a photo accompanying this honor, Gary dips her. She looks nervous, enchanted, giggling up at him. He has one hand on her back, suspending her above the floor, and another clutching her hand, drawing it over their heads forcefully. He is stone-faced, looking directly at the camera rather than at his dance partner. In another photo, they are competing in a bandstand dance-off. Her face is obscured by his long jagged profile. On another page of the yearbook, the class's last will and testament, the pair "leave their acrobatic dancing steps to anyone with the muscles to try them."

Throughout the rest of the book there are pictures of Gary shooting a basketball, standing in the back line of the tennis team, surrounded by a half-dozen girls as editor of the school newspaper. They all show a serious, guarded-looking young man—not at all the class clown I imagined him to be.

"Do you want to know where he lived?" the archivist asks me. She's found Gary's old address. It's just a few blocks up Main Street. I stop at Shish Kebab Grill on the way there. Forking a baba ghanoush sandwich up Old Northern Boulevard, I remember I have cousins who live in Roslyn. If I see them, I will have to explain why I drove thirty miles out of the city to look at photos of a dead man. I'm thinking of writing a book, I will say. Or I will pretend I don't see them.

I've done this before, walked past someone I knew, pretending to be engaged in a focal point to the right or left of his or her face, bracing myself for the moment the person says my name, deflated when he or she doesn't. It's both a paralysis of indecision and a deep insecurity that my face is not recognizable enough to be differentiated from other humans.

Gary's old apartment complex takes up an entire block on either side of Main Street, a few blocks in between the school and the village. The red brick has browned over time and the white icing between the brickwork is ash-gray. Inside there is no common area, just two green doors and institutional-looking stairs that lead to the second-floor apartments.

I walk two blocks north toward the high school, and if you discount the 7-Eleven, the surrounding Victorian homes and manicured walkways make it easy to imagine living here during the Eisenhower era, when an eighteen-year-old Gary Wilensky, with his heavy brow and puffed-up chest, with his tie of tiny swords, walked down this very street. Not the handsomest boy in school, though substantial. An upperclassman, certainly. The basketball star. The best dancer in Roslyn High. *Argumentative.*

It was his temperament that took his friends by surprise—the potential to flip his mood. The danger of underestimating Gary might result in a hostile encounter on the basketball court or worse. A Roslyn High classmate remembers the day one of Gary's girlfriends came to school with a bruised eye. When asked about it, she had said Gary did it, and it wasn't the first time.

I reached out to the high school girlfriend, who would now be in her late seventies, but never heard back. Many are reluctant to speak about Gary, considering the circumstances surrounding his death.

I don't blame anyone for this. I also tried to drown out his memory in the years that followed, but eventually he sprung to the surface.

It was 2008. I was driving to a college reunion with an old boyfriend, Michael. We were both in our early thirties. He was a poet and I worked for a tabloid newspaper. We were hunting for meaning or something to do. A story we could write together about our college experience, the place we fell for each other but never dated, and now here we were heading back to Baltimore.

We traded benign college memories—the frat party where

pledges swallowed live goldfish, the film professor who smoked on the Gilman Hall steps—but were soon onto the more tragic. Addiction, suicide attempts, a murder on campus.

At a Delaware tollbooth, I handed Michael a crumpled five-dollar bill. Then I mashed my palm flat over the door lock—thwarting a sudden impulse to open the door and run. A capsule had been pierced in my brain, and now a memory leaked out. A man in a trench coat with his collar turned up.

Gary Wilensky. I said his name. *Gary Wilensky.*

The syllabic combination, the roll of the tongue, so familiar, so reminiscent of a time I'd buried away, I wanted to keep saying it.

"I have a story, but it didn't happen to me," I told Michael, though I didn't remember exactly what the story was. I knew something terrible had happened, involving a plastic blow-up doll and shackles and a wheelchair. I knew Gary Wilensky was dead, and for a moment I missed him.

Later in the trip, I sat in a campus coffee shop and watched Michael across the street dwarfed by a sculpture of Native American lacrosse players. One bronze player loomed over him, penny-green stick poised to smash his head. Michael leaned against it and scribbled poetry. Again I thought of Gary, a drawing of him in a magazine, dressed in a trench coat, arm raised above his head brandishing . . . What was it? A flashlight? A baton? A cattle prod.

"This is stupid," I'd said when Michael suggested we each describe the statue in our notebooks. "I'll wait for you at the coffee shop."

We'd been arguing the entire weekend. First when my car

was towed, then in front of the statue, and later in a campus parking lot.

"What *is* your problem?" Michael asked, hands stiff in his coat pockets.

"This isn't the story I want to write," I said, because I was frustrated. I had questions that couldn't be answered here, with him. I had a thought that needed to be completed, and everything that didn't involve that thought was a distraction.

"Well, what do you want to write about?" he asked, exasperated.

"Gary Wilensky," I said. I wanted to keep saying his name.

"But I can't write that with you," he said, throwing up his hands. "That's your story. I'm not in that one."

This was how we broke up, in a Baltimore parking lot, arguing about another man. He was right. I wanted to do my own thing, to shake loose the obligation of partnership, to be as alone as I was when I was fourteen. I wanted to be that girl, not this one.

Years later, still alone, I have driven in another car to Roslyn to dig up remnants of Gary Wilensky's past. I am a reporter, I tell myself, because that is better than being a person with an obsession.

I am prone to obsessions. I know this. I fixate on one person compulsively. It is a brand of OCD that involves putting my eyes on every word or image pertaining to a specific person in order to feel in control of other parts of my life.

Jim Morrison came first. It was an obvious choice, an early teenage cult-follower move, spurred on by newbie sexuality and Oliver Stone. Though the obsession was less romantic than it was relentlessly mathematical—always counting the number of pictures of him that belonged to me; always memorizing his poetry, each unscripted moan in his songs; running through the encyclopedic collection in my head; believing that I could put him back together if I just had all the parts. And years later, when I was too old for it to be cute, the target was Keith Moon. Same thing—all the pictures, all the books and stories. Not even the music, this time, but the famed antics, and the photographs of his sticky bangs, his wild, puckish eyes, his glorious, mythologized self-destruction. For a year, I counted the pictures of him on Google Images until I could fall asleep each night.

The infusion of a dead man into my daily routine felt safe and made me less lonely, less desirous of real partnership. It made me feel in control of someone who was legendarily uncontrollable, and in effect braver, more in touch with the wildness inside of me.

By this point, I have spent months coming up with new search terms to enter into a borrowed Nexus account, variations of Gary's name misspelled, and feeling with each discovery—a *Geraldo* transcript! A 1984 UPI article!—that flimsy dopamine drip that squelches from the brain when an addiction has become routine. *More.*

I have already read everything about him on the Internet, which is strange in itself. Had his crime taken place now, there would be personal accounts from his students on social media, essays with click-bait headlines, a Facebook group, perhaps a hashtagged collection of photographs on Instagram.

Instead, the trail of Gary Wilensky on the Internet is led

by two *New York Times* articles and a few archived magazine pieces, a mention of his name in a book about the Catskills, another in a book about predators, and another in a lighthearted book about camp.

He is dead in the truest sense, obsolete, which must rankle his ghost. Alive, Gary Wilensky tacked Gary Wilensky's name on everything—T-shirts, magazine ads, newspaper articles. Dead Gary is barely a few pages on Google.

Nobody cares about him anymore, which makes the fact that I do, feel more significant. The difference between this obsession and the others is that I knew him. I was alive when he was alive. We sat between armrests and breathed the same trapped air. It's different because any worshipfulness I had for him was in the past, and any obsession I have for him now is more inquisitive. I believe that this obsession, this time, could be productive, legitimately enlightening, if I can just stay grounded in the facts.

Here is a fact: In April of 1993, the reporter called. I chewed the rubber coil and paced the white kitchen tile answering his questions. My mother listened on the other side of the swinging kitchen door.

A week later, I found the eight-page *New York* magazine article, "Break Point: A Tennis Coach's Fatal Obsession," on a coffee table in the living room. It opened to a photograph of a life-sized doll with yellow skin and a painted red mouth, slack and open.

Everything but her head was deflated. She was flesh-toned and flattened, folded up from the knees, arms crossed at her chest. But her head was round and human-sized, made of hard rubber, topped with bristly yellow hair that curled at her temples. One of her eyelids was lazily half closed as if she'd been drinking.

"A rubber sex doll found in the cabin," read the caption.

I stared at her until my mother took the magazine away.

"You'll finish this later."

Twenty-odd years later, I did. When I returned from the college reunion, I visited my parents and said Gary Wilensky's name.

My mother placed a finger to her lips and got up from her bed where we'd been sitting. She walked over to her desk, opened the bottom drawer, and removed a blue file folder with his name on it.

Between the flat planes of cardboard was a stack of jaundiced folded newspapers, a brittle *Newsweek* magazine, two invoices for tennis lessons, each with a résumé printed in blue ink on its backside, an index card stamped with the red outline of teddy bears and Disney characters holding Valentine's heart-shaped messages: *Luv U Lots. Be Mine.* On the opposite side of the card was my address, Gary's return address, and a label with the number for his tennis-tip hotline. Resting beneath the Valentine was the *New York* magazine article with the photograph of the blow-up doll. A startling image, still, so many years later.

My mother, the collector, the archivist, the character in the movie who catalyzes the hunt for the killer with a bread-crumb trail of old tabloid headlines. All through my teens and twenties I would scavenge her room when she was away, rifling through cabinets for old prescriptions, jewelry boxes for stale weed, bureaus for packaged tights, and desk drawers—that same drawer—for the manila folder where she kept photographs of two men she almost married who weren't my father. The evidence that she was a young woman once, and I almost wasn't. Strange how I never discovered the folder with Gary Wilensky's name scripted in ballpoint pen until the need to claim her property had been replaced by the need to cultivate my own. All I had to do was ask.

I sprawled out on her bed to read the *New York* magazine reporter's story on the life and death of Gary Wilensky. I looked for my name, but found only penciled-in brackets around two paragraphs on the third page of the six-page article. Brief impressions of Gary from an unnamed student who witnessed his mood shift in his final weeks.

I examined Gary's old invoices, billing my mother for lessons once a week.

"Didn't he coach me twice a week?" I asked her.

"That's right," said my mother. "I paid for the weekday lessons, but Saturdays were free."

"They were free? Why were they free?" I asked.

"Because he thought you were good. He told me so. He wanted to get your game to the next level."

"Don't you think that's weird, Mom?"

"No, you were good," she insisted.

There was the folder with the whole truth about Gary Wilensky laid out on her bed. And still there was some leftover pride separate from the facts, a preserved memory of a phone call between a tennis coach and a mother about a daughter who was special. A part of her still wanted to believe him. A part of me wanted to, as well.

1992

man: portrait

FOLDED IN A BOX INSIDE A studio apartment on Ninety-First Street is a pile of Gary Wilenskys. All of them swinging rackets. All of them pressed in blue ink onto XL Hanes T-shirts.

He'd gone to a caricature artist—the kind who draws oversize grinning heads on pin-thin bodies, a portrait style once reserved for celebrity patrons of Sardi's and now churned out for tourists on the street. It works like this: In exchange for twenty dollars and ten minutes of your time, the complexities of your identity are boiled down to one or two pronounced facial features and a reference to your favorite activity. The result is a blueprint for the dime-store mask of you—the one someone else could wear to pretend to be you. All long-jawed, horsefaced you.

This is how Gary Wilensky would like to be remembered—drawn in blue ink with a Looney Tunes grin, chin dripping from his face, perched on a pile of tennis books with a racket in one hand. He's stamped the image on postcards and flyers promoting his junior tennis program—adopting it as his logo and his brand identity. This cartoon version of Gary, so strikingly similar to the real man that kids who've never met him can recognize him on the street. He has his students to thank for the free promotion. Each one gets a shirt with his likeness emblazoned on the front.

When he dropped off the portrait at the T-shirt printers, he requested that the words *Gary's Girls—Hot Hitters* appear over his head. And below his feet he asked for this: *Big Apple, USA*. There's another version of the shirt that replaces *Hot Hitters* with *Awesome Swingers*. Perhaps someone complained, or he needed a gender-neutral option for his occasional, though now rare, male student.

Mostly they're for his girls. A token of the private club they've joined as members of his program. It matters to them. Gary learned this at camp.

Come June, the New York State Thruway is an express pipeline leading private school girls away from the hard angles of New York City to the lush overgrown upstate forestland.

He was used to getting out of the city in the summer. He'd done the resort scene in the Catskills and then the Poconos. But in the late eighties, when he landed his first gig teaching tennis at Point O'Pines, an all-girls camp in the Adirondack Mountains, something clicked.

Each summer Gary would load up his car and drive along the highway, four hours alone with his own mind, until the road narrowed, the sun fell away, and the mountains rose like whale humps in a black ocean. That meant he was close.

Point O'Pines is on its own peninsula lapped by a lake, staked with pine trees and white clapboard cabins. In their uniform of blue shorts, girls flood the area, popping open their trunks, laying out their bedsheets, rolling their sleeves up to their shoulders, aiming at a bull's-eye, pulling on a sail, pushing against the lake with an oar, flinging their arms around each other, belting out the songs they'd memorized the year before, whispering secrets, formulating opinions, playing all the games girls play.

The tennis program had long been a benchmark of the curriculum. There were plenty of strong players and a few exceptional ones cocking their rackets on the clay courts.

But when Gary wheeled in on his roller skates, a tennis skirt over his tree-branch thighs, he became the star of the courts. Costumes, prizes, private jokes—he was a mobile arcade, a one-man show. Everyone wanted to be in his orbit, whether they were good players or not.

They competed for candy, a coveted commodity for the younger girls, and for the older ones—maybe a secret pizza party? A dirty joke? Of course, they all wanted to win those Gary's Girls shirts.

A few years later, when he was set to arrive in Maine, at Tripp Lake, another girls' camp with uniforms, city kids, and a prestigious tennis program, he had a new idea. In addition to Gary's Girls shirts, he packed his car with trucker hats printed with the words *Player of the Day*, along with T-shirts that read *Player of the Week*, all of them custom made for his campers. After each lesson, he'd choose one winner—someone who had played her hardest, showed promise, or just captured his attention—and gather everyone around to crown her with a hat. The weekly T-shirt ceremonies were an even bigger coup. Everyone wanted to be the player of the week. Girls took pictures of each other in their prized shirts and paraded around camp.

Of course it was a hit. All those girls wore the same exact uniforms until Gary came along and offered them a chance to be different. If you're the kid allowed to wear something special, something you earned, you win the popularity contest. Game over.

It helped that he'd upped the ante on his own costumes as well. Tutus, wigs, full drag, clown noses. That got their attention, but the player pageant really clinched the deal. As the master of ceremonies, Gary saw his stock soar.

Then when parents came to visit, the campers made sure to introduce them to their favorite instructor. That's when he'd tell the mothers how promising their daughters were and maybe drop a mention of his tennis program back in the city. He wasn't pushy. It was always posed as a suggestion—it was up to them if their kids wanted to continue training with him.

Between Point O'Pines and Tripp Lake, Gary Wilensky's junior program in Manhattan was filling up with campers from the city. Through one of the camps, he even landed his first ranked player, a talented girl he privately coached for years. When he got the job, even other pros in the city, who scouted local tournaments for ranked girls, heard about it.

So it came as a surprise when he had to leave Point O'Pines in the middle of summer, when rumors surfaced, when the directors grew more concerned about his favoritism and his temper flared, when the announcement was made that he'd be going home early. But before he left, Gary had another idea. He decided to give it all away—all the shirts and hats he'd lugged in his car from Manhattan.

Cotton pressed with the apish grin of Gary Wilensky dangled from hangers hooked on fences around the courts. The girls competed for the privilege of carrying his memory throughout the rest of summer. He pelted ball after ball, calling shots, naming winners, watching them all as they ran, swung, and sweated to win shirts with his face stamped on them. He might have hoped the game would never end.

girl: portrait

BEFORE WE ENTER THE AUDITORIUM, THERE is an inspection. Collars out, shirts buttoned to the neck, skirts unrolled, sweaters with hints of red removed. "Spit it out." A teacher cups her hand underneath a girl's chin to catch a wad of gum. There are no free passes on Tuesday mornings, when the entire school lines up by grade for prayers.

"Go, go, go," the teacher prompts us when the first notes of Handel or Bach are played on the grand piano, and the auditorium doors swing open. Two by two, but with haste, we arrange ourselves in evenly distributed lines forming an aisle down the center of the room that leads to our headmistress at a podium on the stage, a column of wool pleats, buttons, and bone.

She nods at the music teacher to lay off the keys when she sees all six hundred of us have been organized inside the room.

"Good morning, girls." She is old. Perceptibly, proudly, handsomely old. Not crouched, softened grandparent old, but old enough that it's impossible to imagine what she looked like before she looked like this.

"Good morning," we respond as one big, bobbling mass of girlhood.

There are five-year-olds in the front of the room in tunics, and eighteen-year-olds in the back in kilts.

On either side of the auditorium are scrolls with hand-scripted lyrics to Beethoven's "Ode to Joy," which most of us know by heart at this point. I wonder if our headmistress, who calligraphs a message on each of our report cards, handwrote the lyrics herself or if there's a store—some dusty back room in a West Side office building—where you can purchase your Episcopalian prep school hymnal scrolls.

Teachers stand along the sidewalls, facing us, eyeballing our posture, *tsk*ing any whispers, nodding at us to *Sing! Sing!*

After the fifth "Joy Divine," we move on to reciting the Bible verses and close the morning with a breathy in-unison Lord's Prayer. "You don't have to say any of it," my father had told me once, but some of the teachers look to see that your mouth is moving. They look at me, because they know what I am.

I wear a silver Tiffany lima bean around my neck, but it used to be a gold Jewish star my father had given me. I wore it twice before my mother suggested I save it for *special occasions*. "Too much of a statement for school," she whispered, crinkling her nose.

Too Jewish. Not Jewish enough. The spectrum of belief has no midpoint, and still we're expected to find one.

Screw that. I believe in one man. I mouth his words to the Bible verses during prayers and picture the framed photo of his naked upper half, arms outstretched on an invisible cross, above my bed. I wear his face on an oversize T-shirt when I come home from school, and nobody can make me take it off.

He gazes off in the distance, a wavy shadow in profile, silk-screened on a one-size-only black cotton shirt. *Jim Morrison, 1943–1971.*

But images don't do him justice. It's when he gasped for air between lyrics onstage, eyebrows helplessly upturned, screaming *Yeaaaah*, and dropping his head so that his hair tumbled over his face while his leather legs writhed. He was drowning in those moments, demonstrating his own fate. He knew he would die, and he wasn't afraid. I want to trap and swallow him so I can be fearless, too.

In my room are shrines—behind a cabinet, a Case Logic cassette case dedicated solely to Doors material: all seven studio albums, two compilations, a live album, and a posthumous recording of Jim Morrison's poetry set to jazzy background music. On a shelf above my desk is *No One Here Gets Out Alive*, the biography of Jim Morrison, along with *Wilderness: The Lost Writings of Jim Morrison*, and a thin poster-sized book of photographs of Jim Morrison with the Doors.

Beside it, I have placed a red candle shaped like a bear, a secret Santa gift my sister had received from a classmate. I carved *Jim* into the belly with a kitchen knife.

This "obsession," as my mother calls it, began when I was twelve, before the movie came out, I swear. I saw the real Jim perform on a PBS documentary my dad was watching and bought the paperback biography of his life, which is better than the movie. It's about how he grew up in a military family and had to be clean-shaven, stiff, and obedient. But one day he drove with his family past a Native American man dying on the side of a highway and was possessed by the man's spirit. Then Jim moved to Venice, California, met Ray Manzarek, dropped out of school because nobody understood him, overcame his shyness, tripped in the desert, met his soulmate, became a rock legend and a bunch of other things. The whole time, you know he dies in the end, but you don't believe it until the last few pages. And even then you feel that he is still alive, living inside you, just as the spirit of a Native American man lived inside him.

When I think of Jim living inside me, I feel free. I feel as though I'm walking through a dream he is having, and that his reality is more real than my own. Everything that's expected of me, everything I'm failing at, is meaningless, because it'll all go away when he wakes up and I disappear. This is what I think when I look at the poster of him hanging over my bed.

But there is another poster tucked underneath my bed, one I don't want to see. In it, he is sitting in a car, staring dazedly out the window at his fans. I'm on his lap, in a white button-down shirt, lips over braces, age twelve, facing the camera. The black-and-white image is mounted onto cardboard and surrounded by colorful handwritten messages. *Mazel tov!*

A year ago, I stood on a podium in my sister's black velvet Laura Ashley dress, safety-pinned at the chest with socks, and read Hebrew words I had already memorized from an unrolled scroll. Then we rode four blocks scrunched in a taxi to Maxim's on Madison Avenue.

It was dark red inside the nightclub. The heels of my pumps sunk into the carpeting. The walls were the color of black cherries, affixed with pink petal sconces and mirrors shaped like partially blown bubbles.

My mother had something to show me before the guests arrived, and led me to the cocktail area, where two poster boards rested on easels. On one was a blown-up photograph of all four members of the Doors, and standing behind them, a superimposed image of me, taken the year before by a professional photographer my parents knew. On the other easel was the poster of Jim and me alone together.

It was the greatest gift my mother had ever given me. After a year of trying to break the spell of my infatuation, she had given in and reversed course. She brought Jim and me together. My mother was the best mother.

Guests started to trickle in, and she went to make the rounds while I stayed by the easels and waited for my friends. The room filled with relatives, my father's clients. The men wore tuxedoes, the women wore velvet dresses or silk pant-suits or sequined two-piece numbers with shoulder pads and pumps. "Do you remember me?" an old lady said, holding a cocktail napkin and a toothpick. "I'm your so-and-so's so-and-so." An aunt gave me a wet kiss, then licked her thumb and rubbed it along my cheek. Everyone's breath smelled of temple, that parched devotion, mixed with hot-dog burps and stale lipstick. A woman in a pink suit whom I'd never seen before stopped in front of one easel and then looked at me. "Is that you?" she asked, throwing her head back in a cackle. I wanted to shove her mouth full of pigs in blankets until she choked.

When the girls from my grade arrived, I led them to my easels, and after they'd all signed them, we huddled together so I could run down the list of boys who'd RSVP'd. Most were from out of town, camp friends I'd invited to up the male head count. A few were from Hebrew school and an all-boys school on the Upper West Side—many of whom I'd frantically invited in a last-minute effort to even the ratio.

"When are the boys coming?" all the girls kept asking.

"When are they going to play 'Me So Horny'?"

"When are they going to play 'I Wanna Sex You Up'?"

The band played Billy Joel, so much Billy Joel, and sequins

slow-danced with silk tuxedoes while we snatched abandoned cocktails off tables.

We made music videos at the make-your-own-music-video station, until the woman who laughed at my poster announced that it was "adult time" and kicked us out.

"Are more boys coming?" Bianca asked. There were seat cards in front of untouched plates with boys' names written on them. "When are the boys coming?"

In my left shoe were two Benadryl; in my right was a third. I went into the bathroom and dug them out, then hid in a stall until my sister came in to say the band was calling my name. A brass-based "Let's Get Physical" transitioned into "We Are Family," which meant it was time to light the candles on the cake and call up my relatives one by one, while holding a microphone in one hand and a wild flame in the other. Applause. Percussion. An expanded accordion of *awww*s.

The night blurred with cherrywood and fire. My father gave a speech. He said I was his favorite. My sister cried in a bathroom stall. My mother fumed. I danced with my father to "Wonderful Tonight" and wished everyone else in the world would go away.

At the end of the night, when the guests had cleared, my sister and I stood in the lobby holding bags of silver Tiffany pens and envelopes stuffed with checks. The two poster boards of Jim and me, now covered in writing, leaned against my leg as we waited for my father to settle the bill.

My mother stood a few feet away from us, talking to a friend of my father's. He was the photographer who took the pictures of me they used for the posters.

"When she's a little older, she's going to have to get that fixed," he said, nodding in my direction.

"I know," said my mother.

In the cab home, I asked her what he meant and she told me. She said she saw it right when I came out of her, when the doctors placed me in her arms, and my newborn skin was still translucent. There was this twisted bone inside my nose, the same as my father's and my grandmother's. She knew then I'd have to have *work done* when I was older. "A man can get away with it. It's harder for a girl."

I want to peel off my face. Something is wrong with it.

"When you're fifteen, when your face stops growing, that's when we'll fix it," my mother says.

"So I was always like this?" I ask her.

"It wasn't so noticeable when you were younger," she says, looking at me, but not at my eyes. She sees that something is wrong with me, but she is looking in the wrong place.

"Don't worry," she says, "we'll fix it."

But I don't want to be fixed. I want to be dead.

When I turn sad for no reason, my mother says it's because I'm moody. "Got the blues again?" she asks. I don't know what I have or don't have. I only know of dangling my feet out the window seven flights above the concrete, imagining what it will feel like when I land.

I bet you don't feel it when you've hit the ground. It's the falling you have to worry about. All that time to reconsider, to remember, to paddle through the air and change direction, to remember some more.

I hope to remember that when I smile, my nose twists, that

they want to shave it off me, and that it will only make the ugliness burrow deeper inside.

It's in me—I am the twisted bone through and through. It isn't the blues I have, it's something else.

Tantrums boil up and sprout coils at my temples. When I can't contain them, I write them down, hoping to relieve the pressure. *Pressing her arteries between my hands, squeezing all the blood out from her neck.* My mother found my most violent notebook. She knew it was about her. "You left it out for me to find," she screamed. Maybe so.

I'm an airtight jar of carbonated steam. Throw me out the window and watch me burst—all crystal spit and heat.

Inside a drawer is my suicide note. It is written in pencil on white stationery framed in lilac vines and addressed to my parents. The last line reads, "I'll be watching you from above," a lyric from an Escape Club song that made me think of sitting on a cloud looking down and shaking my head at mortal failings. It's outdated. My handwriting, along with my position on the afterlife, has changed now that I'm fourteen. I used to want to die to punish my parents; now I want to die to punish myself. I need a new note.

Here's what it will say: *I am ugly. I am selfish. I am lucky and ungrateful. Nobody will ever love me. The only person who could love me is dead.*

girl: kiss

TONIGHT WE ARE GOING TO AN Upper East Side club. I'm
wearing a pair of silk bloomers with lace trimming that Sarah
brought home from Hilton Head. Weeks ago, when she laid out
the delicate blouses, lingerie, and floor-length dresses on her
bed, she let Bianca and me each pick out one item. I imagined
the rest she would resell with a Manhattan markup—to whom,
I didn't ask.

Ever since middle school, Sarah detected a profit in fads.
Back then it was oily stickers. Now it's designer clothing. Same
difference.

She has a hustle I admire, the kind that comes with an innate
confidence, a faith in her own moral code, a belief that one can
be scrappily resilient and a good person at the same time. And
in Sarah's case, this is true.

It was particularly true when she laid out those satin black
shorts, which were technically lingerie. I snatched them up
before Bianca could get her hands on them. When I tried them
on over a pair of sheer black tights and we all gathered around
the full-length mirror in Sarah's bathroom, we marveled at my
legs as if they weren't my own. They were narrow, delicate at
the calf with tiny muscles blooming around the thigh.

We took photographs with my disposable camera, glamour
shots, sucking in our cheeks, parting our mouths, doing our
best impression of a dead-eyed Kate Moss in those Calvin Klein

ads. I stood while Sarah and Bianca crouched so I wouldn't look so small. I bent a black nylon knee as if captured in a sultry walk to my boudoir.

That was the test shoot. Tonight I am wearing those shorts for real. Sarah and Bianca have agreed to meet at my house to get dressed. Because my parents are out for the night, there will be no approval of our outfits before we leave the apartment. I have paired my shorts with my favorite top—Bianca's gray ribbed sweater with a deep V-neck. Underneath is a black push-up bra. On my feet are platform foam sandals that lift me up off the floor by three feet—the influence of rave culture has helped correct one, but not all, of my physical imperfections.

My hair has been blow-dried by a man named Tony. My mother sends me to him every Thursday night to straighten my curls for the week. She demands the bottom be curled under, rather than blown straight, though the moment I step out of the salon, the under curl flips out, Annette Funicello style.

I don't fight her on it. My hair has belonged to my mother since I chopped it off at age five for a game of make-believe in which I played a boy. That night, after my mother calmed down, I sat on the toilet as she folded what was left of my hair into hot curlers, and made it clear, with each pin she fastened into place, that she was the boss of my hair, and would be for as long as I lived in her house.

Tony, who I must request when booking an appointment at European Hair Design, is Serbian. This is all I know of him, apart from what I've observed. He handles his blow-dryer like a power tool. I watch him in the mirror, his forehead scrunched, as he tugs my knotty bird's nest into smooth strands with a round brush, hot air, and muscle. At times he looks like he's untangling himself from the grip of an octopus.

In the mirror, I watch him and wonder if he pulls as hard on my mother's hair when she comes in for her own weekly appointment. I wonder if he kisses women, and if, when he does, he kisses them with the same forceful, intense expression, never looking into their eyes but down at their lips, poised to unravel the next tangled thing.

I am sorry, I want to tell him when he switches the blow-dryer to cool air and waves it at his face like it's a gun.

I'm sorrier still when he is done and I look up at my own reflection, disappointed that my hair will never be, no matter how many men pull on it, the texture of really straight hair. "Can you get it any straighter?" I'll sometimes ask, because if I go home with tight little knots of frizz at my temples, my mother will send me back. "This is just, you know, your hair," he will say, inspecting the roots. And then, seeing my eyes welling up, he'll say, "I'll try, I'll try," because he is a patient man and I am a child monster.

When he is done, I hand him the sweaty piece of green paper my mother has given me. The entire time in the chair, I keep the bill crumpled in my fist, nervously anticipating the moment my hand touches his. The slick act of sliding a tip to someone else is so out of my league, small, breast-budded me presenting a secret gift to a full-bodied man, something he needs that I have. I am sorry for it all.

When Sarah and Bianca arrive at my house, they immediately empty their knapsacks filled with going-out clothes onto my bed. The dog jumps back onto the floor and curls up outside the room with her back to us. We are too much for her.

I pull a dress from my closet for Bianca to wear—a thigh-length black apron that wraps around your backside for slightly more coverage than a standard waitress's apron. She wears a white tank underneath it—a wife-beater, it's called, which means ribbed tank top.

Sarah pulls on an outfit I assume she borrowed from her mother's closet: a strapless black jumpsuit that flares at the legs and shows off her tanned, bony shoulders.

"Are my arms disgustingly skinny?" Bianca asks, straightening them out and walking her hands, palms down, across my vanity. "Look, they're like Ethiopian legs."

I laugh because that is part of the pact between best friends. You're allowed to make offensive comments, as long as you're putting yourself down in the process.

"My hair is right out of a 1950s senior class photo," I lob back at her, though I'm not sure if the reference lands.

"My nose is like André the Giant," she returns. I don't talk about my nose.

"Shut up, everyone," Sarah says. "You're both lucky. We're all lucky."

Sarah struggles with her hair in my mirror, forcing two strands behind her ears, moving a shorter piece over her forehead, and then brushing it all out with her fingers. I imagine she hates something about herself, too, but can't say it out loud now.

"Come here," I say and they follow me into the library—the dog, too—to the closet where my parents keep their liquor. The room is lamplit with dark wood shelves that rise to the ceiling. There is a green Turkish rug that covers most of the floor. The dog resumes her nap on it. My father's mahogany desk is stacked with envelopes. The stereo system behind a cabinet door is full of buttons and green waves of light. We need going-out music, so I put on Z100. Snow rattles off "Informer," and we approximate the lyrics we don't understand. *A-lay-key-boom-boom-now.*

We sit on the floor facing a lit closet full of wine bottles. There are handles of vodka and gin, a blue bottle of Bombay Sapphire, a bottle of my father's Crown Royal preserved in its velvet bag. Forget those. We go for a dusty brown jug of peach schnapps. I first discovered it years ago, when my mother rubbed a schnapps-soaked Q-tip on a sore on my tongue. The taste—syrupy, pungent, buzzy—was everything ice cream had been missing.

This is my bottle, the one my parents have forgotten about, and we swig from it before returning to my room to stash a mess of clothes in my closet. We take one last look in the mirror, first at ourselves, then at one another.

We wear our coats open down Park Avenue, miniature backpacks strapped to our shoulders and stuffed with allowance, Marlboro Lights, coffee-bean Revlon lipstick, and concealer. My backpack is black suede with a high zipper count. Bianca's is an Agnès b. Lolita and I want it. It's nothing much—a small black fabric satchel with two black ties to put your arms through—but written across the back in white script is the name Lolita. All the pretty girls have one. When I ask to try it on, just to see how it feels, it's like strapping on an internal organ I've been missing.

We're in the taxi headed toward the club, which is actually a rented event space, formerly known as a den of debauchery for another generation. Surf Club, Tropicana, Country Club, one of them. Who has the flyer? Sarah has the flyer. She says "sir" when she gives the driver the address, and then asks him to turn on the radio. We roll down the windows. "Can we smoke in here?" But we're already lighting up. Sarah is reading off names on the flyer. When the Pharcyde's "Passin' Me By" comes on, we have to scream the lyrics without taking a breath until the chorus.

As we stream down Park Avenue, the taxi windows wide open, the breeze blow-dries our foundation and scatters wild sparks of hope, setting off an electric charge that runs between the three of us. This is my favorite part, when we are so close to the destination, but not there yet, when there are still a few minutes left to believe that this night will be the one that changes everything.

Sarah knows the thing to do is walk past the line standing behind the red rope and head straight for the promoter.

"It's just three of us," Sarah says, negotiating our entrance. We air-kiss the boy who tells the bouncer to let us in and walk up a narrow set of stairs. There is always a narrow passageway and there is always a cool older-looking girl sitting at the top of the stairs with a box of money and a stamp. We each hand over our ten-dollar bill, half the amount our parents gave us for the night. It is just enough to get us in, split a cab both ways to one of our houses, and walk home from there.

Inside, the club is lit with neon streaks underneath banquettes, roped around the dance floor. The room is nearly empty. It's early still.

In other clubs around the city—Limelight, Tunnel, Club USA—men wear angel's wings and shimmer with glittered lips under strobe lights. Marky Mark and Deee-Lite huddle in VIP booths, while Julia Roberts tousles her red curls on the dance floor. I've seen them all pressed into newsprint and the back pages of *Paper* magazine.

But those clubs are different from our clubs. Here, only girls wear glitter, and only just a light dusting on their eyelids. The famous faces are familiar from tennis lessons and walking up and down Park Avenue. The boys wear baggy khakis that dig below their Calvin Klein elastic underpants bands. They sidle into booths, shoving backpacks stuffed with graffiti canisters underneath their legs.

They say, "Come sit on my dick." What they mean is "Want to sit on my lap?" Their laps are hammocks spread over mysterious pocket bulges—the hard edges of beepers and resin-scraped bowls. A secret language of pokes shared between two bodies, but only for a few seconds, before a hand is pressed to your back, pushing you off, bored in the aftermath of a dare accepted, disgusted by the intimacy of what it entailed.

Sarah plucks drink tickets from her purse courtesy of one of the promoters and heads to the bar for three sex on the beach cocktails.

Bianca and I eyeball the entrance, sizing up the miniskirts, the sheer black legs underneath them. When she turns back to me with pertinent information, she makes a wall with her hand, so that my ear and her lips are in a private room. *She went to Nightingale, but now she goes to Riverdale. He's dating so-and-so, but he used to hook up with so-and-so.*

The flutter of air tickles my ear canal.

"Is my breath bad?" she asks, pulling away, crinkling her face.

"No." It is sweet, like a cherry Life Saver. "Is mine?" I exhaust in her face.

She shakes her head, but I'm not sure I believe her. She'll never shame someone else unless she herself is shamed first. The bond between two girls surrounded by boys is so fragile, always threatened by embarrassment, especially if that embarrassment isn't shared.

"There's—" whispers Bianca.

"I know," I say.

We are both looking at the girl standing near the entrance. She wears a thigh-high flapper number that fits tightly around her hips and chest but dangles loose, shimmying fringes in all directions. She glistens in the dark club, like her thick black hair glistens when she gathers it to one side.

She opens her arms to a girl with a slicked-back ponytail. They hug like it's a camp reunion, rocking back and forth, touching each other's hair, until another girl comes along to receive a hug.

As the room fills, the music gets faster—a mix of hip-hop and seventies disco. "I Will Survive" comes on, and we join the rest of the girls in the club on the dance floor in a collective moment of solidarity, our feminist credo against the boys who otherwise dominate the room, apelike and intimidating. We are mouthing the lyrics to each other, not so much dancing as facing our respective female friends, holding each other's hands, talking through the song.

Our hands are broken apart. A boy has entered our three-person dance circle. His name is Matt. I know that he was kicked out of a good prep school and enrolled in a bad one. I know he has carrot-colored hair under his baseball cap, and that he is facing me, but he is so tall, I can only see *Hilfiger* emblazoned across his chest. He grabs ahold of my backpack straps and pulls me toward him, spreading his legs wide apart so he sinks down to my face. His lips are on my lips, and his tongue is jabbing around inside my mouth.

I'm thinking of those wriggling, bloated creatures that graze the ocean floor—the ones with prehistoric names. A glow-in-the-dark slithering living muscle with a wide unblinking eye, always searching in the darkness for a smaller creature who will fit inside of him.

When the boy lets go, he slaps his friend's hand and laughs— they both laugh. They are two tall, laughing boys. I need Sarah or Bianca. I need them to cover me up, but I can't see where they went. I push past the bodies and bodies. Gloria Gaynor's lyrics give way to the part of the song that disco-ball swirls in circles, like my head is swirling. I elbow my way into the bathroom and into a stall, where I sit on the toilet with my head between my knees, because it happened. I had my first kiss. And he was popular.

I am full-body trembling. Micro-shivers radiating from a core, pumping an organ in the thick of my chest, deep below the two small mounds that pressed against the boy's hands. I'm afraid of the boy. I'm afraid he'll want more. I'm afraid of how tall and forceful he was, and how he laughed like he knew it was my first time. I'm afraid of what he might do to me next. I'm afraid he'll leave without getting my number. I'm afraid he's already left.

It's nearing curfew. I've got to find Sarah and Bianca, to

tell them what happened, and with whom. They'll recognize his name, of course they will. They'll want to know if he got my number. I shouldn't have run away. But he was laughing. It wasn't that he liked me. He kissed me as a joke. A dare. *I dare you to kiss the shortest girl in the room*. That was it. *She gives blow jobs standing up*. I won't talk about it with the girls unless they bring it up. And if they do, I'll laugh, too.

I scan the room for them, but stop when I see the older girl in the fringed dress again. She is still receiving adoration, this time from a boy who looks like a man. He wears a suit. A goatee frames his mouth. She is holding his hand as his lips tell her ear a story. She breaks away to laugh, flipping her head down so her hair swings like the fringes on her dress. When she pulls her head back up, I picture a thin line of blood running from her nostril into her mouth.

She is the one I hit with my tennis racket. It was an accident.

girl: new lesson

"GARY, CAN WE STOP AND GET candy?" we ask on the way to the courts. Gary reaches into his pocket and hands us each five dollars to spend in the corner bodega.

We take his money and eat the candy. If he asks us to buy something for him in the store, we'll do that. If he doesn't, we won't.

Now we are playing against him. Hitting a forehand and a backhand. We are working on control, so Gary offers up his body. "Hit me! Hit me!" he says after each ball he tosses. So I do, right between the legs. And he twists one leg around the other and spins in a circle, like he's a human jackpot. "Good!"

Built into every lesson are pauses when you have to clean up the mess you've made. "Let's get 'em up," says Gary, and we break off to all sides of the court. Me at the back, Gary at the net, Emma on the other side of the court. Tara doesn't play with us on Saturdays.

I squeeze a ball through the wire bars of the tennis basket. I crash a basket on the little yellow heads. At the net, Gary paddles more balls in my direction.

"Heads-up," he calls out, lobbing one in the air. It flies over my head and thwacks the canvas wall, ricocheting back toward Gary.

"Thanks for all your help—it really makes all the difference," I say, because sometimes I can't control my sarcasm, but also because Gary doesn't mind it. We've got a shorthand. I gently rib him, he returns the favor. He calls me Piper-ooni. He lets me sit shotgun whenever I beat Emma. I'm almost certain he prefers it when I do.

The basket of balls has become too heavy for me to lift. So I use my racket as a platter, loading it up with balls and then dropping them into the basket. Half of them don't make it in. They bounce and roll back toward the net to where Gary has just cleaned up.

Emma's side is almost spotless. She has fewer balls on her side, so it isn't fair.

"Watch it," says Gary. He comes up behind me and grabs the basket from my hand, easily lifting it.

"It's not that heavy, see?" he says.

"I'm a whole lot smaller than you, Gary."

"You're not that small," he says. I wait for a smile, some suggestion of his own sarcasm, but nothing. It might be the first time anyone has said that to me and meant it. I am grateful, flushed with embarrassment.

It was only two years ago that my mother took me to the bone doctor to see if I was going to eventually grow to make it to her height—five feet even. Since I was a toddler, she's worried I wouldn't pass the four-foot range. She made sure I had three glasses of milk every day for the last fourteen years to keep my bones strong and stretching. She had warned me of another possible measure that an unusually short boy, the brother of a girl in my class, endured: daily injections to keep his growth steady. We went to a specialist to see if such measures should be taken with me. I wore an apron lined with lead and laid my hand on a mat. Afterward, the doctor hung a photograph of a skeleton's five fingers on the wall and said that it was me. "Not to worry," the doctor told my mom. "She's going to be just as tall as you." Then we took an elevator down to the street and walked for blocks against the wind. My mom's short black hair was blown back, and her cheekbones rode high. Inside her face was a skull, part of a skeleton, too.

Our Saturday lesson is halfway done. During the week, it's all practice, practice, practice. Hit a forehand, a backhand; now run to the net, hit a volley, and get back in line. On Saturdays, we focus on technique and the game itself. Today we're working on our slices—tricky maneuvers, cheap even, designed to fake out a player. Standing on either side of the half court, Gary lobs us rounds and we cut through the air with our rackets, grazing the ball, hammering down at an angle like we're peeling the skin off an apple. Most of our balls go into the net, but a few bounce on Gary's side, springing upward and then sideways. "Good!" he says. And sometimes, "Excellent!" I get one excellent and a good. Emma gets a good and two excellents.

When we are on opposite ends of the baseline, Gary looks much younger. He is wrapped in loose-fitting neon athletic gear. He holds his body in a gawky teenage shrug. His hair appears darker. His voice, nasal with traces of his Long Island upbringing, sounds as if it hasn't fully dropped yet.

But standing closer to the net, I can see the deep indented waves in his forehead and the parentheses around his mouth. His eyebrows spring white, curly hairs. When he smiles, his teeth are the color of sawdust.

He is older than my parents, though this is hard to understand. They are the bosses, but Gary is somehow not.

"Ready to play a set?" he asks.

"I want you to focus on your backhand follow-through," he tells Emma, miming a slow-motion stroke. His whole body twists, Gumby-like, limb over limb.

"And you . . ."—his chin points in my direction—"you don't worry about hitting your serve so hard. Just focus on getting it in. Consistency—that's what we're going for, okay?" He claps his hands and jogs courtside.

I ignore Gary's instruction and slam into the ball as hard as possible. It hits the net and drops dead.

"Consistency," Gary shouts between two cupped hands.

So this time, I toss the ball and tap it gingerly.

"That's in," Gary confirms as Emma, with her long, skinny legs, lunges to return it. Soon we are running each other all over the court, screaming "Out!" and "Fifteen–forty!" and "What's the score?" and "Ad in." Sometimes, when a ball lobs over the baseline, we don't even make a noise. We just hold up one finger in the air to signal it's out—so very out, it isn't worth announcing. This is one way of showing your opponent you barely have to lift a finger to win a point. It jostles their nerves and throws them off, but it's a dick move to use on a competitor you like. And Emma and I do like each other.

Playing with her isn't like playing with that racket-tossing girl from school. We congratulate each other on a nice shot and agree, when we switch sides, that one side of the court feels darker than the other, which was why each of us lost one game on that side. Emma hands me two balls and gives me a huge, gummy grin. Her whole face squints when she smiles. I find it endearing.

She is laughing about something, that kind of laugh that's more physical than audible. It sounds like swallowed hiccups. Although I'm not sure exactly what the source is, I start laughing, too, because I think it's related to Gary. He is squatting on the clay ground, riffling through his double-sized racket bag. Emma and I are having a fit now, finding each other's eyes to make sure we were laughing about the same thing, and still unsure, laughing even harder because each of us wants the other to feel supported.

"What's so funny?" Gary wants to know and we both respond with "Nothing," which may actually be true.

"Are you girls laughing at me?" Gary gives us a toothy grin. He is in on the joke. And now we're bent over holding our stomachs.

"It's me, isn't it?" He smiles, the hole in his front teeth wide as a doorway to Narnia.

Then he looks at his watch and claps his hands. "Okay, we've got five minutes. One more quick game. Who's serving?"

The score is four games to three. "FOUR–THREE!" I yell so Gary can hear that I'm winning. I look at Emma on the other side of the court in her school gym shorts, her skinny legs pocked with bruises, her hair knotted in a lopsided bun, and I regret tainting what we just had with a reminder of competition.

I toss the ball overhead and tap it lightly so it goes in. She returns the serve harder than usual—a clean blow to the sweet spot of her racket. I watch the ball land inside the sidelines and hear Gary slow-clapping. "Gorgeous shot, Emma!"

Love–fifteen. Stalling, I tap the sides of my Nikes with my racket. Tufts of chalky green powder and clay pebbles fall off. Love–fifteen.

I'm about to toss a ball into the air when two middle-aged men wearing tennis wristbands and white shorts pull back the canvas flap behind Emma.

"We have this court," the shorter of the two shouts in Gary's direction.

Gary looks at his watch. "We have four minutes," he shouts back.

But the men stand there, blocking Emma from drawing back her racket. I'm all ready to pack it in. Two confident, business-like older men with wristwatches and tennis sweatbands have confirmed we're all done here. That's good enough for me. I start picking up balls and putting them on my racket when Gary raises his hand.

"Piper, wait, wait, wait," he says. "I want you guys to play one more point."

"We have this court," one of the men repeats, growing frustrated.

I'm not sure whose side to take in this standoff, but I settle on the men I have never met, because they seem in charge. If this had been a movie, they would be the boardroom bosses and Gary would be the child trapped in an adult's body who is forced to work for them.

Gary decides to give in, too. "Okay, girls, let's clean it up," he says, not looking at the men, who are already taking their places on the court as we gather our balls.

Through the revolving door glass, I see Gary clenching his

jaw, the bone in his cheek moving up and down, like a parasite pumping iron under his skin. When we get back into the car, he is silent, so we are silent.

I hate those kinds of men. The ones who flick their silver wristwatches, who snap their money in Tiffany clips, who dismiss someone like Gary as hired help, who think anyone that works with children is lesser than they are on some masculinity pyramid. To such men, Gary is not a man at all.

I let Emma sit shotgun, even though I won. I'd rather sit in the backseat today. Gary puts the car key in the ignition. He is wearing a fluorescent pink hat, and from where I sit, it looks lopsided. I lean forward and squeeze his shoulder. He looks at me in the rearview mirror with a flat expression. It seems for a moment that he doesn't recognize me. Then his eyes dart to the windshield. "So where should we eat?" he asks.

WILD-HAIRED BARBIES hang from the ceiling fan, a sign on the wall reads LIFE'S A BITCH. There are side-by-side signed head shots of celebrities. Billy Crystal. Joe Piscopo. Chips and salsa before we've even ordered. This is my kind of restaurant.

Gary is leaning against the wall with one foot on the seat beside him. He looks cool, like he's a regular here.

"Get whatever you want," he says. He'll just have some chips. He's watching his figure. Wink.

There is that wink. So intimate and fleeting, it almost feels imagined. It deserves to be accompanied by the ping of a triangle, or some other sitcom device that suggests magic is happening.

I used to believe in magic. I thought I possessed it. *You're special*, my parents had told me, which was further confirmation. It seemed likely, considering how many fictional characters possessed supernatural powers in one form or another, always changing up time by snapping their fingers or rubbing an amulet, sticking a quarter in a fortune-telling machine, wishing on a shooting star and believing hard enough. I took wishes seriously, using birthday candles, loosened eyelashes, and fountain pennies to wish for the same thing—that nobody I love dies. When they hadn't, I believed it was because of me.

That faith in magic dwindled over time, as competition heightened, parental compliments lost their value, and teachers introduced new scales of measurement, assessing my abilities as decidedly average, devoid of that special quality. I guess this is their job, to help kids grow up and stop believing in magic, anchoring them instead within the business of hard work.

Still, there are those rare teachers who do just the opposite. They are the ones who don't judge you by a set of numbers, but by an emotional quality they see in you but not in others—a quality they recognize in themselves. They have a secret they want to tell you so badly, but they're not allowed. Magic is real. They have it, and so do you.

It's just a wink, an aside. A nudging reminder that someone who isn't your parents still believes you are special. Not just special, but the most special.

My sister had a drama teacher who made her feel this way. Her teacher didn't wink; instead, she asked my sister to feed her cats. She handed my sister her house keys. The invitation alone was flattering, but the keys, their brass puzzle-piece edges, were so intimate, so twinkling with promise. It meant the teacher trusted my sister over all the other students, to cross into her personal world. The framed photos, shelves of books, kitchen odors, drawers of secret histories, were all laid out for my sister to absorb, because she was the chosen. More than that, she was the best actress in the whole class—she had to be. She had the keys.

But when they were taken away and handed to another student, a younger one cast as the lead in their next play, my sister came home and cried on her side of the white wall. She pulled at her own hair. She went over again and again what she might have done wrong. She worked harder, focused more, asked for private guidance after class, and did anything she could to win her teacher back. Only she saw my sister's magic, and only she could see it again. This is why, I learned, you have to choose who chooses you. It must be the right magical teacher. They must know that once they've made their choice, they can never change their minds.

After dinner, Gary drops Emma off at her building first and then pulls up to my awning. When he puts the car in park, it rocks back and forth. I don't want to get out yet. "Gary," I say, and then "Never mind." *Am I your favorite?*

man: favorites

GARY WILENSKY HAS HIS FAVORITES. THEY know who they are. Sometimes he calls them on the phone just to talk. He'll speak with their mothers, too, offering progress updates or confirming what they want to hear: Their daughter is promising.

When he talks to his students, he is careful to listen, to purse his lips around his teeth and keep quiet, storing the information they provide so he can ask them about it later. He wants them to feel heard, to know they can confide in him, can trust him with their secrets. He hopes they see him as more than just another teacher—as a friend, a surrogate family member, the only adult in this world who takes them as seriously as they take themselves. He tells them as much, in his way.

You're growing up to be quite an attractive young woman. The girl is in the passenger seat of his car headed home after a lesson. She was ten or eleven when he began coaching her. Now she is thirteen. Her hair is frizzy at the roots and pulled back in a bun. When she smiles, her pink gums show.

Another night, another student. No lesson today, just dinner. Mom approved. When the little girl gets inside his car, he reaches over to pull her seat belt across her chest and snap it tight in the corner of the seat. He drives slowly and parks in front of his own building. Outside the Ruppert Yorkville Towers, Fuddruckers's yellow-and-blue pole says *come inside, come inside*. At a table for two, he shows the girl a trick he once learned with two forks and a quarter. She likes it. *Magic*, he might say if she wants an explanation. *The young lady will have*, and *For you, sir*, and *Be careful, it's hot*, and *Are you going to eat all that?* And all that. Then he gets serious, sad even.

Gary Wilensky is heartbroken and he wants to talk about it. He loves someone, he tells her, and it's not working out. He wishes she'd love him back. When he finishes with his story, he waits for her response. The girl forks her bowl of bow-tie pasta. She is ten years old, delicate and small-wristed with thick black hair. She is mature enough to grasp their unusual shift in dynamics, but still too young to know how to respond. *It's okay, Gary*, or *Are you okay, Gary?* Perhaps, something along those lines.

Sometimes he doesn't talk to them at all. Instead he follows from a distance and then captures them with his long-lens camera, freezing them in time, collecting their images like playing cards. In his apartment, pictures pile up of all his favorites. He has many favorites, but there is one he favors the most.

He started teaching the Daughter about a year ago. The Mother was looking for a private coach. Gary Wilensky came recommended.

It was a coup to land a private coaching gig for such a talented young player, who was quickly ascending the regional tournament ranks. She'd recently placed in the top twenty in her age bracket, in the eastern district. This was an opportunity to do his preferred work, providing one-on-one guidance to a gifted young athlete. Professionally speaking, it gave him more credibility as a coach. He was an athletic trainer. A mentor. A private coach of tournament juniors including eastern and nationally ranked players. Those were the words that went on his résumé, which went on the back of the receipts he sent out to all the parents of his students.

It's been sixteen months since he began coaching the Daughter, and now she is seventeen, in her senior year of high school and on track to attend an Ivy League university. She is sporty and smart, well liked in her class. Sometimes she wears her brown hair in a ponytail and pulled through the half-moon hole of a baseball cap.

The Mother is close with the Daughter. She is also compassionate, a good listener. He calls the Mother on the phone and asks to speak with the Daughter. He calls the Daughter and asks to speak with the Mother.

Perhaps, if he was asked about his plans for the holidays, and if he said he had no plans, he'd be invited to join them for Thanksgiving. *Uncle, grandpa, good old Gary—never says no to a home-cooked meal. Poor Gary, always so alone.*

He is a teenager back in Roslyn, where the windows of Victorian homes along Main Street flicker with television light and the burnt orange halos of candle flames. He has just seen a girl he likes to dance with. There will be talk of her bruised eye at school, and his name will be mentioned. He passes the clock tower at the center of town, a granite and sandstone memorial erected in the last century for someone else's mother. The inscription above the doorway reads *She fell asleep*. His mother is dead, he once said, although this was a lie.

He buys the Daughter gifts, little tokens of affection. He makes mixtapes. On a label, above a list of song titles, he writes "Favorites," but there is only one.

The Daughter tells her mother she is no longer comfortable around Gary. The attention, the phone calls, the gifts.

The Mother is a mental health professional. She wrote a book on why some men can't commit. When she lets Gary go, she suggests he seek treatment.

He is cut off. Fired. Though this is not the first time. He was fired from Point O'Pines; from the resort in the Catskills; from Midtown Tennis, the very first club that hired him. In the past two decades he's been let go plenty of times. *His temper. Hard to manage. Playing favorites.* He's always found other work. He has good references from other places, and it's rare that anyone would dig deep enough to find the bad ones.

If they do, he might be able to rationalize his departure. He didn't want to work for anyone else; he wanted to go out on his own; they didn't understand his progressive coaching methods; they were threatened by his success; and so forth.

Still, this time is different. This is not about an argument he has had with a boss or a difference of opinion. This is his undoing: He went too far, he felt too much. He lost control of Gary Wilensky—the teacher, the surrogate, the man. He lost the job, but maybe he senses a deeper loss, a betrayal by the Daughter for not understanding his desires, for breaking an unspoken contract he believed they shared.

Before the year is over, Günter Parche, a stalker obsessed with Steffi Graf, will stab her competitor, Monica Seles, during a tournament. "She is a dream creature whose eyes sparkle like diamonds and whose hair shines like silk," Parche will say of Graf in court. "I would walk through fire for her."

"She didn't give me a fair chance," an unnamed man will explain in a case study on stalkers.

"The male ego perceives some obligation from the woman to allow him [a] 'fair chance,'" author J. Reid Meloy will write in

The Psychology of Stalking. "The need for revenge or to 'teach that person a lesson' becomes a preoccupation."

Meloy will also link depression and low self-esteem to fixations on fractured relationships, when a rift is mistaken as the source of one's suffering, and rectifying it is the only cure. "Such depressed individuals may be involved in cases of stalking, especially those entailing workplace violence," he will write, in the first book-length survey of stalking behavior. But that won't be published for another six years.

For now, Gary Wilensky has his own books: *Final Exit: The Practicalities of Self-Deliverance and Assisted Suicide for the Dying; November of the Soul: The Enigma of Suicide.* He might read, study, or make a plan, or he might lie in his bed and stare at shadows. This world is better off without him, and all that.

2014—2016

child allies

FOR ME, THE LIFE AND DEATH of Gary Wilensky took place over one year, the same period my own mind became the most dangerous it has ever been. At some point both our stories nearly overlapped, though not entirely and certainly not neatly.

It began inside his car. Mixtapes in the armrest, Red Vines candy on the dashboard, roller skates and Marx Brothers glasses in the trunk. The internal clutter of Gary Wilensky's sedan purposely defied the pristine expectations outside it. Here was a place to remove the *good girl* costume, if only for an hour or two.

In his car, girls could be sticky-fingered and snort when they laughed. They weren't chastised for being too loud or shamed for hog-chewing gum.

His was a sanctioned area for childish impulse and indulgence. It'd been a while since I'd listened to my instincts or felt the spike of confidence that comes with having those instincts validated. *You like that? Open it.*

Maybe I am making more of it than it was: a drive between Manhattan and Queens for a tennis lesson, but for a brief time, those rides offered a break from trying so hard.

We'd showboat in his car, roll the windows down and request Grey Poupon from taxis waiting for the light. Gary never told us to stop. He wasn't opposed to confrontation, double-honking, and cursing at drivers who got in his way. His tiny explosions

were startling, and then, after a beat, hilarious. He wasn't trying to set an example. He was one of us.

At a time when the world was still divided between adults and
kids, this seemed significant enough to devise a new category
for men like Gary. I called them child allies, and I watched for
more. You could spot them all around, if you knew the markers.

They used winks and elbow nudges to establish a private
communication, reminding you, after letting you sip their drink
or steer the driver's wheel, not to get them in trouble.

Their pockets were stuffed with tokens, little oddball gifts
that didn't require verbal conditions like *please* and *thank you*.
You'd never hear them call you *kid* to your face, or refer to
themselves as adults because they didn't believe in labels.

They never shushed you or told you to be patient or revoked
a promise because of your *attitude*. That was the most important
condition of a child ally: He or she could never say no.

Gary never did, though now there are other terms to better
explain his behavior. *Grooming* is one. Another is *deceptive trust
development*—a series of manipulation tactics used in the pre-
abuse stages of grooming to gain a child's allegiance, secrecy,
and compliance.

Stalkers establish private time with a child separate from
other adults—at a restaurant, in their car—to engage a child
in her interests, offering tiny bribes that translate into secrets
shared and squirreled away, so that a child feels a sense of
obligation to the adult. She might protect him or believe she
owes him something, and eventually become dependent on his
attention.

"I definitely remember him giving us money to buy candy,"

Emma, now a mother herself, recalls when she and I speak for the first time in years. "Was that part of the fee?"

I tell her it wasn't, and she pauses for a moment. "Yeah, it's weird. But you know, your parents trust this guy, so whatever he does is fine."

Gary lured with cheap sugary snacks—hiding gummies in the side panels of the car, handing us five-dollar bills for bodega sweeps while he idled outside. But it was his figurative treats that reeled me in—the implied freedom to curse, binge, and act out without punishment. We didn't have to hide anything from him.

"He'd always listen," one of the high school students he coached at Brearley told the *New York Post* in 1993. She claimed he would call her on the phone to discuss her personal life, her friends, her boyfriends, any problems at school.

"They are very good at talking to children," says Dr. Eric Hickey, a criminal psychologist who specializes in sex crimes and profiling predators. "They talk at their level. They're almost one of the kids themselves, and their potential victims think they're a wonderful person who understands them."

Hickey classifies Gary as a hebephile—someone attracted to pubescent children, rather than prepubescents, and who craves attachment and closeness to his potential victims.

And for a while, at least, it seemed Gary was satiated by those fleeting suggestions of intimacy—creeping up to the line without crossing it.

"They're looking to see how each child responds," says Hickey. "It gives them a little thrill."

Jane was a preteen at an all-girls private school when Gary

was her coach. Her mother had taken lessons with Gary, and then signed her up for his junior program. Now a nonprofit coordinator based in Brooklyn, she sits across from me at a bar in Fort Greene, breaking off pieces of her grilled cheese.

"I don't remember much," she says of the two years she took lessons with Gary. She does recall his humor, and one night when she was alone in his car. She was in the passenger seat, age twelve, when they pulled up to her apartment building.

"I remember him commenting to me 'You're turning into an attractive young woman,'" she says. His statement had made her blush. "I had started taking lessons with him during an awkward phase, so when he said this I felt, like, complimented. To have an adult say I was becoming attractive felt somewhat good."

At the camps where Gary taught, he developed a reputation for picking favorites—establishing a hierarchy with prizes and a weekly T-shirt giveaway for the girl of his choosing.

As much as it motivated young tennis players, it also elevated Gary's influence. "He literally walked on water," a former camper recalls. "If he said hello to you, it made your day."

Kate, a camper turned student, compares the competition born from those prizes to beauty pageants. "If you won one of those shirts or hats, he'd parade you around the courts," she says. "How bad it must have made the other kids feel."

At the same time, it drove her to play harder. "You wanted to do well so he would be proud of you," says Kate, now a television producer. "I had never before felt like that about a coach."

We are sitting in Starbucks in Union Square. It's been one week since the first blizzard of the season. A protest at the park across the street is just wrapping up. A young woman shuffles toward the register with a sign that reads ENOUGH IS ENOUGH tucked under her arm, like a handbag.

Kate is small-boned and a fellow short girl. When she twists her hair with two hands, I see the ding of a tiny diamond in one ear. She was eight or nine when she first met Gary at camp. Like other former campers, she remembers his costumes—the clown nose, the tutu, and the roller skates—but it was his perceived vulnerability that hooked her and balanced out their age difference. As much as she craved his attention, he seemed to need hers as well.

"It never felt inappropriate in a romantic way," she says. "It just felt like an older friend who shared a lot with you."

It's the first time I've heard someone speak of him this way. I'd seen a similar side of Gary, and it also drew me closer to him. I wanted to help him; it made me feel good that he thought I could. I ask Kate if she thinks this was a tactic he used on certain girls, if he could detect that need in us, the same way he sensed his costumes would appeal to other students.

"Maybe," she says.

After camp, Kate continued playing with Gary in the city. Twice he took her to dinner, just the two of them. She was ten, he was fifty-six. On a Sunday evening, Gary picked her up from home and took her to Fuddruckers, the restaurant in his building.

"As soon as I got in the car, it hit me that I was alone," Kate says. She remembers him reaching across her body to strap on her seat belt.

"Like this." She swings an arm down to her opposite hip.

"I remember being sort of, like, maybe this is weird, maybe I shouldn't have come."

Before our meeting, Kate called up her mother to ask her why she felt comfortable sending her off to dinner with Gary.

"You guys liked each other," her mom said, and she was right.

At dinner, Gary showed Kate a magic trick using two forks and a quarter. Later on, his mood changed. "I have a memory of him talking about his love life and some girl—how it hadn't worked out," she says. The conversation had made her uncomfortable, less with him and more with her own lack of experience.

"I remember sitting there thinking, 'I'm not equipped to give him the advice he needs,'" she says. "I felt like I didn't have the tools to tell him what he needed to hear."

Still, this was the side of Gary she connected with, even at age ten.

"I think the loneliness spoke to me the most, and something about feeling special," she says.

Another former student who played with Gary as a teenager, Sam, recalls driving in his car, not knowing the exact location they were headed. Of course they were going to play tennis, but it didn't matter where. There was an understanding that he would take each of us to the place we were supposed to be and return us to our parents when we were done. And that is what he did, always while sprinkling sugar. "I remember that, and he always came up with funny nicknames for people," Sam says. "And those shirts, the caricature of him is what he looks like in my mind." But she also recalls how on occasion, Gary's mood would change.

"He had a streak when he got angry with you—maybe because it didn't happen very often, but when it did happen, it was, like, yikes," she says.

It reminds me of something Emma had mentioned when we caught up on the phone.

"Not long before everything fell apart, he was coaching me so I'd get on the tennis team and he was really, really hard on me. He was so hard on me that he made me cry at a lesson," Emma said. "Do you remember that?"

I do, but that comes later.

reporters, survivors,
old flames

IN 1993, MICHAEL STONE, A REPORTER for *New York* magazine known for his coverage of the Preppy Killer case and the Central Park Jogger, wrote a story about an Upper East Side girls' tennis coach called "Break Point: A Tennis Coach's Fatal Obsession." Of the hundreds of articles published on Gary Wilensky that year, Stone's profile stands out as the most comprehensive and thoroughly reported. It is also the only official record of my personal reflections on Gary at age fourteen. My mother had heard, through a chain of private school parents, that Stone was looking to speak with Gary's students for the story.

We talked on the phone, off the record, which my mother decided was preferable to having my name in print.

"Even the ride to the court would be a laugh, with games and music in the car."

"Some of his young students sensed his unhappiness, and he told one that he'd watched all these girls grow up in front of him, passing him by, and that he wanted his own child."

"He seemed preoccupied and snapped without provocation."

These are the traces of what I told him the night he interviewed me. My mother, who had listened to our conversation, penciled brackets around the lines in the article to remember what I had said. The faint gray lines are proof that I was part of this story, and that I wasn't.

Now Michael Stone is an author. One of his books was cowritten with the artist Eric Fischl. My mother kept a book of Fischl's artwork on our coffee table. I used to pull it on my lap and flip to the picture of a naked woman lying in bed, with one foot resting on her thigh, exposing the triangle of darkness at her center. In the painting, the light through the blinds zebra-streaks her body as she gazes at a boy, whose hand has slipped into the fold of her purse. *Bad Boy: My Life On and Off the Canvas*, it's called.

I call up Michael Stone to ask him questions about Gary Wilensky, two decades after he called me to do the same.

"As I recall, my editor called me as soon as the news had occurred and wanted it for the next week," he says. "I played [tennis] but not professionally, but I knew a lot of people in the New York tennis scene, so it wasn't hard for me to network."

Gary, he learned, was a large figure on the scene. "I'd never heard of him, but a lot of friends and people I played with, pros, clubs I played at, certainly knew of him," Stone says. "His reputation, as I recall, was pretty good. No one suspected he was leading this dark life. He kept it pretty well hidden."

What was the larger context of this story? Why did it matter? I ask, but not like that. More like a stumbling, twisted request for direction. A help-me-figure-out-why-this-still-matters-to-me statement that ends with a verbal uptick suggestive of a question mark.

He notes the intense competition among New York private school students at the time, and how that intensity translated to their social lives, where access and privilege were more instantly rewarded and less likely supervised. The phenomenon of teenage girls becoming tennis stars added another layer of pressure and exposure.

"How you tie that all together I don't know."

Before we hang up, Stone offers a suggestion.

"I don't know how much of this is a memoir and how much is crime reporting," he says. "But if it's even partly the latter, you've got to talk to her."

Her. The Daughter. The victim of Gary's attack.

THE FIRST time I reached out to the Daughter, early on in my investigation, I sent a long email that said very little. She wasn't sure what I wanted. Neither was I. I just wanted to talk, I suppose. I can't bring myself to pull up that email or the second one, which was sent a couple years later—more succinct but still expectant, filled with the ignorant sentiment of someone who believes her experience in any way compares to the experience of a trauma survivor. Maybe the emails weren't that bad, but my lack of consideration before I sent them was. Of course, she would want to talk about what happened, I thought, because I wanted to talk about what happened.

It wasn't until she politely turned down my request to speak to her that I realized the extent of my privilege.

What's most insufferable about privilege—whether white, wealthy, physically able, or free from the trauma of abuse—is the denial of its existence. The assumption that we are all the same. That some small emotional bruise you once had is comparable to the jagged head wound another endured, the memory of its stages—watery, crusted and matted, clean and indented but never entirely gone.

While each individual's experience is unique, post-traumatic stress disorder is common among victims of stalking, with some citing the impulse to go into hiding and the enduring fear that their predator will resurface. Stalking victims also frequently report depression, nightmares, anxiety, and flashbacks. And most of those victims—four out of five, according to statistics—are women.

The majority of stalkers are male, and many are triggered to act on their impulses when faced with real or perceived rejection by a female.

There is a quotation from Gavin de Becker, author of *The Gift of Fear: And Other Survival Signals That Protect Us from Violence*, that surfaces repeatedly in victim-related Internet communities. "Stalking is how some men raise the stakes when women don't play along. It is a crime of power, control, and intimidation very similar to date rape."

Today such Internet communities are providing outlets for survivors to share their stories. There are support groups, treatment methods, and mounting psychological research on the impact of stalking on victims. But in 1993, little was known about stalking behavior in general. It wasn't until 1998 that *The Psychology of Stalking*, the first summary of scientific research on the topic, was published, and even within those pages, victim accounts were scant.

What is as true now as it was back then is that we look to survivors of trauma for personal insight into ourselves. We read their books, watch their network interviews, and try to isolate what it takes to overcome the unthinkable. To survive—not simply within a traumatic circumstance, but all circumstances. We turn them into superheroes in order to believe that we, too, can fight death, when in fact those who've survived trauma may be more in touch with their own mortality. But this is all a generalization. No matter how many studies I cite, I can't know what the Daughter endured, and it isn't my right to know.

She wants to be left alone, a classmate told a newspaper when she returned to school in late April of 1993, captured flash-eyed in a baseball cap. But they wouldn't leave her alone, not for weeks until new stories came along. And perhaps she was finally given the space she deserved, until I emerged years later, wanting something, too many things. Insight, approval, trans-ference of experience, a survival story that would teach me a profound lesson in overcoming my own hurdles. But survival is earned, not passed down from hand to hand like so many other things.

"TURNS OUT, I'm not a very good reporter," I tell Michael, my old college boyfriend the poet, who was with me when I remembered Gary Wilensky.

Now Michael and I are middle-aged. We sit across from each other in the backyard of a coffee shop. He is a college professor with a wife and child. There are ten blocks of Brooklyn between our two homes. His downstairs neighbors complain about all the footsteps his family makes.

I remember one night in my own apartment, in bed with a different boyfriend, while two friends from out of town slept in the living room. There was a feeling of fullness, like the apartment would burst with the affection I felt for all the people inside it. All of them together because of me. *This must be what it's like to have your own family*, I thought. I didn't think about Gary. How he wanted a family of his own, too, and believed he could have it. As if it were something you could strangle into submission. Maybe it was. Not family, but the decision to have one. An idea floating past you that you either choose to grab or let move away, believing at some point, when you're ready, it will circle back again. When it doesn't, what happens to you then?

"Is that what you're doing? Reporting?" Michael asks, his wide blue eyes still the same eyes I remember, but his face, once gaunt, has filled in around them. He has become substantial, like a grown-up, I think, and wonder if he thinks the same of me or if men think about this differently. If they think, she's gained weight.

"I don't know. I'm looking for answers. I thought maybe the Daughter would want to speak with me, but I understand why she doesn't. It was stupid for me to assume."

"You should try her again," he says, but I won't.

"I'm not even certain what I'd ask. What is it I'm looking for?"

I met Michael when he was a senior in college and I was a freshman, at a Halloween party where he dressed like the Mad Hatter, but with his neck-length dyed-blond hair and his skeletal paleness, he just looked like Beck, who crooned "Debra" through someone's bedroom speakers. The rest of our college encounters were equally worthy of eye rolls. We took a film class together and went to the library to watch *Persona*. He lay on institutional carpeting in the dark AV room, and I rested my head on his chest, listening to his insides shoot air bubbles, pump fluids, rise and fall. The proximity of love, of finding out what love would be, was so perfectly placed in that moment. I could still make out the shape of it without feeling the flattening weight of a thing with dimensions. Just the outline, suddenly visible enough to believe it was coming. A moment to have and never have again.

Now Michael speaks of his marriage and how it came to be. They lived in different states and had limited job mobility. But he decided to make it work early on, without even mapping out a plan, because he loved her, and soon he discovered she loved him back. "You just have to decide what you want and you can have it," he says.

He was always generous, always a collaborator, always driving toward the shared story, not turning around to find the one he had missed.

"You're so good at relationships. I think I'm bad at them," I say, because I assume this is what people think when a woman is single and childless in her mid- to late thirties. But also because I think it's true.

"No," he says, "you're just good at being alone."

I wonder if this is something you can be good at. Maybe it's like being good at discount shopping or finding a parking spot, the kind of thing you tell yourself you're good at so you'll find the reward in commonplace things. Or maybe it's like being good at finding a vein, or sleeping in, or holding your liquor, or not letting other people's feelings affect your decisions—things that are only good in the moment and ultimately harmful.

"Maybe it's not my right to tell her story. I wasn't Gary's victim."

"But you're not telling her story," he says. "You're telling your own."

"And Gary's," I remind him.

"Piper," he says, his voice rattling with some throat-trapped fluid, "this is your story. Don't forget that."

1993

man: movie character

IN JANUARY, AN AMERICAN PRESIDENT IS sworn in, a Serbian village is attacked, Monica Seles beats Steffi Graf, a deranged fan plots revenge. There are protests in Turkey, a civil war in Sri Lanka, an art exhibition in outer space, a slight dip in homicides in New York City. Elvis is on a stamp; Michael Jackson is at the Super Bowl. Two movies about Amy Fisher are broadcast at the exact same time on different channels. There is a song called "I Will Always Love You," a song called "Deeper and Deeper," a song called "I'd Die Without You." Astronomers believe 97 percent of the universe is dark matter. A group of sixth graders at an all-girls school in Manhattan are collecting Absolut Vodka ads. A group of Ku Klux Klan members in Florida are protesting Martin Luther King Jr. Day. A movie star has died, a ballet dancer has died, a jazz trumpeter has died, a Supreme Court justice has died. A poet stands at a podium overlooking the country and speaks of a "piercing need."

Late in the month, Gary Wilensky drives thirty miles north of Manhattan to White Plains to accept an award. The USTA's Eastern Tennis Association has named him the coach of the year. His colleagues from two decades on the tennis circuit are at the event. Arthur Ashe, the first African-American man to win a Grand Slam singles title, is being inducted into the Hall of Fame. It's one of his final appearances before he succumbs to AIDS the following week.

There is dinner at the ceremony. Trophies are handed out at a podium. But Gary is immune to the celebration. Scrawny and slunk in his oversize suit, a shadow of gray stubble around his jaw, he seems funereal.

"What's the matter, Gary?" Those who know him are concerned.

What can he say? He says this: His father's health is declining. He's worried about him. And all that shuttling back and forth from Manhattan to Long Island to care for him is exhausting.

This isn't entirely a lie. Irving Wilensky, now in his eighties, isn't in the best health. So much time has passed since their picture was taken on the tennis court of the Catskills resort. Dressed in white tennis shorts and a velour V-neck, Gary had a crown of wavy brown hair and bulbous muscles above his knees. His father, who drove upstate to see Gary, the big-shot tennis director, in action, was still a sharp dresser in dark glasses and a mock turtleneck. The two men were flanked by a few name-brand tennis stars and a storied Catskills entrepreneur who had recruited Gary. When the camera flashed, Irving stuck one hand in his pocket and smiled with the sturdiness of a man who'd just completed his job.

Irving Wilensky, who will die in a year's time, is still, in January of 1993, a proud father. Of course he's heard Gary speak of regrets—that he couldn't make his marriage work, that he was too involved with his career, that he never settled down and had a family, that he was lonely. But Irving believes his son has other reasons to feel good about his life. He's become a shrewd businessman who earns a healthy living playing a sport he loves. And through his work, he's made a difference in so many kids' lives. That's something. Still, there are some things Irving doesn't know.

Inside a studio apartment, twenty-nine flights above the street, Gary Wilensky is making Valentine cards for his students. He sits cross-legged on the hardwood floor listening to one of his soft rock mixtapes—"Favorites." Laid out before him are index cards, a red ink pad, and stamps shaped like bears—each one holding a heart with a message: HANDLE WITH TLC. BE MINE. LUV YOU LOTS. There is a Mickey and Minnie stamp surrounded by fluttering hearts, and one Gary had custom made—the cartoon version of himself.

There is more work to be done. He writes letters. Three in total. When he is finished, he pulls out his tape recorder and reads them aloud to himself as two spindles roll round and round.

HAVE YOU SEEN ONE OF THOSE FILMS WHERE SOME GUY IS TRYING TO EXPLAIN SOMETHING THAT THE AUDIENCE KNOWS TO BE TRUE BUT ALL THE SCREEN CHARACTERS HAVE A DIFFERENT PERSPECTIVE AND WON'T BELIEVE OR UNDERSTAND THE TRUTH UNTIL THE END OF THE MOVIE?

MY INSATIABLE NEED OF A FAMILY AND THE IL-LUSIONS AND FANTASIES THAT I LIVED THROUGH A FAMILY I LOVED TO BE WITH AND ADMIRED MORE WITH TIME AND WISHED I COULD BE A PART OF . . . BUT TOO WELL ALWAYS UNDERSTANDING THE FICTION OF IT ALL . . . TAKING THE SWEET BUT ONLY FLEETING SPORADIC MOMENTS . . . AND THE INEVITABLE CRASH

LANDING OF REALITY WHEN "GOODBYE UNTIL NEXT
TIME" WOULD ARRIVE. I WISHED THAT ALL THE TIME
I SPENT WITH ALL OF YOU WOULD NEVER END . . . AND
WHEN THAT SAD TIME FOR ME ARRIVED, BE IT THE
LONG RIDE HOME ALONE OR THE LONELY CAB RIDE TO
MY APARTMENT AFTER THANKSGIVING . . . OBSESSION?
MAYBE SO . . . DANGEROUS? CERTAINLY IF I LAID ON A
SEVENTEEN-YEAR-OLD'S MIND . . . GUILTY BY CONNO-
TATIONAL PARENTAL LAW.

I LOST CONTROL AND I AM SORRY . . . I KNOW I HAD
NO RIGHT TO PUT [THE DAUGHTER] THROUGH ANY
OF THAT . . . BUT PLEASE BELIEVE ME THAT I NEVER
MEANT TO HARM [HER] . . . EXCEPT FOR YOU . . . I PROB-
ABLY LOVE AND GENUINELY CARE ABOUT [HER] MORE
THAN ANYONE ELSE SHE KNOWS . . . I JUST COULDN'T
HANDLE THOSE FEELINGS CORRECTLY BECAUSE OF MY
BACKGROUND AND I AM CURRENTLY TRYING SO HARD
TO MAKE UP FOR THE DAMAGE I'VE DONE BY TAKING
YOUR ADVICE, AND HOPEFULLY LEARNING HOW TO
DEAL WITH MY PROBLEMS SO THAT I NEVER ENDAN-
GER THE WELFARE OF A CHILD AGAIN.

YOU DON'T OWE ME ANY COURTESIES AFTER WHAT
I HAVE DONE . . . BUT I'M ASKING ANYWAY . . . PLEASE
LET ME KNOW ON OCCASION HOW [SHE] IS DOING . . .
COLLEGE ACCEPTANCES . . . TENNIS TOURNAMENTS . . .
RESULTS . . . HEALTH . . . STATE OF MIND . . . KNOWING
I HAVE NO POSITIVE VALUE IN [HER] LIFE IS UNBEAR-
ABLE PUNISHMENT . . . AND IF SHE SHOULD EVER SPEAK
A WORD, A PHRASE, A SENTENCE THAT PERTAINS TO

ME POSITIVELY ... PLEASE LET ME KNOW ... FOR THAT
WOULD BE A WONDER DRUG FOR MY CONSCIENCE.

PLEASE ACCEPT MY APOLOGY FOR EVERYTHING
WRONG I'VE DONE ... I PRAY EVERY NIGHT TO A GOD
I WANT TO BELIEVE IN FOR HER HEALTH, PEACE,
AND HAPPINESS ... I LOVED YOU ALL AND I'M JUST A
LONELY MAN WHO LOST HIS WAY ... AND MAYBE I'LL
SOMEDAY BE FORGIVEN AT THE END OF THE MOVIE.

When he has recorded it all, he stops the tape, folds the letters, and writes out the Mother's name and address on the front
of the envelopes. He slips them each in the mailbox and waits.

Maybe what he has written will lead to a reconciliation. If
not, he has spoken his truth, groveled, and unloaded. It's all
there.

His apology: He lost control and is sorry. The explanation:
He's just a lonely man who lost his way. His defense: He's not a
villain, but a character who's misunderstood. His promise: He's
seeking treatment. His plea: Open the door a crack and let him
back in. His warning: *Dangerous?*

This is his testimony. The paper on which it is written is
for the Mother, but the tape recording is for his own use. A
goodbye to his moviegoing audience, all the mothers and their
daughters. A blueprint of his own fractured mind, to be studied
after he's gone.

From the letters, Dr. Eric Hickey, a criminal psychologist who profiles child predators, will later surmise that Gary
Wilensky was "delusional but not insane."

"If he was a psychopath he would not write the letters," he'll explain. "He registered right from wrong, but was in denial of the harm he'd caused. This rejection he experienced when he was fired wrecked him and ended his fantasy world. He needed to fix it. When you get to that delusional place, you'll do anything to protect your own delusion."

Whether or not Gary believes he is in the wrong, he knows enough to concede to it, to declaw himself with a sympathetic explanation and a promise to change. Yet he can't help revealing that he hasn't. As much as he tries to reframe his passion for the Daughter as fatherly, his desperation to hear from her ("a word, a phrase, a sentence that pertains to me") shows his lack of control. If a part of him recognizes this, if he hesitates before he includes such a request, he is overridden by another impulse to feed his own obsession.

He imagines the ending, the moment he's validated, wherein his behavior, and the confusion surrounding it, suddenly make sense—it is coming soon.

"Maybe I'll be forgiven at the end of the movie," Gary says into a voice recorder. He speaks in monotone. All of his playful inflections and audible winks, the tinny nasal pitch, that hint of a Long Island accent, have been replaced by an unrecognizable voice. A man in a mask. *Dangerous?* Maybe so.

girl: x-rated

WHEN THE BOY IN THE WINDOW flicks his bedroom light on and off, it means pay attention. My own bedroom window is maybe sixty feet from his—too far to make out precise facial features, but close enough, hypothetically, to toss a rope of tied-together bedsheets through his window.

He must be a teenager, because he lives with his parents. They spend most of their time in a kitchen, two windows to the left. They are squat and old, and he is taller than them, with a mop of brown hair, thick thighs, and a big nose. It's the protrusions that stand out the most from this distance.

He's watching my parents, too. I know because his lights always flicker after they've fallen asleep. In the den, David Letterman talks to my snoring dad on the sofa. In my room, it's the boy's show: He wears a yellow T-shirt with no pants, and uses one hand to caress himself while the other brushes his hair. He acts like he doesn't see me watching, but this is just part one of his act. He puts down the hairbrush and picks up a blow-dryer on the bureau. Then he puts down the blow-dryer, walks to the window holding himself with one hand. He waves with the other.

His is the only penis I've ever seen, and it appears to be half an arm's length, rubbery and the color of a blood orange. He is instructional in the way he touches himself—as if he's teaching a group of students the techniques of a sport. It's all about form, control, consistency.

I used to watch him from my window seat in the dark so I wouldn't be seen, but eventually he'd wave to remind me I was there. If I ignore him, he switches his lights on and off and won't let up. Besides, I want to look, not so much anymore at the thing he's showing off, but at his face, which from this distance is just the general idea of a face. A face before it's been properly wired to a brain, an outline of what a face will be before the painter fills in the defining features, a Mr. Potato Head fitted with only a nose and a wig cap.

I have seen this boy's most intimate body part countless times. I know the layout of his bedroom, where his parents eat dinner, the fogged glass of his bathroom window, the one room in his apartment where the lights are always off, but I've never seen him blink. If I squint one eye, I could crush him between two fingers. He is like a tiny rubber doll with all his parts. It's strange how at a certain distance, people become objects.

"He's a pervert," my mother had said the first time we spotted him, months earlier. But first she had covered her mouth with her hand, because the whole thing was hysterical.

I was having a sleepover with two other girls from school when he made himself known. One girl spotted him first: He was brushing his hair, naked from the waist down. We thought we were spying on him until he walked to the window and waved his arm like a windshield wiper. We screamed and flopped on my bed, then dropped to the floor as if we were under attack and got to our knees to make sure he was still there. He waved again. When my mother heard our squealing and came into my room, we pointed to the window. I loved her for laughing, like she was one of us girls. And then she closed the curtain for the night.

When the first girl fell asleep, the rest of us decided to rub Vaseline on a phone cord and place it on her neck. "The penis is attacking you!" we chanted until she woke up. It was hilarious. Euphoric.

But it's different now, on these nights alone with him. It isn't funny at all, but instead generates an urgent, disgusting, rage-inducing, oily sensation. Is there a word for a fantasy you don't enjoy, a waking dream that you didn't have, but rather it had you? There is this teased-up version of me who wears a short denim skirt and has a nest of wild, curly hair and a gum-smacking painted-on mouth that spews the word *fuck* into his face as he presses this other me against the brick wall in the alleyway between our buildings. I hate them both. I want to drop an air conditioner on their heads and flatten them out. I want to make him feel as monstrous as I do.

It's an act of revenge, I think, no more than that, when I flick my own lights. I've stuffed a hot pink satin bra from my sister's drawer with balled-up tissues and tightened the leather strings on my suede hot pants. The tape deck plays recorded air until the first chords of "Break On Through (To the Other Side)" chase a bouncing ball into my room. Now I'm the ball, erratic and buoyant, a slippery hot pink target that shoots up to the bed and back down to the floor, flying, dropping, shooting up again.

I am Jim Morrison dancing around a fire pit. I'm Jim Morrison's Wiccan reporter girlfriend in the scene in the movie where they chase each other around a candlelit room covered in their own blood.

When the song is over, I drop to the ground, still pulsing.

Heavy on the knotted blue carpet, tissues unpacked from my bra in one hand. For a moment, my heart is the only organ in my body, and it's lodged in my ear canal. But soon it sags back down to my chest, and my brain takes over. *What did I just do?* Something I couldn't control, something I won't be able to back up.

Across the alleyway, the boy flicks his lights fast and furious. A silent applause.

girl: candy man

ON WEEKENDS, THE ENTRANCE TO THE Popover Café on Amsterdam Avenue is jammed with people listening for their names. You have to weave through the narrow spaces between bodies to reach the hostess stand. I'd done that once before, on another day, in other company, but the wait for a table was too long. *Gary, did you make a reservation? Gary? Gary?*

The outside of this restaurant, with its checked window curtains, is modeled after a homey coffee shop in a small country town. On the inside, it's a sleek red-and-black bistro with the hallmarks of every other popular brunch spot in the city. A book-sized reservation list, servers forearming platters of cream-sauced eggs, a waiting area crammed with pointy elbows, pricked ears, and darting eyes. A stagnant rage is reserved for those already seated, and a fresh hell-fire fury for each person who approaches the hostess stand.

Some tall lady with her hands on her hips stands between Gary and me, intentionally taking up space. I watch him talk with the hostess through the triangle in her arm. She is showing him a clipboard, and he's nodding. His smile is the shape of a croissant. The room smells of sweet, flaky dough. A hundred conversations braided together sound like one, a breathless monologue spoken by an alien in his alien language. No way we're getting a table.

Gary looks over at Emma and me, chucks his chin up, and signals with two fingers to follow him. He's got it all figured out.

We follow, believing we're being shown the bathrooms or maybe a back exit. But the hostess places three menus at a four-top and Gary pulls out a chair. He seems pleased as he settles in, but unforthcoming. If he explained his magic tricks, then they wouldn't be magic.

A waiter comes by and places a puffed pastry the size of a knuckled fist on each of our plates. In a ramekin on the table is a smooth, creamy scoop of strawberry butter. We dig it out with tiny knives and smother the steaming hollow insides of our pop-overs. Gary holds his pastry in one hand, but doesn't crack it open yet. Instead he watches, nodding, as I cram my mouth full of sweet, crusty bread. He wants to know what I think. Is it as good as he promised? Willy Wonka, I think when I look at him.

With an arm slung loosely around the back of his chair, he sinks into his seat sideways. His long legs, crossed at the ankle, extend beyond our table, creating a booby trap for waiters to trip over.

We talk about movies. Gary loves movies and so do I.

"Gary, tell us the ending of *The Crying Game*!"

Nope, he can't do that. It's a secret.

"Come on, please?"

Later.

"Gary, I saw *Alive*."

"The cannibal movie?"

"Yeah, it's a true story."

"Did you see the part when they eat their friends?"

"Yeah. It wasn't as scary as I thought it'd be."

"Anyone see *Body of Evidence*?" Gary's eyebrows rise mischievously.

It's a Madonna movie so it's supposed to be sexy. In October, her book, *Sex*, came out. The books came wrapped so you couldn't look inside. But there was a display copy in a music store by my house. I paged through the black-and-white photos, waiting for someone to scold me, but nobody did. There was a picture of her nude on a highway. A blond Marilyn Monroe wig on her head and a black strip of hair between her legs. In another photo, Vanilla Ice pressed into the side of her breast with his thumb. His diamond watch hung loose on his wrist.

Body of Evidence. It had the sound of a grown-up movie, like *Final Analysis. Double Impact. Basic Instinct. Fatal Attraction.* Always a combination of words that imply both legal proceedings and shadowy bedroom scenes. In the trailer for the movie, Madonna crawls over a courtroom table. Adult sex is so serious in the movies, catalyzed by murder or a grueling life-or-death trial. The men are always strong, battle-hungry, defiant in the courtroom—their only weakness the sight of an untrustworthy woman in a negligee. The act itself, the woman always on top of the man, turns heroes into hostages.

"I want to see *Groundhog Day,*" I say.

"What about *Falling Down?*"

I saw it with my parents. It wasn't like other Michael Douglas movies. There was no sex. Only guns. He played a man on a rampage through Los Angeles, enacting his own brand of justice. An *antihero,* my mother had called him when, in the end, we learn his violence was all an attempt to get to his daughter's birthday party. The hero-hero was a cop with my father's mustache, who was about to retire when he heard of an armed vigilante.

Gary knows the actor who played the cop. He's played tennis with him before. *Great guy.*

After Gary pays the bill, Emma and I are ready to get back in the car and head home, but he has one quick errand to run. We groan, we protest, but we're going anyway.

"Didn't I take you to the Popover Café?"

Yes.

"Didn't I manage to get us a table?"

Yes.

"Now it's you girls' turn. Come on, that's how it works."

The windows of the shop where Gary takes us are covered by black curtains. If there's a sign above the door, I don't notice it. Inside, it's a bakery, a glass-cased museum of chocolate figurines, glistening braided bread, pastel-glazed cakes and cookies. It cracks open older memories of other bakeries, walking into a kaleidoscope of unknown flavors and having to choose just one thing, the decision informed not by experience, but pure magnetism. What colors do you most want to taste? What reminds you most of your favorite things?

Everyone knows Gary. He is talking to the lady behind the bakery counter. She wears her hair in a head scarf ironically, and has dark brown lipstick and an iron-on baby tee. The way Gary is leaning down with his elbows on the display case, paying attention to her, bothers me. She tosses her head back and laughs at whatever he's saying. Why the hell did he bring us in here?

Emma is standing at the display case on the other end of the shop. "Look." She points to a selection of chocolates. "Penises," she hisses. Right in front of us is a row of pointy chocolate statues mounted on two small hills. We look at each other and cover our mouths to catch the noises. I point to a row below the chocolates: challah bread in the shape of vaginas. On closer inspection, all of the pastries behind the glass are shaped like genitalia or nude statuettes or couples naked and intertwined, bulging chocolate veins.

Emma's face is pink. I'm covering my mouth so it doesn't explode.

Gary is at the door holding a cake box. He's ready to go.

"What's so funny?" he asks.

"Nothing," I say. I'm trying to read his expression to see if he recognizes the mistake he's made, going to a bakery like this instead of a normal one.

We are standing in front of the display case so he doesn't see what's inside it. And now we are following him out the door.

"Something's funny," he says. "What is it?" But he's smiling, like he knows.

When I get home, I don't tell my mother what I saw. Gary was testing our maturity. It was a privilege to enter an adult space without being chased away, to not have to listen from another room while they cackled, to join them in their conspiracy. I was not about to lose that privilege by acting like what I saw was a big deal. And it confirmed what I already believed: The realm of adults, when they're not around children, is more perverse than they let on.

I've seen the newsstands' plastic-wrapped magazines tucked inside their slots. Their names in fluorescent bubble writing—*Juggs, Bazooms, Screw*—as cartoonish as candy wrappers. I've passed Chippendales on First Avenue, and learned that although it bears the name of two Disney characters, it is not a place for children. I've seen a woman in a licorice bikini on a birthday card in the adult rack of the stationery store, before being shooed away by the store clerk. And now this, a whole bakery of sex. This is the secret adults don't want us to know: They are just children with sex. It is not at all like the movies where they move slowly in the shadows between satin sheets. When we are not around, they gorge on candy and comics and dirty jokes, just as we do, only more so. There is nothing mature about their desires. Their mouths are rimmed in chocolate. They writhe in whipped cream. They fuck like Willy Wonka.

And Gary let me see. He didn't shoo me away. He wanted me to know their composure—their rules and manners—are all lies. They tell us no, and they do worse. They even eat sex.

A VALENTINE from Gary Wilensky sits on top of our mail pile. It's mine, so I take it into my room and study it for secret messages. Some kind of code, a private joke, an authentication that suggests this index card was designed specifically for me. But it's just a bunch of red stamps for little kids—teddy bears and Mickey Mouse. Gary's face is a red stamp, too. On the other side of the card, there's a telephone number for his tennis-tip hotline. And his address. And my address. And that's all.

girl: storm

ON A SATURDAY AFTERNOON, THE SNOW starts falling in clumps. From the living room window, we watch umbrellas turn inside out. The sky is the same color as the street: charcoal burned white. "They're saying it could be the worst storm we've had in a century," Mom says. "Nah," says Dad. "They're just trying to goose you up."

"They" are the weather forecasters who talk over each other on two TVs—one in the library, the other in the kitchen. *Cyclone . . . The coast of Florida . . . Winds approximately . . . Hurricane . . . Snowfall up to . . .*

Emergency supplies wait on the coffee table. Long candlesticks, two flashlights, Trivial Pursuit.

A brick of meat loaf roasts in the oven. Water bubbles on a burner.

The sky cracks in half. A blue bolt aims at a skyscraper but misses. The dog whimpers and flattens into a black-and-white puddle on the floor. This is not her night.

When the room shudders with blue light, it reminds me of watching through a window at someone else watching TV. How lonely it feels from the outside.

My bedroom window rattles. The wind sounds like a giant insect rubbing its legs together. When I press my palm against the cold glass, it presses back. All the lights are on in the building across the alleyway. Everyone is home together, waiting out the storm or watching it. Even the boy across the way is with his parents, huddled at a round table in his yellow-lit kitchen. He sits with his father, while his mother darts in and out of view, fussing about.

We eat dinner with the newscasters. *Gusts seventy to a hundred miles an hour . . . Evacuation plan.*

When my father speaks, my mother shushes him and turns up the volume. He waves her off. "I want to hear this," she explains.

After dinner she asks "Who wants Tasti D-Lite?" and all is forgiven. A frozen low-calorie dessert shop has opened on Lexington Avenue and now our freezer is packed with plastic tubs of an off-white chalklike substance. The flavor choices are eggnog, pumpkin spice, or cheesecake, but they all taste like frostbitten vanilla.

A piece of paper attached by a magnet to the fridge reads *Thin tastes better*, the motto of a well-known Manhattan diet doctor my parents went to a few years back. Each week after they visited his office, they returned home with a new audiotape of motivational one-liners recorded in a man's thick Queens accent. Now they spray butter-flavored liquid on their toast and squirt fat-free blue cheese on their salad. They spoon cold white shavings into their bowls and call it dessert.

Life is what happens when you're making plans reads another piece of paper buoyed by a magnetic pig in a chef's hat. The words are written in black felt-tip and traced over a second time, as if a mistake has been corrected.

After dinner, Dad is laid out on the sofa intermittently snoring and waking up to flip the channel. I am beside him on a love seat, dressed in my mother's silk pajama suit, waiting for that moment we were promised, when the lights quit, the refrigerator stops humming, the TV goes dark, and the only people in the whole world are us.

Mom pads to the doorway in her slippers to say she's going to bed. My father snorts alive, gives a drowsy good night, and goes back to sleep.

"I love you," she says to me, which means be careful or goodbye or, in this case, good night.

"Mom?" I ask. "What does it feel like to love something?"

She is tired. This is not the kind of question someone should field right after she announces she's going to bed. But she is up for the challenge, rattling off a bunch of adjectives I've heard before to describe a mother's love. Still, that's not what I want. I want evidence that love isn't just a word we substitute for other words, but a sensation. She nods, taking a moment to find a comparison I can grasp.

"You know how you feel about the dog?" she says, answering one impossible question with another.

The dog has a black mask over her eyes and a long white nose. The underside of her body is white as well, and there are brown speckles on her raw pink belly skin.

The way I feel about her makes my teeth mash as if I were flattening bits of her for digestion. I want to pop her with my incisors to make the feeling go away. Recognizing this urge, she keeps her distance. My mother is the dog's favorite. She reinforces this fact by following my mother out of the room.

When my parents fight, it's about the dog. She is untrainable and leaves puddles around the apartment when everyone is away. Each one blames the other for her accidents. Someone didn't walk her enough; someone was too lenient with punishment. My mother hired an animal therapist who said the dog understands what's right and wrong, but suffers from anxiety. The fear of being bad when she's left alone.

At a loss, my mother has been known to lock the guilty party in the hallway outside my bedroom in the hopes that solitary confinement is rehabilitative. She'll close my door and warn me that *under no circumstances* . . .

On those nights, the dog will shove the black tip of her nose in the space underneath my doorway. A paw pokes through, searching with its hooks for an escape route to dig. I wait for the footsteps in other rooms to subside before opening the door to let her in.

When I do, she moves into the room slowly, guiltily, planting herself down on the carpet and tucking her limbs under her body, nose to tail, forming a tight circle of shame. I pound the mattress, pleading with her to come up on the bed, to be bad, to understand that they're wrong, not her. But she won't budge. She wants to make it clear: She is waiting for someone else, someone more important than me, to forgive her.

But tonight she isn't looking for forgiveness. She was good today, and free to follow my mother into the master bedroom. She flattens out beside my mother's bed and rests her head on one paw, raising it each time a heavy snowflake smacks the glass. Now her concern is the world exploding outside. Mom is above her, asleep with a *People* magazine in an A-frame on her chest. On the cover is a picture of David Koresh with the headline "The Evil Messiah." He looks like Jim Morrison. I pull the magazine off her body and take it into my room.

On another Saturday night around this time, I was at a suite in the Regency Hotel. A boy who liked Bianca was living there temporarily, though we didn't ask why. A renovation, a divorce, something to do with money and sadness. We brought a six-pack of Rolling Rock and placed it on the coffee table alongside a plastic bag of weed and a plate with a few stale fries half covered by a silver room-service top. As the boy licked a rolled joint, he closed his eyes and his long eyelashes jigsawed together underneath a twisted backward baseball cap. I pictured his tongue on top of mine, and then I pictured holding him while he wept about his sadness into my shoulder.

He pulled Bianca into a bedroom and took the joint with him. I sat on a chair in the living room facing a muted episode of *Saturday Night Live* and waited until it was time to go home.

"So?" my mother asked later that night, eating a Mallomar in her nightgown at the kitchen table. "Meet any nice boys?"

Then a few days later, when the phone rang, my mother answered it in the kitchen and called my name. "A boy," she mouthed, trying to restrain a smile. She pitched herself on a stool at the kitchen island and pretended to flip through a catalog, fooling no one.

It was the boy with the lashes. His voice was deeper than I remembered. My mouth became a dried-up scab and my tongue a Band-Aid that peeled off it each time I spoke. He said he lost my number and it wasn't easy finding it again. He asked me what I was doing. I told him nothing. He said he wanted to see *The Crying Game*, even though he knew the ending. I said I wanted to see it, too. I took my mother's diet soda from her hand and she got herself another one.

"Well, why don't we see it together?" he said and then he

made a joke about how we could take along my short friend and buy her a ticket to *Aladdin*. This is how long it took for me to recognize his mistake.

"I'm the short friend," I said. "No, you're not," he insisted, and I wished he was right. When he asked about the color of my hair, the other line beeped. I clicked the receiver and pushed the swinging kitchen door again to stand in the dog's hallway. My mother yelled something about me ripping the phone cord. It was Bianca on the other line. When I told her what was happening, I held the receiver with my neck so I was free to dig my nails into my wrist.

"He thinks I'm you," I said, heaving quick Lamaze breaths to simulate laughter. When I clicked back to the boy, he'd been replaced by the flatline alarm of a dial tone. I let it flatline a little longer so I could say a fake goodbye, and unknotted the phone cord, placing the receiver in the cradle with immense concentration. I wanted to stay a little longer inside that moment and not the next one, when I had to turn around to face my mother. "So who was that?" she asked, her mouth still delighted.

Worse than knowing you're unlovable is believing, momentarily, that you are not. In the old apartment, I would watch from the bedroom doorway when my sister's boyfriends came over to pick her up. They'd stand in their overcoats, shaking my mother's hand. Then they'd take my sister's hand, and her silver bracelets chimed as she walked out the door. Fairy dust.

When my parents are asleep, I can sit on my bathroom sink and smoke a cigarette out the window. The storm is still alive. It coughs snow in my face through the open window. I pull on a Dunhill, hard enough that it burns. Bianca says I smoke too loud. Maybe so. I wish I was an easier person to love.

A lemony light flickers from a window in the building across the alleyway. Maybe it's been flickering for a while, and I hadn't noticed. Through the white scrim, I think I see the boy walking toward the window, though it's hard to tell if he's exposed. His whole body looks like a shadow, a black piece of paper cut out in the shape of a boy. There is his torso and his big oval head, tilted slightly. And there is his hand, all five fingers, flat on the glass. The cloud of weather between us is soft and twinkling. I place my hand on the glass, too, and leave it there for a moment.

man: storm

ON A SATURDAY NIGHT IN MARCH, a cyclone banged on Gary Wilensky's window and lit up his studio apartment in a spastic blue light. Snow spitballed in every direction, and thunder gave way to an achy, wind-borne moaning. Other families in other apartments huddled together behind windows, and those who lived alone watched them through a white veil.

The next day, ice clinked against window glass. The airports were closed. Ten inches of snow piled up in Central Park. Governor Mario Cuomo declared a state of emergency. Newscasters prattled on about the Storm of the Century and the Great Blizzard of '93. All the shovels came out and the digging began.

Now it is Monday, and Gary Wilensky is getting himself a gun. Not a real gun, but a movie prop. Still, the one he rents from a shop that services set designers is a real .38 caliber revolver. It's just been modified to fire blanks. The pistol is heavy in your hand, like a trophy.

Like that silver little Smith & Wesson Michael Douglas finds at his feet in *Falling Down*, a film that's spent the past two weeks in the number one box office spot. Douglas's character—an unemployed engineer with a flattop and Eisenhower glasses—blazes a warpath through the streets of Los Angeles, amassing an arsenal and taking out his frustrations over losing his job and family on anyone who interferes with his mission to attend his daughter's birthday party. "I'm the bad guy?" he asks the cop who catches up with him at the end of the movie. "How'd that happen?"

On Thursday, when the snow has turned to cliffs of packed yellow ice all along the sidewalks, Gary makes his way to his therapist's appointment.

He'd begun treatment shortly after he was fired by the Mother. Maybe he thought if he got help, he could wipe clean his past and all would be forgiven. It had worked once before, but that was long ago. Anyway, he's of another mind-set now.

Today, in his therapist's office, he has news: He's done with treatment. He's going to try something else.

A few days later, Gary has changed his mind. He needs a real gun. So he drives an hour east to Farmingdale, Long Island. While it's gotten harder to purchase a gun in the city, between stringent permit requirements and the prior year's ban on assault rifles, there are still loopholes to the law if you drive out of Mayor Dinkins's purview in any one direction. There's talk of the Brady Bill being signed into law, mandating federal background checks, but that doesn't concern Gary. He'll be long gone by the time it's passed.

Right now, what matters is directly in front of him—the Long Island Expressway and the choices that lay ahead. Remingtons, Colts, Smith & Wessons. And real ammo. No blanks.

He is a different man than he was only two months ago at the awards ceremony. If his mood was leaden then, now it is jet-fueled.

And if he passes exit 37 on the right and sees the exit sign for Roslyn, there's a version of Gary Wilensky who might blaze out the window, over the loose, shimmying trees and back into his old high school gym, where "Long Tall Sally" would clatter as he twirled and twirled his dance partner, all sweaty-palmed and buzzing, pulling her close to his chest and tilting her over the dance floor.

American Outdoor Sports is an emporium of weapons: pump action, single shot, bolt action, semis, slugs, choke tubes—even fixed blade knives and spear points. But it's the Cobray 9mm semiautomatic carbine that hooks him. In February, the *New York Times Magazine* had a feature on street guns and the benefits of a 9mm semi, which is lighter than a revolver and easier to handle. But the standout feature of a weapon like this particular Cobray is the way it looks. It's long, T-shaped, and bulky—a little bit *Scarface*, a little bit *RoboCop*. They call them "ugly guns" on the street because of how absurdly large they are compared to pistols.

It looks just like the "ugly gun" Michael Douglas whips out in *Falling Down*, when he demands the manager of the burger chain serve him breakfast during lunch hours. "Ever heard the expression 'the customer is always right'?"

Sold. Gary will be back in two weeks for a shotgun.

In the meantime, there is more to buy. Disguises—a fake mustache, a pile of wigs. Copper red, medium brown, sandy blond, and one wig that's grandma gray with tight little roller curls. Somewhere along the way he picks up a white rubber mask—the kind a horror-movie villain would wear to hide his charred and pulpy face. Even on its own, laid out on the floor, without a human face behind it, it is the boogeyman, shaking awake that dormant fear from childhood of the faceless man—who, up close, looks as if he's standing far away, his expression unreadable. A masked man who wants something, but what?

Downtown is where all the kink shops are, and Gary has a grocery list of items to buy, though get him in any shop and he'll go off book, clearing out shelves and loading up baskets. He's a salesclerk's dream, blowing through thousands of dollars in a clip. He can't stop. If he's curious about something, if he wants to take an item home and try it out, he'll buy it—full price.

Forget what he buys in sex shops. It's what you'd think, only the most expensive versions. Each silver link, each instrument of pain and restraint, will serve as visual symptoms of his disease.

Is there a name for what he has? There is a boundlessness to his energy. He is flooded with new ideas, new items to scrawl on a pad, new supplies he needs to buy in order to quiet his mind. There is always more to buy. He can't stay still: bouncing uptown, downtown, east toward the shore, and soon north toward the mountains. But there is also a certainty to his mission, an inevitability that lurches him forward.

He makes lists, charts, preparations. He returns to his studio with fistfuls of shopping bags and turns to his list to check off more items. He is trying to stay organized. His mind veers. Despite attempts to categorize items in columns on the page, he can't seem to stay on track. WHEELCHAIR is in the same column as LAMPS and SEXY NIGHTWEAR. SANITARY FOR GIRLS is in the same section as HAMMER and WINDOW BARS. RAZOR BLADES is circled with an arrow that points to BLOOD CATCHER. He writes NO TRESPASSING. He writes NIGHT TELESCOPE. He writes CARBON

MONOXIDE. He writes KINKY and underlines it, adding six items beneath it. He starts a column just for food items, but forgets to fill it in. He puts a checkmark next to SLEEPING BAG, writes BAG FOR HEAD, and then begins doodling cursive letters on the other side of the page.

He starts a new section: MEDICAL SUPPLIES. He buys medical supplies. He's found a place on East Seventy-Second Street where he can purchase a wheelchair. Also on the list, BEDPAN.

Finally, there's SpyWorld. Forty-Ninth and First Avenue, across the street from the bus stop. Gary knows the area well. In an unremarkable building just a few blocks north of the United Nations is a toy store full of expensive traps. SpyWorld's owner claims to be a former wire expert for the NYPD, and through certain channels that haven't been named, he has acquired the kind of military-grade spy gear you wouldn't think existed outside of movies.

These are not dime-store gadgets for peeping at your neighbor, but cutting-edge technology worthy of the store's clientele: government agents, Interpol, billionaires, embittered spouses. There are long-range tracking devices, voice-altering machines, police scanners, pin-drop-sensitive security monitoring systems, a pair of $1,500 binoculars outfitted with microscopic microphones, a $1,200 parabolic laser device designed to pick up conversations from a mile away, a few $6,000 fax machine interceptors and scramblers, a set of $8,000 night vision goggles courtesy of unnamed sources in Russia. And here a James Bond section, with hidden microphones disguised in Rolexes, beer cans, and silver coins.

Gary was once so giddy while shopping here, he posed for a picture. At the time, his hair was still dark. He wore a fluorescent blue windbreaker over a fluorescent blue pullover. A mustache ran straight across his face as if it'd been stuck there with adhesive glue. Maybe it was. Eyebrows arched, smile naughty, he stood before a wall taped with articles. The most visible one being a photographic spread of semiautomatic rifles.

But that was another trip at another time. This time he's prepared to spend five figures. Tracking devices, voice altering machines, an array of hypersensitive security monitoring equipment and a pair of night vision goggles—like the goggles Buffalo Bill wore in *Silence of the Lambs*, when the audience sees Clarice through his eyes, filtered through green light, feeling her way around his dungeon. "You don't know what pain is," he'd warned.

Outside SpyWorld, the bus stops across the street. Five years ago, Gary visited that spot every morning, camera in hand, to film two boys, eleven and twelve. But first he'd tuck in his hair and tighten the laces of his black leather mask, becoming the shadow of a man. Not the Gary Wilensky who dresses in tutus and laces up his roller skates, or the cartoon one on the T-shirts, but the one who covers his face in animal skin and presses his eye to a glass square closing in on two young faces, imprinting them onto thin plastic sheets of tape, and then sealing each tape in the trunk of his car until the day came when they were finally discovered. Now here he is years later, not a new man, as his court-ordered therapist was led to believe in 1988, but an old one with a new mask.

girl: breakup

BY NOW WE HAVE A RHYTHM. We speak in light flickers when the lights in other rooms have gone dim. Sometimes I flash my lights. More often, it's him flashing his. Sometimes, though, his window is dark, his blinds are down, and all I can see is a nose poking through. He is watching, waiting. Other times he has hoisted the blinds way up and his room is lit in a theatrical spotlight. But tonight there's something new. The bottom half of his window is covered up. There's a large white sheet of paper pressed against the glass. And there is writing on it—big loopy letters and a tilted question mark with a hollowed-out dot. *What is your name?*

Four words. Words. He has words. Now there is language, not just muted signals. And a public acknowledgment of what we've been doing, that it hasn't been something acted out in a semiconscious dream state or something we can each pretend the other has misconstrued. Now there is no denying what we've been doing. It's been written out and made official: *What is your name?*

Something about his handwriting frightens me. It slants to the right and seems urgent. The bellies of his As are perversely elongated. The W is disproportionately large—a result of over-eagerness, poor spatial judgment. And that tilted question mark with the emptied-out dot—that's just silly. *What is your name? What is your name?* What does he want? What is it he needs from me? I feel drenched in ectoplasm or some kind of clear viscous glue that insects shoot out to trap a mate.

I want to pull down my curtains, but they're billowy and large and really not meant for practical purposes, rather to frame the window in scallops. Pulling them down is like bringing a sailboat to shore—you really have to know what you're doing, and there are a ton of ropes involved. But if I manage to pull down the curtains, it's worse. I can't acknowledge that I've seen his poster. He can't know that I am a person who reads and feels things and reacts. We are only the outlines of bodies and the skin-colored approximations of faces. We are dollhouse characters for each other; that's what we were supposed to be. I thought we had agreed this wasn't actually happening. *What is your name?* When did such a simple question become so hard to answer?

For three days I crawl on the floor to hide from the boy and his sign. I do my homework cross-legged on the carpet under a dimly lit halogen lamp. I will not respond. I have to respond. I could write my name. I could ask for his name. I could tell him to meet me in the alleyway, but I would never do that. But I could.

When my mother walks into my room, she turns up the light to full blast. "Why is it so dark in here?" Another question I can't answer. I point to the window. To the sign. She moves closer to it and squints her eyes, reading each word aloud. *What. Is. Your. Name.*

It doesn't register with her at first. The last time she had seen the boy was the first time we had both seen him, months ago. Then her whole posture changes. Her chest puffs out; her hands on her hips triangulate at the elbow so her body takes up more space. When she looks at me, her brow furrowed, I want to be see-through. "This is still going on?" she says.

It's not clear to either of us if she's angry with me as she hoists the scalloped curtains down and clack, clack, clacks out of my room.

A call is made in the kitchen with the door closed.

"Hi . . . favor . . . daughter . . . going on."

I am a disgusting person with disgusting thoughts.

A few hours later, she's back in my room holding a poster-sized sheet of blue cardboard paper. Written across it in black marker and traced over a second time: *You have been reported to the police.* She tapes it to my window, and in the morning when the light comes through, all I can see are her big black backward letters and the vague outline of windows that all look the same.

At breakfast, she tells me what else she has done. A friend of hers—a former cop who was a bouncer at one of the teen dances she used to organize—is taking care of it. When it's dark again and the boy's apartment is drenched in yellow light, I watch from the bathroom window. There is a man sitting with his parents at the kitchen table. Then he is gone and the boy's parents are in his bedroom. His mother points to the window. His father raises a fist and pushes the boy so hard he lands on the bed and bounces. Although he's bigger than both his parents, he looks shrunken when he gets back up, his head hanging low, his arms slack at his side. His mother walks to the window and closes his blinds. Then the boy, with his head still hung, disappears.

girl: love songs

I KNOW GARY'S SECRET. I'VE SEEN the playlists on the covers of his mixtapes, and I've been in the car alone with him when he let the radio knob ease from Z100 to 106.7 Lite FM. I've watched him as he waited for the light, resting his head back and closing his eyes to the pastel sound of Peter Cetera. And I felt it, too—that longing.

This is private music, the kind you're supposed to groan about when flipping through stations. You're supposed to press the scan button as fast as you can to obliterate it from the air, and replace it with something younger, harder, more guarded, less earnest. There is nothing cool about a heartbroken man singing in falsetto or a woman harmonizing with him. It's a weakness. I have it and so does Gary.

"Next Time I Fall," "Don't Know Much," "Somewhere Out There" (the theme from *An American Tail*), "All Out of Love." "One More Night."

It's a mistake to call these love songs. They are the musical architecture of tears, the slow-dripping sounds of losing someone. They are not about love, but about the agony of separation embedded in the code of love. They are about me and my mother.

I discovered this when I was in third grade, racked with compulsive thoughts of her death. Whenever she would leave me, even to go to the grocery store, I would score my emotional state with one of those songs, not because it made me feel better or braver, but because those songs, as overwrought as they were, expressed exactly how it felt when we were apart.

The doctor called what I had separation anxiety. I call it mourning. It wasn't the fear of losing my mother, it was the awareness that I had already lost a part of her—the part of her arm that balanced me, the part of her lap that fit my body like an armchair. "That hurts," she began to say when I'd crawl onto her seat in the car. "You're getting too big." That was supposed to be a good thing, I understood that. But I also understood that with each new moment, two new versions of us shed two older versions. The more time passed, the further the distance between us and them, between the two of us now. I couldn't crawl into the front seat with her anymore. That part of life was over, and every day we moved further away from it, until one or both of us would eventually disappear.

So I began the grieving process in advance, to prepare for what the pain might consist of, the sickness it carried with it. It felt like melting—all the fluids in my body were draining out of me—and it sounded like Linda Ronstadt and Aaron Neville, like Peter Cetera and Cher, like Phil Collins and REO Speedwagon, like Lite FM.

Even now, while we are inside Gary's car, the opening keys of the synthesizer on "One More Night" bring me back to when I was most agonized, and in a way, most in touch with my own existence, with hers. My mother. My first love. The first person I couldn't afford to lose. As the song drifts between our headrests, I wonder if Gary is thinking of his mother, too.

2014—2016

mothers, fathers, others

GARY'S MOTHER, EDITH WILENSKY, COULD BE the daughter
of a Connecticut socialite. She could be the sister of a war hero
who died in combat in 1948. She might be the daughter of a
Russian Jew or a Polish Jew. Or not a Jew at all, but likely a
Jew. She could be Edith Fox, or Edith Parks, or Edith Wolfe.
Or Woolf. Or Wolf. Or Wulf. I've gathered leads to all these
surnames, though I'm uncertain which one, if any, would have
led me to her.

In Edith's day, a man was given a name. A woman was given
a temporary tag to be traded in for the prize of a romantic commitment. Any vestige of her old self was bumped to the middle
slot, and any middle name that once filled the slot vanished, as
was expected of women's middle names. Maiden names are only
slightly less obsolete—they're for password verifications and
deep genealogy dives. Maiden names are designed like disappearing ink, dissolving a former identity as easily as a felt brush
wipes a blackboard clean of a lesson plan.

What happened in Edith Wilensky's life before she took the
name Wilensky and then after she removed it? The original
surname given with the hope that it would one day be replaced,
the married surname taken with the hope that it wouldn't. But
when a marriage fails, the assumed last name isn't really hers
anymore either. Maybe this is why Edith Wilensky changed her
name after her divorce, or maybe she remarried. Either condi-

tion, combined with the years that have passed, has made her a
challenge to locate.

What I know for certain is that Edith was born in 1918 in
Hartford, and took the last name Wilensky by the age of
twenty-one. Her husband was a Jewish salesman eight years her
senior, named Irving Wilensky. They lived on Ocean Avenue
in Brooklyn, home to a cross section of working-class Italian
and Jewish immigrants. Irving pulled in around $130 a week
hawking textiles for dresses, while his wife stayed at home and
cared for their only son, Gary, born September 1, 1939.

In that same year, in Queens, the 1939 World's Fair was
erected. The fair, with the theme World of Tomorrow, offered
44 million visitors a glimpse into the future—a promise of a
bright new post-Depression era—never mind the barrel of a
second world war. What mattered within the parameters of
Flushing Meadows, which would later become home of the US
Open, was the prospect of an automated highway system, dish-
washing machines, mechanical pets, cigarette-smoking robots,
and a historic dedication by Franklin Delano Roosevelt, marking the first televised broadcast of an American presidential
speech.

That same year, Irving announced the launch of Gary Junior,
a firm manufacturing junior dresses for wholesale buyers, in the
March 31 issue of *Women's Wear Daily*. Quilted taffeta, nylon
cord, gold leaves embossed on cotton swing skirts. Sketches of
slender women with cinched waists and skirts that belled out
over Barbie-slim legs, daintily shod in ink-drawn pumps, all
accompanied ads for Gary Junior in the trade paper throughout
the early 1950s. Irving, who was first and foremost a salesman,

recognized early on that messaging mattered. He gave each pattern a name—"Thunder and Lightning," for a rayon taffeta print. A striped chambray skirt and rope belt, he called "The Skirt That Sells on Sight."

In 1949, he placed a full-page ad that was prescient of a *Mad Men* era. The image was simply a giant hollow exclamation point. The large display text read "HEY." In smaller print, potential buyers were invited to visit their showroom.

Two weeks later, another full-page ad featured a giant question mark, with the words "AND WHERE HAVE YOU BEEN?"

The ads were aggressive and hard to ignore. It didn't matter if buying dresses wasn't your business, the message was for everyone reading the paper: Pay attention, remember the name, Gary Junior.

It worked. The company, which had its offices on West Thirty-Fifth Street in Manhattan, continued to expand and won two major contracts totaling 30,000 dress orders less than two years later. There was enough brand recognition (and money spent to develop it) that by the early fifties, when a fourteen-year-old Gary suffered from appendicitis, *Women's Wear Daily* wished him a speedy recovery in their pages.

By 1950, Irving, Edith, and Gary had moved to Hewlett Harbor, Long Island, a South Shore alcove encircled by placid shorelines. Developers at the turn of the century erected Gold Coast–style mansions for local magnates, and returned in the forties and fifties to build sleek single-family units for the upwardly mobile middle class. Advertised as the area's most exclusive community, Hewlett Harbor became an instant subur-

ban oasis for commuters to the city, with brand-new homes—
sold prebuilt—averaging $35,000 complete with dropped living
rooms, General Electric appliances, thermopile insulation, in-
frared and ultraviolet lamps, and built-in liquor cabinets.

Irving's wages also went toward a first-class cabin cruise
to the West Indies for husband and wife aboard the SS *Nieuw
Amsterdam*, a luxury ocean liner.

But the following year, Gary Junior's reputation took a hit
when the Federal Trade Commission charged the company
with mislabeling the wool count in their dresses. The complaint
against Wilensky and his partner, Oscar Zinn, was eventually
dismissed on the grounds of insufficient evidence, but a year
of negative press took its toll. Irving sold his Hewlett Harbor
home in 1952, and by 1954, Gary Junior had become Galy
Junior, still a dress manufacturer but with a new, nonfamilial
name. Soon Irving's partner, Oscar, sold his stake in the company and joined a competing label.

Edith and Irving were through as well. A teenage Gary
Wilensky moved with his father to Roslyn's newly built Silver
Hill apartment complex, a multiunit efficiency that looked like a
redbrick high-rise chopped down to the trunk.

Roslyn was an idyllic hamlet trimmed by leafy tree branches,
lined with a grassy park overlooking a pond, and cinched at the
waist by a street-long village with a soda shop and a post office.
The local news in 1955 centered around parking disputes and
a protest by a group of students against what was described as
"horror" content, prompted after a reading of *The Blackboard
Jungle* in class. When they weren't promoting "self-censorship"
of books, students at Roslyn High waged a war, via pamphlet,
against girls wearing too much makeup.

Still, there was no censoring one of the most prominent and tragic headline news stories of the year. A recent graduate of Roslyn High was brutally raped and murdered in Greenwich Village by a convicted sex offender who spotted her on the street and followed her home. Much coverage was devoted to the search for the suspect and his drawn-out trial, in which his lawyer claimed his sexual urges were "so overpowering that he became a wild man."

Meanwhile, Irving's Galey Junior had sold $1 million worth of merchandise in a single season. Running a small company in high demand might have meant long days in Manhattan and nights commuting home to Roslyn, but Irving spent as much free time as he could with Gary, often on the tennis courts. He'd taught his son to play at age five and continued to practice with him regularly.

There are questions that might be asked: Why didn't Gary live primarily with his mother? How often did he see her? Where did she go?

According to *New York* magazine, she moved to a home nearby, but that is the extent of what I know. A few of Gary's high school acquaintants told the magazine that he reeled over his parents' split and blamed his mother for leaving him. He told two classmates she was dead after suffering a long illness.

Gary's high school friend Neal Pilson can't recall ever meeting Gary's mother, which was odd, considering their tight-knit community. "I knew everyone else's mother," he says. "Come to think of it, I don't even know where Gary lived."

It's tempting to assume Gary's relationship with his mother was fractured by his parent's divorce. In one small scientific analysis, adult stalking behavior was linked to separation from a primary caretaker in early life. This perceived rejection, when coupled with other mental disturbances, might resonate in later life when the person is rejected again. Their obsessive and, in Gary's case, violent behavior might be rooted in a unresolved desire to change the past, to recapture what was lost so long ago. But even if this was true of Gary, there isn't enough background on his childhood to fully substantiate it.

In 1957, a year after Gary graduated from high school, Irving Wilensky, then forty-nine, remarried; his new wife was a thirty-five-year-old woman with a daughter from her first marriage. They eventually moved to Port Washington, the next town over from Roslyn, while Gary moved south to attend the University of Alabama. Though the South was still entrenched in Jim Crow racism—only two years earlier the university accepted the first black student, while still barring her from dormitories and dining halls—the school had made a surprising push for more Jewish East Coasters, reportedly trying to attract a competitive applicant pool. The school was cheap and easy to get into by East Coast standards. He joined Sigma Alpha Mu, a Jewish fraternity with a reputation for parties, alongside fellow New York–born pledge Bernie Madoff.

But Gary didn't stay in Alabama long enough to leave an impression on his frat brothers. (Nobody I spoke with remembered him.) After his freshman year, he transferred to Rider University in New Jersey before dropping out.

The year was 1958, when Sophia Loren and Tab Hunter landed twenty miles from Roslyn in Long Beach to shoot *That Kind of Woman*, Sidney Lumet's film about a sophisticated Manhattan mistress who falls for a young paratrooper. After a locally publicized call for young extras, over five thousand teenagers stampeded the seaside town. One of the six chosen for an extra role in the film was a seventeen-year-old boutique model from Roslyn named Judy. She left such an impression on casting directors, she was recruited to screen-test for Paramount. That was the girl Gary Wilensky would marry. (Judy did not respond to my request for an interview, so my research is largely limited to public records and reporting.)

By the time they wed in 1969, Judy had put aside any Hollywood aspirations and was pursuing a law degree, while Gary taught tennis in midtown Manhattan.

Their marriage lasted only six months. After their divorce, Judy got married again, this time to her law professor, and together they started a private practice representing musicians—Frank Sinatra, Luther Vandross, Don Henley, the Beach Boys, Michael Jackson. Their firm went on to win precedent-setting judgments on behalf of artists in binding record contracts.

Gary never remarried. Irving Wilensky would tell reporters Gary's marriage failed because he put tennis first. He wasn't ready to start a family and wanted to focus on growing his career instead. But this could have been a father's perspective on a son he only partially understood. In fact, another source had heard that it was Gary who wanted children. (His ex-wife never returned my repeated requests to speak with her.)

In 1973, Gary looked like a seagull, with matchstick legs and his white Adidas parted in a V. As the cameras flashed, he dug a silver shovel in the Catskills dirt to cement the opening of the Concord Resort Hotel's new indoor courts. Gary's smooth dolphin sonar could simultaneously signal the most important person in the room and the cameraman to converge wherever he might be standing. Shoulder to chest with Pancho Gonzales at a charity tournament. Knocking an elbow against Bobby Riggs after an exhibition match. Edging into a semicircle with John Dockery, Marty Glickman, and Red Holzman while wearing a sweater covered with finger-sized tennis rackets. He could talk his way into any inner circle, and he would, if it meant a photo op.

"Gary wasn't a world-class player, but he had the ability to talk to people, which is sometimes more important than playing," says Fredo Weiland, a tennis pro who worked at Midtown Tennis alongside Gary in the 1980s.

He used the press to gain traction, just as Irving had done so many years before. In 1974, Gary posted a quarter-page ad in *Women's Wear Daily*— the fashion trade paper where Irving's business ventures played out in print—advertising his very own tennis gift shop. "Gary Wilensky Tennis Lover," the ad read in three-dimensional Yellow Submarine font. Crouched above the headline, as if resting on a cloud of letters, was a photo of Gary in a butterfly color, his smile parenthesized by a long trail of mustache hair.

"If You're a Lover, Don't Be a Stranger," read the text beside his head.

Dad must have been proud then. Gary's Tennis Shop did little more than spread his name around the city before it closed, but he was never short on new ideas.

"He was good with the gimmicks," says Fredo. "He thought outside the box."

Gary was a champion performer, if not at tennis, then at public entertainment. He zigged and Zelig-ed his way through pop culture, modulating his act to suit each era.

In the seventies, the age of mimes and stuntmen, he donned his roller skates and challenged a unicyclist to a well-advertised tennis tournament. In the eighties, he appeared on an episode of *To Tell the Truth*, a remake of the fifties game show that challenged B-list stars to pluck the actual roller-skating tennis pro from a series of imposters. And in the nineties he kicked off the decade's obsession with televised true crime.

"He was a showman," says Erica Goodstone, his former student and friend. "Even his death was a show."

At his core, he was a salesman like his father. Always staying on trend, always modifying the merchandise to suit demand— and as was true of his father, who manufactured textiles for juniors, Gary's niche was also the junior circuit.

"He had hundreds of students over his career and was a pro at many camps, at Central Park, and at numerous clubs," Irving Wilensky told the *New York Post* in 1993, after his son had died. "He taught a lot of students who were five, six, and seven years old and followed them through their graduate years. He was one a father could be proud of. He did not seem like the kind of guy who would do something like this."

After Gary's death, eighty-five-year-old Irving was interviewed by the Associated Press, the *New York Times*, the New York *Daily News*, and the *Post*. In a photo in *Newsday*, he is slouched in an armchair. His arms sag from the short sleeves of a thin button-down shirt. He has scruff on his chin and his mouth curdles as if he has tasted something rotten and is searching for the language to describe it. His eyes rest on a point below the camera's lens.

In his son's final days, Irving claimed Gary called every day, sounding frustrated. He could tell something was wrong by the sound of Gary's voice, but he didn't know the extent of his son's issues.

"I am shocked," he told the *Post*. "[He] never confided in me that anything was troubling him. I wish he had."

The only trace of Edith Wilensky in reports came from Irving himself. He'd broken the news of Gary's death to her by telephone. "She took the news the way you'd expect a mother to," said Irving.

Edith, who by then had changed her last name to Wolf (or Wulf or Woolfe or Wolfe), attended Gary's private funeral, a gathering of about thirty friends and family in Long Island.

When contacted, one of Gary's closest living relatives turned down my request for an interview, citing a wound still too damaging to revisit. "Gary's final days caused a great deal of pain to [his father]," the relative wrote in a follow-up email, adding, "Gary was adored by his mother and father, and remained close to them all his life."

Irving Wilensky died in 1994, less than a year after his son. If she is alive today, Edith would be nearing a hundred, but the last time Gary's relative saw or heard from her was in 1993 at Gary's funeral.

collectors, photographers, stalkers

THE SCANNER GROANS AS IT MEMORIZES the contents of the folder my mother gave me. My living room floor is a patchwork of brittle newspapers, magazines, and stale papers, each one placed on glass and pixelated for posterity, or just to subdue the recurring fear that they will all be burned up in an electrical fire. The headlines read "Tennis Pro's Dark Secret," "Coach Would Kill to Keep Sex Slave," "Stalker Hired Despite Warning."

The salacious coverage had flooded every newspaper in the country before washing over into *Hard Copy*–style news programs and the midsections of magazines.

But it's the clips with smaller headlines and shorter inch counts that contain the subtler clues to Gary's past.

In response to *People*'s feature story on Gary ("Stroke of Madness"), a Manhattan couple wrote a letter to the editor that the magazine published. They'd known him for ten years—their daughter was a former student. Gary had even cared for their dog when they went away on vacation. Reflecting on his kindness, they recounted how Gary called them crying when their dog was stolen under his watch. He offered to pay a stated ransom fee of $1,000 to ensure the pet's safe return. This story is supposed to offer a counterpoint to the media's villainous portrayal.

"How could this kindly, sensitive man degenerate into dangerous madness?" the couple writes. "In judging Gary Wilensky, we know there was a very nice person, then something unfathomable happened."

The letter's defense of Gary speaks to his evident ability to charm parents, or if nothing else their willingness to dismiss the severity of his crime. But reading into the letter, knowing Gary's conflation of violence and compassion for young girls, I find it reasonable to assume that the kidnapper of the girl's dog was Gary himself. He was possibly intrigued by the emotional torture he could inflict on his student, and later guilt-ridden and remorseful, concocting a story of heroism to cover his own tracks.

Another article, published in *Newsday* titled "It's Just Not Their Kind of Problem," calls out "parents of privilege" who have chosen to brush aside the Wilensky case as something of an inconvenience.

In the piece, parents of students interviewed on the condition of anonymity reflect a lack of concern in the wake of his crime. "It's not changing our lives," one parent who sent her daughter to Wilensky told the paper. "There's no change in terms of protecting the children."

A former student had a similar reaction. "We're not dwelling on it."

"We don't even want to think about it," another student told the *New York Times*, again on the condition of anonymity. "We're in no-comment mode," an administrator at the Brearley School, where Gary coached the varsity team, told the same *Times* reporter.

But farther upstate, hundreds of miles from the Upper East Side, a local paper published an op-ed from a concerned parent who'd sent his daughter to camp with Gary. She'd told her dad what a nice guy her coach was, and how he'd even invited her for pizza and movies in his cabin.

"We put our youngest child in his care," wrote the girl's father, Richard Grossman, in the *Syracuse Post-Standard*. "He is every parent's nightmare. And now he is ours."

"Was it your nightmare, too?" I had asked my mom after reading this article. "Is that why you kept the folder?"

"I kept the folder because it was something that happened in our lives," she'd said. "It's like the photo albums we have in the house. They're just memories."

But memories hold meaning, even those buried in a drawer for years. I want to know why these memories were forgotten, why they matter now, and whether the answer to both questions is the same.

I flip an article from the *Troy Record* facedown on the scanner. The headline reads "Stalker Wanted a Family."

"Do you have kids?" the sex therapist who knew Gary Wilensky had asked me during our interview. When I told her I didn't, she asked if I wanted them. I don't know, I responded, I guess I was waiting for the decision to be made for me. I'm still waiting, though at thirty-eight, not deciding has become a decision in itself.

I had expected motherhood to develop inside me, the way puberty had—without my input, and within the same time frame as others my age. Uncomfortable initially, the alignment with other women experiencing the same stage of maturity at

the same pace eased the awkwardness of transition. Motherhood seemed the final step to becoming a woman, and like all
the others, mostly required time. But it's not children that usher
in maturity, it's the ability to make decisions.

"Are you a reporter?" someone else I interviewed had asked.
Yes? No? For a decade I've been writing and editing wom-
en's lifestyle content for major news outlets. Reporting was an
aspect of the job, but what constitutes women's lifestyle hovers
between news and entertainment. At each publication, the crite-
ria for women's content have been carved into categories: food,
fashion and beauty, relationships (though limited sex), health
and diet, and parenting. Politics were filtered through the lens
of fashion (what [insert first lady's name] wore to the state dinner), entertainment through relationships (what we can learn
about love from [insert celebrity divorce/romantic comedy/
Oscar speech]), news through parenting (how to talk to your
children about [insert headline-grabbing tragedy]). Service, I
learned, was key to any women's story. What she can take away
from this story on [insert interview with cookbook author],
how she can improve from reading about [insert hair trend/diet
trend/fashion trend]. We can always be better.

When a new generation of young women became the target
audience, and the Internet provided more accurate measure-
ments of interest, political action, feminism and intersectional-
ity, body image, and cultural appropriation were shoehorned
into the same categories. There were countless debates about
whether a story about body shaming belongs in the section
marked fashion, or whether campus assault could be filed under
health. The labels were useless, outdated, but still slow to be

replaced. As an editor, I could have fought or merely suggested a change. But there were more pressing priorities, and I still believed that such categories appealed to women, even if they didn't appeal to me. Whoever invented them knew what it meant to be a woman more than I did. I believed this in the same way that I believed that women cared about gift guides, fashion week, and viral proposal videos; in the same way I made a nasal prolonged sound when someone showed me their baby's picture or their engagement ring or a story about a man who did something nice. I was covering up the fact that I didn't feel anything. I was pretending to be a woman, in the way women are perceived, in the hopes that it would quiet the girl inside me who resisted.

More scanned articles. *Albany Times Union*. The *New York Post*. *Newsday*.

"Meanwhile, police searched Gary Wilensky's one-bedroom Upper East Side apartment and found binoculars, porn videos and photographs of young girls." This line appears in a *Newsday* article about cops searching Gary's Manhattan apartment after his crime. I've read the article before but never noticed the line. Another article about the raid of his home also mentions these other photographs. He was following multiple girls before he died. I wonder if I am in his photo album, too.

detectives, talk-show hosts, defenders

THE FIRST TIME I SAW STEVEN Heider was on the cover of the New York *Daily News* in 1993. He was squatting next to a pile of cuffs and shackles laid out on the floor.

The second time was years later, when I found a YouTube clip from *The Maury Povich Show*.

In it, Heider has sandy blond hair, a pair of square science-teacher glasses, and a full mustache. So that is how I imagine he looks when he picks up the phone, more than two decades later. When I press my ear to the receiver, I listen for his mustache hair bristling into the mouthpiece.

"Obsession, that's what this was all about," he says. He speaks slowly, with the reflective swagger of a man rolling a toothpick in his mouth. It's been years since he's discussed Wilensky with the press, and still his sound-bite assessments flow easily.

"I don't think he knew what he was going to do. He was obviously disorganized in some respects," he says. "But obviously he had developed a fatal obsession."

Fatal obsession. I'd seen the words before in the headline of the *New York* magazine article. I wonder if the reporter had borrowed the phrase from Heider.

When the Wilensky case broke in 1993, Heider was the

detective assigned to handle the flood of media that poured into the small upstate town of Colonie, just outside Albany. It was an unlikely spot for Gary Wilensky's final resting place—three hours north of Manhattan, four from his hometown of Roslyn, and almost two hours south of North Creek, where his deserted cabin was found strung up with chains, shackles, and security equipment. Colonie was only supposed to be a stopping place for Gary, not a final destination.

But parked in an empty lot on Wolf Road, just down the street from Colonie's police department, Gary left his plan behind. And left Heider to answer questions about it.

The area had its share of local crime, but this case presented a bizarre set of circumstances new to the department. Not only did the case continue to unfold after the perpetrator was deceased, but the wave of attention from national and even international media outlets was unprecedented.

Heider fielded a barrage of calls and interviews from newspapers and TV stations, both during and after the investigation.

"This was right after Waco, Texas, and there was a lot of national news attention to twisted cases like these," he recalls. "I think that this was bizarre enough where it appealed to people's sensational tastes, so to speak. You don't end up on the front page of the *Daily News* every day."

A local reporter called him Hollywood Heider. Now everyone just calls him chief, or Colonie chief of police, a title he'll continue to hold even after he's retired from the role. He's done remarkably well for himself in the years since he last spoke of Gary Wilensky. And speaking with him, I can see why. His instincts are spot-on.

"Why are you investigating this case?" he asks, with a sudden gentleness reserved for an answer he's already inferred.

"I was his student," I say.

"How old were you then?"

"Fourteen."

"Were you ever interviewed by a police detective?"

"No."

He waits for my next thought. "If I were, I would have defended his character," I say. "That's kind of what I'm interested in most. Why I was so protective of Gary, why I felt so connected to him, even after his horrific crimes were committed."

There is a pause on the line while Heider considers this, and I worry I've said too much.

"What you describe is his exact MO with many young women," he says. "He's what we call in my business a predator."

Back in 1993, Heider's specialty was crimes against children—from physical abuse to sexual assault. This was not his first case involving a coach and his student. In fact, he'd seen many adults in positions of authority exploit children left in their care.

"The classic case of a child abuser is not a stranger in a black van," he says. "It's a very friendly person who uses their position to gain the trust of young people and get them to do things they wouldn't normally do."

These predators use their authority to make children feel special, and in turn earn the children's allegiance, he explains, and then pauses.

"This must be very cathartic for you."

I agree with him, without considering if it's true. I'm still craving more information—hard evidence of what Gary left behind at the scene of his crime. I know there were tape recordings of Gary reading the letters he'd sent to the Mother and the Daughter.

"What about the cassette tapes? What was on them?" I ask.

"Hours and hours and hours of him talking about things," Heider says. "Some of it was talking about the victim and his obsession with her."

"And the photographs? I read that police found photographs he'd taken of other students without their knowledge."

"We recovered some photo evidence that appeared, that may have—" Heider hesitates, taking care with his words as I steer him in this direction. "Throughout Manhattan he was taking pictures of various girls he had coached," he says.

I want to see these photos. I want to know if I was in one. But the request requires tactfulness. Asking for access to Gary's stalking photography feels like its own perversion, an admission of guilt, as someone who still desired a child predator's approval. A co-conspirator at worst, an unhinged reporter at least. So instead of asking to see the photos, I pose a more general, professional-sounding question.

"Is there any additional evidence from the case I can access?"

I learn I have to file a Freedom of Information Act request. Shortly after we hang up, I do.

The package arrives only a month or two following our call: a manila envelope marked *Piper Weiss*, containing a series of tan filing folders pressed over fresh Xerox ink. No photographs. Just documents.

There are dozens of articles—some I've read, many I

haven't—and a stack of police reports from that evening and the following days: found items belonging to the deceased; a sketch of the suspect; two press releases about the crime—one with scant information and a second more detailed write-up of the hours in which Gary's attack, death, and subsequent plans were uncovered.

There is a copy of a check from his checkbook with a picture of a log cabin on it ("Scenic America"), and lease for a house "off Cemetery Road," with some chillingly prophetic stipulations. "[The tenant] shall conduct himself in a manner that will not disturb the neighbors' peaceful enjoyment of their premises. The tenant further agrees that he will not use or permit said premises to be used by any person in any noisy, dangerous, offensive, illegal or improper manner."

A series of witness accounts are included. One woman who saw him twice in the parking lot of the Colonie Sheraton Airport Inn, just before the incident, noticed his long, oversize coat, knit wool cap, and "intense-looking eyes." A hotel desk clerk who witnessed the crime described Gary as wearing a "scarf around his neck" and a "sea captain's hat." Both witnesses noted the wheelchair beside his car. Later, an officer saw "the shine of a gun barrel."

There is a record of his rental car, the address of a medical supply store where his wheelchair was purchased, and the floor plan of the Sheraton Airport Inn in Colonie. Also included in the package are excerpts from the letters to the victims that Gary wrote and recorded on an audiotape before tossing them behind the Turf Hotel parking lot.

Each slip of paper helps piece together an account of Gary's final hours, but only a few provide a window into his mind. Between the articles and police reports, in no particular order, is evidence of an internal chaos. They include frantic, handwritten to-do lists and a record of supplies, a stalking timeline, and a series of questions he intended to ask, presumably, once his victim was captured.

1993

man: new home

GARY KNOWS WARREN COUNTY WELL. SO many times, packed into his car along with boxes and suitcases, he slithered up the thruway to Point O'Pines, where he'd be swarmed by a hive of snap bracelets and rainbow shoelaces, a twenty-four-hour twittering of girls around his orbit, all of them sharing the same home base. No goodbyes for weeks.

The thruway is different than it was back then. It's late March and the trees are still wounded by the blizzard. The mountains, which bob up three and a half hours into the drive, are still in their winter white caps.

Twelve minutes from Brant Lake is Chestertown, not much of a town, but standards shift here in the North Country. Barren restaurants, one-room post offices. It's easy to forget, winding through the resilient clusters of trees, the human struggle to survive among them.

It was only hours ago that he was in the city, where the only trees are planted and staked with CURB YOUR DOG signs. Now here he is, high in the ear-popping mountains, pulling up to the Realtor's office and the woman with the keys to his future.

He already laid the groundwork with a phone call and his living requirements. He wanted something extremely private and available immediately. Don't worry about his price range, he'd told the Realtor. She had faxed him a few options and today he's all ready to lock this down.

From house to house and between them on the winding roads, Gary plays a city guy who's earned himself a getaway, a little R&R in nature, away from all the stress.

Deeper into the woods they go, twenty-five minutes from Chestertown into Johnsburg, which is less a town and more a cluster of hamlets centered around Gore Mountain in North Creek, a major upstate skiing destination—but a joke for his clients who do Aspen or the Swiss Alps on holiday. They would never come up here.

North Creek is barren in between seasons, but in a few months the river will be loaded with rafts and kayaks. If Gary worries that this area will be too populated, his concerns must have diminished when they turned onto the isolated Cemetery Road. Past the headstones and half a mile down a dirt road, Gary finds what he is looking for.

This is the one. Gary drops $2,500 on the spot, just to show how serious he is. When he is back in the city, he meets his future landlord, a New Jersey man around Gary's age. All the landlord knows is that Gary Wilensky is a low-key recluse looking to escape Manhattan, and that he's prepared to hand over six months of rent, $11,500, up front in exchange for a one-year rental. They meet for a moment—a hello and handover of cash. The offer is too good to pass up.

Before Gary came along, the owner's plan was to sell the house, and after Gary leaves, to put it back on the market, but after Gary, the house won't sell— not for at least two years. It will become the notorious cabin off Cemetery Road, the "house of horrors," as *Newsweek* will call it. Even the owner's wife will refuse to go back inside.

Gary Wilensky scans each musty room, minding the windows, the doors, the exits and entrances. On a pad of graph paper, he takes notes. LIVING ROOM. CABIN DOOR: SMALL WOOD MAT—BLANKET. PATIO DOOR— LARGE WOOD MAT. VIDEO CAMERA—WINDOW— GARBAGE BAGS. DINING ROOM—GARBAGE BAGS? KITCHEN—DOOR—MAT.

The cabin itself has a simple layout. Two bedrooms, a dining room off the kitchen, and a den/living area. He works through the night boarding up the house, setting up his equipment. Gary the builder. Gary the woodsman.

He lays out his spoils from SpyWorld—gadgets with pages of instructions—assembling each one, running wires throughout the house. Gary the electrician.

Outside the house, he climbs a tree and strings more wires around branches, holding a camera in one hand, like a technological Tarzan.

Then there is Gary the party animal, who makes sure there are wine coolers in the fridge. Mixtapes and porn on deck.

Gary the movie star, who writhes around on the bed, rustling the bedsheets, posing for the camera.

Gary the nurse, who tucks in the bedsheets, prepares the bedpan, and lines up his medical supplies.

And Gary the architect of this plan, the darkest of them all, who handles each cold chain link, fastening them with hooks, testing the pulley, tightening the restraints. He's the one who scribbles down items on a graph paper pad, adding to his master list everything that Gary Wilensky still needs before time runs out.

girl: new friends

THIS IS THE WEEKEND OF FROST Valley—our first co-ed class trip with the boys' school on the Upper West Side. We're all on three buses headed to someplace with snow and cabins. Bring warm clothes, the teacher said. Bianca wears two tight sweaters. One is camel colored, one gray. Around her neck is a spit-thin silver necklace with a bean and a longer silver necklace with two charms: a heart and a lock.

My hair won't lie flat. There is one tight curl at the root in the back of my head that Tony must have missed. I keep feeling around for it the entire bus ride.

This is the trip where three girls in my sister's grade were suspended for smoking pot. I smoke pot in the woods with three boys. I am trembling from the cold, and from putting my lips around the thin wet paper where their lips have been.

We walk through the woods surrounding the campgrounds. Someone says, "This is where they shot *Friday the 13th*." Someone else says, "*No way*, they shot it at another camp, in another place." Someone says, "Check this out." A tree has fallen, ripped from the root. All the wires of its base are in a tangle and there is a hole in the earth where it came unattached. It looks like something you should turn away from. "'If a tree falls in the forest,'" someone says. "How does the rest go?"

The zip-line plank is too high, so I turn around and walk back down the ladder. One boy plucks me from the last step and carefully sets me down on the snow. The other two clap for me even though I didn't do anything.

In the bunk we run through the names of the boys who are now our friends. Tim. Jordan. Max.

Then we run through the DJ names the boys gave us. B-side, Sarah Stylze, Phiphedog.

A science teacher leads a nature walk in which he tells us the names of all the trees. The snow comes up to my shins. One of the boys rips a lone hanging leaf off a bare tree and hands it to me. We sit by a campfire cross-legged and watch the flames while our knees touch. He is wearing corduroy. I am wearing boot-cut jeans. This is what it feels like to be normal.

On the bus home, the boy promises to make us all mixtapes, which he does. There's "Bianca's Pop Mix," "Sarah's Hip-Hop mix," and "Piper's Folk Mix." On it, there's a song called "Helplessly Hoping," a song called "I Want You," a song called "Tears in My Eyes."

THE BOYS from Frost Valley don't go to clubs. They have house parties. One of them called Bianca and gave her the address.

In a lobby on Central Park West, one of us says a last name and the doorman nods. Kids have been saying that name all night. Elevators are this way.

Sarah and Bianca are both wearing jeans with clogs. I'm wearing a black minidress with overall suspenders and a white baby tee underneath it. And clogs.

There's a mirror in the elevator. Sarah makes her mirror face and tucks her hair behind her ear. Bianca tilts her head to see what she looks like tilting her head. Pretty. Her eyes catch mine in the mirror. I look back at my own face. "I'm Danny DeVito," I say, because in the mirror I'm so much shorter than the two of them and it should be acknowledged. We laugh. We watch ourselves laugh. The elevator door opens and we can hear the party from the hallway.

We debate who should open the door first, and finally Sarah says, "I'll do it. Let's just go in already." The door opens to a foyer, which leads to the living room. Two girls from another school are on the leather sofa. A boy is on an armchair flipping channels on a mute TV. An older-looking boy is sitting at a long dining table rolling a joint. Three others watch him. We don't recognize anyone.

"Let's try the kitchen," says Sarah, and we link fingers walking in a line toward the room with the yellow light. Max is looking in the refrigerator. When he sees Bianca, he smiles and then gives us each a Rolling Rock.

"More people are coming," he says. Then he interrupts whatever he was about to say to mouth, "One two three and to the fo'," because the song just came on. The volume of the music suggests there's more people here than there actually are.

Now here's Jordan. Hugs for Jordan.

"You guys remember Connor, right?" says Max.

I don't remember Connor, but I know this is his house. Connor's hair is sand-colored and almost short enough to be a crew cut. He's got a compact wrestler's body and thin pink lips.

"Do your parents know you're throwing this party?" I ask.

He gives a little smile and shakes his head no. I want him to open his mouth so I can watch his tongue move.

He leans down to speak into my ear. Heat, a light sprinkle in my ear canal that raises the hair on my arms. He smells like sweat and underneath it, soap. More hairs stand at attention.

When I ask him another question, I cover my mouth with my hand in case my breath is bad. I'm dry-mouthed, cotton-tongued. More beer.

"Come with me into the other room," says Bianca. Something about whether Max is cute or not, and something about a question he asked her and what should she say. I don't know. The diamond stud in her ear twinkles. Saliva on her front tooth twinkles. The green part of her eye twinkles.

I wander from room to room. The apartment is a maze of off-white walls and doors. This one is a closet, here's another closet, and the bathroom. This is an office, that's his parents' room but don't open that door.

In Connor's room, a group is sitting on the floor passing around a blunt. Above them on a shelf are wrestling trophies. No posters in here. Just blue bedsheets with thin yellow lines. A window faces the stone wall of Central Park, and beyond it, the shadowy outlines of trees.

The same song that was playing in the kitchen is playing in this room, too, but from a different stereo. The bright green bars in the display go up and up. *It's like this and like that and like this and uh*. Someone taps my shoulder, hands me the blunt. It makes me cough, which makes other people laugh. I can't control the coughing. I will cough like this forever. Beer. *It's like that and like this and like that and uh.*

Connor's CD tower is taller than me, which is funny. "What's so funny?" Jordan is standing beside me. His hair is parted in the middle and two short brown wings frame his fore-head. There is a space between his front teeth where you can see his tongue.

There is a line for the bathroom. The party's filling up with people holding red cups. Sketchy punch. Connor walks by, we toast red cups. I follow the shoulder blades in his back through his white T-shirt. Also wings.

I don't remember where I put my clogs but it doesn't matter. *It's like this and like that and like this and uh.*

I'm in the doorway of another room with a dollhouse, a wall of ribbons, and a picture of a girl on a horse in a gold frame. I'm deciding whether to go in or not. A boy tries to sit on a minia-ture chair. A girl on the bed laughs. It is like looking into a big dollhouse room, I want to tell somebody.

In the corner of the room is the boy who made the mixtapes. Tall, curly brown mess of hair, forehead long like the rest of his body. "He's the smartest in the whole class," Jordan had said. He is standing by a bookshelf, flipping through a children's book. Beside him is a girl with blond hair from another school. He is reading to her. *Tears in my eyes.*

Where is Connor? I want to find Connor. I go into the living room to find Connor, but Jordan waves me over to the couch. It's not leather, the couch. It's soft suede, all lived in and cush-iony. "You can put your feet on me," he says, so I do. Jordan's lap is khaki-colored. One of my feet is in one of his hands. He squeezes it.

"I'm so high, are you high?"

He nods yes like he's a zombie, and then we both crack up. "Where are Bianca and Sarah?"

He shrugs. I get it. We are playing a game where I ask questions and he answers them without using any words.

"What movie is playing on the TV?" He points to a DVD case of *House Party* on the coffee table. "Is there more beer?" He points to the kitchen.

I've got one he'll have to explain. "What is that a photograph of?" I point to a framed picture on the window of a bride and groom kissing. He squeezes my foot; his smile straightens a little as he looks at me. My heart thumps.

"Turn off the music," someone says. "Turn off the music." It's Max. He's standing at the front door. His blue polo shirt is splotched with red paint. His hair is a mess, like he's been rolling around on a bed with someone. He looks cute, I think.

"The cops are coming," he yells.

I sit up. Bianca and Sarah are huddled by one window. Other people are crowding around the window next to it. "What are we looking for? Cops?"

"Connor," someone says. "Connor got stabbed!" Max is saying Connor got stabbed. "Stabbed?"

Red lights are flashing in the window. Red lights on Jordan's face, in the hollow space between his two front teeth. Red lights on Max, his two pinprick pupils. He needs to tell Jordan what happened. Jordan will know what to do next. "What happened?"

Max and Connor had gone for a beer run. Right in front of the building, a group of kids were fighting, and when Connor tried to break it up, he ended up with a knife in his side. That is one version that surfaces in the chaos of the party. Another faction claims it was a planned mugging turned violent. "These guys were waiting for people to leave the party so they could jump them," someone said.

"Are there more?"

"Is it safe to leave?"

"Can I call my dad?"

My father pulls up to the building in his winter hat—a cowboy-style Stetson, which usually embarrasses in the company of friends. Tonight, though, all I notice is how handsome he looks under the curve of its brim, like a real cowboy. His car smells of genuine leather. Heat pours through the vents. The radio speaks softly of other events in other places.

We wind through the park, and for a moment it feels like we're deep in the woods.

Then the world lights up again on Fifth Avenue. The awnings glow, and light rain makes the avenue look like it's writhing in crystals. Next is Madison with its gilded storefronts and then Park. First we drive south to Sarah's and then north to Bianca's. Finally we circle back, around the green mall that runs down the avenue, to our own building. Home.

Mom is upstairs in her nightgown and slippers, two pairs of reading glasses on her head. We eat Mallomars and drink Sleepytime tea in the kitchen, speaking softly of what happened.

"He was just outside the building. These kids he didn't know were fighting and he tried to break it up. Someone stabbed him. I didn't see any of it. The ambulance had taken him by the time Dad pulled up in the car."

She nods along, asking questions, but not too many, enough to keep me talking until I can't keep my eyes open any longer.

In bed, I hear her feet pattering on wood, roaming the hallway, closing doors, snapping locks. She opens my door, and I pretend to be asleep. She stands there for so long, I actually do fall asleep. In the morning, the door is still as open as she left it.

By Monday, Connor is recuperating in the hospital. At school, I sign a card that says *Feel Better!* The prognosis comes down the pipeline: He's lucky.

"I keep telling you the Upper West Side is dangerous," says my mom in the kitchen, stirring a pot of carrots. "You know why, it's because they come from the park. Remember the Central Park Jogger."

"*They* come from the park? Who are *they*, Mom?"

She looks at me as if I'm the one who's ignorant.

Later that night after dinner, when we're loading the dishwasher, we pick up the conversation again.

"I'm just saying, you have to be careful in that part of town," she reiterates.

"How is the Upper West Side any different from the Upper East Side?" I ask, because aside from opposite entrances to the park, they are exactly the same.

"It just is," she says, exhausted, and walks out of the room.

What she means is that we are safer than other people. This is something she needs to believe.

girl: man trouble

"WE LOVE YOU, GARY."

"Yeah, we still love you, Gary." One of us has to say it, and then the other one repeats a variation. Gary needs to hear it today.

He'd had so many plans for us, a new restaurant, maybe catch a movie. He'd reserved all of Saturday to hang out, and instead, I dropped the ball. I couldn't go out after tennis. I had plans with Bianca and Sarah.

I kept missing them when I came home late after Saturday lessons. Even if I beeped Bianca, I didn't always hear back until it was too close to curfew. They were meeting new boys without me.

These weekend nights are crucial in terms of making connections, and opening doors to opportunities—a boy, just one boy, who might like me. The anxiety of missing a fated meeting tears at my stomach in either direction. Still worse, the fear that I'm losing Bianca and Sarah. Each new private joke I don't get, each new friend they'd made on a night I missed, tightens the bond between them, pressing out the space where I once belonged.

They're outpacing me, and the pressure to keep up is too much to ignore. All I want is to eat quesadillas and ice cream cake with Gary and Emma, but that is lazy and immature. It's how you lose relevance and friendships. It's how you never cross bases, never grow up, and wind up alone.

So I nix our post-lesson plans, and then Emma says she's busy, too. Gary turns cold. All the way to Queens, he is quiet—eyes on the windshield. The silent treatment. Emma turns back to me from the front seat and rolls her eyes.

"Come on, Gary. Turn on the radio, Gary." He does, turning the volume knob up high, but his silence makes it clear he's just following orders.

girl: shame

ALL THE PRETTY GIRLS IN THE upper school are in the dance club performance. It is an opportunity to wear a leotard with a sheer fairy skirt and to extend your nylon legs underneath a spotlight while everyone sits in foldout chairs and stares.

I'm in the second row holding two roses. One for Bianca and one for Sarah. This is one of several activities they perform as a twosome. They were best friends first. I get that. They have a secret language of tallness and romantic maturity I will never understand. I get this, too, but it makes me nervous. I've lost my rhythm with them, and I have to put in the work to regain it.

Tonight they are doing a dance to a Sting song. The dance is a slow meditation on friendship and becoming your own person. They crawl through each other's legs, circle around each other, make a side-by-side bridge with their two raised hands and then pull away. Now Bianca is extending one leg on the floor and Sarah is creating a halo over her with her arms.

The last dance I choreographed was for a middle school talent show, a series of swimming gestures set to the Beach Boys' "I Get Around." I wore goggles and orange flotation cuffs on each arm. We're so much older now.

It took so long and then happened quickly. Eighth grade was the beginning. Our first year in upper school, our first year in kilts. Our first year smoking cigarettes in diners and using my sister's old ID to buy booze. Our bat mitzvahs. When we started to wear real bras with lace. When our parents started leaving us alone for the night in our apartments, and when we started boiling our own pasta, buying our own coffees. When we switched from hot coffee to iced coffee.

Eighth grade. Last year. The same year Bianca first kissed a popular boy. The same year he died. There was an accident at a beach house; bones were broken irreparably. Bianca found out a few days before the memorial service, which took place at our temple, where we had gone with him to Hebrew school. The whole city of eighth graders was going, though no one had specifically invited us.

We debated if we had any right to go. Bianca could go, of course, but she wouldn't go without us. *Are these things even by invitation? Who do we know who's going?* And soon I began to wonder what I should wear.

So we took the day off from school and dressed in black miniskirts. When we got to the temple, we were already late. No one could agree who should walk in first and we stood at the entrance asking each other pertinent questions. *What if everyone turns around and stares at us? What if people are mad that we don't have an invitation? Are we awful people for coming at all?*

We figured we should talk this over some more at the diner around the corner. We ordered cheese fries and Diet Cokes, and by the time they were put in front of us, we were laughing at ourselves, how we'd gotten all dressed up and never even went inside the temple. The absurdity of our insecurity. The fear of what was behind those doors. The lie we told ourselves about returning. The melted cheese over hot fries. The thought of math class happening while we sat in a diner. The giggles, uncontrollable, springing from my stomach, worsened by how wrong it was to have them.

Then Sarah's face dropped. She knocked Bianca's arm. Bianca kicked my shin. Outside a stream of mourners were passing by the diner. Some resembled kids we knew, only their hair was flatter. Their faces slack and uninhabited. One boy looked right at us through the glass. He saw us dressed in black with our plate of french fries. He saw me laughing.

He was one of the boys from the roof that night. Dressed in an oversize gray suit he might have borrowed from an older brother. I want to say he looked at us behind the glass, but that wasn't it. His head turned to us, but his eyes registered nothing. His eyelids, pink and swollen, blinked involuntarily, as if their operator had slipped away, leaving the motor on. If anything, he was showing us his face, and what a face looks like when the person who wears it disappears. It looks like a mask.

This was why we didn't go inside the temple. It wasn't that we feared embarrassment; it was that we feared the moment it no longer mattered. Behind those doors was a truth we weren't ready to witness—the gruesomeness of grief, its dripping desperation, the collapse of posture and order, the obliteration of the bubble that's been blown up around us, leaving us raw and unprotected.

A boy had died. I hadn't understood what that meant. I still didn't understand. But I'd seen his friend's face in the window, and now I wished more than anything else that I had gone inside the temple. I wanted to be brave enough to open those doors and mature enough to handle what was behind them. I wished I could share his grief, so that he didn't have to carry so much of it. I wished I could be the kind of person who didn't care about outfits and guest lists. I wished I hadn't laughed like an asshole. I wished I wasn't so self-absorbed, but instead was more compassionate, more comforting to others, and less shallow. I wished I was on the outside of the diner's window walking alongside the mourners, and not on the inside watching them pass. But it was too late. The service was over. I walked home in my platform heels and miniskirt, pressing through the brightest part of the day, wishing I wore a mask, too.

At the end of their dance, Bianca and Sarah stand side by side linking arms and leaning in opposite directions. When the music fades, they extend one shimmering leg in front of the other, pointing a toe and setting it down, pointing and setting. You are supposed to clap and woot so they hear you in the audience. You are supposed to believe as they're followed by a spotlight offstage, their necks elongated, gazes fixed on the path ahead of them, that they are headed toward some gauzy endless horizon and not the flat, sealed doors of the auditorium.

girl: brave

MY SISTER CALLS FROM COLLEGE TO say she's never coming home. She had a fight with my parents during her last visit. It was about her new boyfriend. They think he's disrespectful. He didn't shake their hands when he met them. And there were other things. She had just gotten out of the shower. They were on the bed when Mom walked in. "But we weren't doing anything," my sister says. "They are crazy," she says. "I'm finished with them."

"How am I going to see you now?" I ask the pinholes in the phone. A small volcano rises in my throat.

A few months ago, we all drove upstate to move her in at Vassar. Mom put the sheets on her bed. Dad unloaded the rest of the suitcases from the car. I wandered the dormitory hall, sliding my hand along the smooth surface of the wall, peeking into other rooms where other students were unpacking. Meanwhile, my sister sprayed her old boyfriend's cologne on her sheets, a ritual she invented for another boyfriend two summers before, when we dropped her off at acting camp. "So I can smell him in my sleep," she had said.

I hate her boyfriends. I hate them all. They keep her from me.

"Slut," my mother called her once—the word from her mouth so sharp and shrill, I could hear her epiglottis vibrate. We were on Fire Island a summer ago and my sister was dating a lifeguard. The house where all the lifeguards lived for the summer had a strict policy: no female visitors. But she had visited her boyfriend, and word traveled easily down the wood-slatted paths from one beach bungalow to the next until it reached my parents.

"Slut." The word traveled from my sister's room down the hall to the living room, where I sat on the couch, trying to absorb *The Golden Girls* in their Florida languor. All pastels, breezy swinging doors, and satin robes. Every third line a joke.

My sister's bedroom was narrow, shrunken by an el of twin beds, a chest of drawers, and three bodies behind a closed door. My mother, my sister, and my father. Every third line a joke. I listened for it. I tried to silence the alarm going off in my brain as their tempers rose to piercing levels.

The anti-harmony of their enraged voices, the slanted orchestra of hurled curses crashing and clanging against each other. It was frightening. Almost more frightening from afar than up close—the distance blunting meaning, turning screams into vibrations, tremors you could feel with your feet on the hardwood floor. The dog curled tighter, neck to tail. The TV spasmed with laugh track.

Down the hall, they boomed and thundered, knocking limbs against furniture. A closet door swung and screeched, books tumbled off a shelf in a hammering succession, the bedroom door buckled. I ran to it and pushed it open. It hit my father's elbow. He turned to face me, teeth clenched. My mother's jaw jutted out, her eyes widened—a threat to scram. My throat hitched, but I didn't move. *Stop it!* I must have screamed, though my ears roared in their canals like the ocean down the street. *Stop it. Stop it. Stop it.* Their faces drained of pink. We stood encased in an icy silence for seconds, minutes. Hearts belted. One last book flung itself off the edge and landed split open, facedown. My father left the room, my mother following, slamming the door behind them. I was left alone with my sister, who was curled up on the bed. A spasming laugh track drenched in tears.

"It's okay," I said, climbing on the bed and covering her with my whole body, but I was thinking of myself, of what I'd done, trying to understand it. I'd overpowered them. I'd shut them down and made them listen to me. This is what it took: a willingness to walk inside the rage. An attraction to the danger. Bravery, is that what it was?

On that first ride home from my sister's college, I watched the number signs on the side of the highway count down from a hundred, each one marking her distance from me. Back at home, her room still held her sleepy smell. Even the bed, the jewelry she left in a box by the window, the sweaters in her trunk, were still warm with her impression.

Now it is colder in her room, and quieter, too. I watch the ticker run across the TV with my father. I load the dishwasher with my mother. I swallow my temper and wait until everyone falls asleep.

The wooden block that holds the kitchen knives. The black plastic knife handle. The place behind the armchair beside the heater. The chalk-white scratches on skin. The thin beads of blood that bubble up. Always looking for new, clean surface areas to carve and chisel.

Sometimes I imagine I'm cutting the pretty faces of boys; others times I imagine they are cutting me. There are cuts for each mistake I've made, cuts for how lucky I am, how much I have that I don't deserve, and for each bone that twists inside me, each imagined fantasy, too dark even to scribble on paper. And then come the research cuts: How hard is it to cut through skin, how deep can you dig, how close to the vein can you get, when does the pain become unbearable, what are you so afraid of?

After, there is a good burning. It feels like opening a tightly sealed jar, screaming as loud as you can without making any noise.

2016

cutters

THERE IS A STUDY THAT CLAIMS the teenage brain develops at the rate of a baby's brain—which is to say, the fastest rate it will ever grow. The difference the second time around is that you are both physically mobile and mentally more aware. You know that something is happening within you but not within your control. This is your new body, you're told, but don't touch it. Don't use it yet. It's dangerous. It's not finished cooking.

The frontal cortex, where logic resides, is busy mapping a route to the amygdala, that gumball-sized emotional center in the brain's core that still leads the teenager's decision-making process without mediation. Feelings override reason. There is only instinct and the sparkling sensation of epiphany. You are a genius; you are an animal. You are a walking fetish—a child in adult prosthetics. You are a sensationalized news story. ("Shocking transformation: Underage teen sprouts sex organs.") You are hideous. You are alarming. You are famous. All around you, they purr and coo, they *psst*. Your body brings out the worst in them—fear for your safety, fear of their own perversions. You can read their minds.

For these reasons and others, teenagers are human oddities. Everyone is watching them, or it feels that way, because of the flood of oxytocin, but also because everyone is watching them. Corporate entities have deemed them mystics, tapping their cultural prognostications and rapturous tendencies to fuel economic growth. Courtrooms, doctors, and parental figures have labeled the same tendencies satanic, idiotic, dangerous, or borderline.

What we know is that teenagers are capable of anything—from setting Olympic records to suicide—and when they recognize the extent of their newfound potential, they are primed, biologically, to act on it.

This may be why the doctor told me to wear a rubber band on my wrist and snap it whenever I felt the urge to cut. He was bargaining with my teen brain—which couldn't be talked out of its cravings, only talked into alternative methods of relief.

I began cutting at fourteen and entered treatment the following year, after my mother saw the marks on my arms as I dressed for school. By that point, the cuts had become so much a part of my skin I'd forgotten they might be alarming. I didn't even know why I'd made them. But when someone asks you for a reason, you're expected to provide an answer.

In case studies, adolescents have cited stress relief, the desire to feel something, and self-punishment. There is a theory that self-injurers have decreased opioid receptors and the pain stimulates opioid production. Another claims self-harm releases euphoria-producing endorphins. If this is true, cutting isn't *like* an addiction, it is an addiction—something to which teenage brains are particularly susceptible.

"My mind slows down, I stop crying, and I just feel better," a fifteen-year-old girl explained in a 2008 case study on self-harm, published in the journal *Psychiatry*. Later she was asked by a psychiatrist what coping mechanism she used before she discovered cutting. "I don't know," she said. "I never hurt then like I do now."

Since the nineties, rates of adolescent self-injury have spiked as high as 38 percent, though that could be attributed to raised awareness. Back when I started, nobody talked about it. There wasn't even a name for it outside medical journals. I first heard the term *cutting*, after I'd mostly stopped, on a 1998 episode of *Beverly Hills 90210*, when Donna Martin's assistant revealed the cuts on her arm and muttered something about not being a supermodel. This was enough to put me off the practice. It was all so silly, so melodramatic. Just another weird thing girls do for attention.

The myth that cutters do it for attention isn't surprising considering the higher prevalence of the practice among adolescent and teenage girls. The explanation that "girls crave attention" has been used for almost every broken taboo adults can't or don't want to understand. If anything, many girls at that age feel too scrutinized and search for ways to counterbalance the attention they're receiving.

For me, cutting was a secret I knew better than to flaunt—bleeding is supposed to be prevented, not stimulated. But the hidden nature of the act was also part of the appeal. I had something separate from others—an intimate way to commune with my own body, its limitations and potential. And more than that, I was reclaiming my body, which had begun to feel like it didn't belong to me. It was always being inspected, judged, explained, warned against, praised, feared, perfected, touched, and protected from touch.

Cutting began as an act of revenge on a body that didn't belong to me anymore, but it became a reminder that this same body could bring me relief.

I was easing out the air pressure—the way you do with a

bottle of seltzer before you open it so it doesn't explode. I was building up my pain threshold to do away with the little girl who was so afraid of everything. I was punishing myself, punishing others—whoever deserved it. I deserved it. *Little fucking rich girl with everything. Ungrateful selfish bitch.* Each phrase matched to a notch on my skin, each notch a mark of forgiveness. A meditation on violence, a sacrifice to mitigate the harm I wished on others, a ritual to both feed an emotional restlessness and prevent it from boiling over.

This is not what I told the doctor. Instead, I told him what happened at tennis camp the summer of 1993, three months after Gary Wilensky had died.

At camp, there were three popular boys from New York City. They knew Bianca. I'd hoped by the end of summer they'd know me, too.

Camp was at a resort in Florida. To stay cool, we hunted for shadows on the court. We filled up little paper cones with water until they softened into tissues. We swam in an Olympic-sized pool, surrounded by deck chairs splayed with the ghosts of our parents, who'd vacationed at this resort in cooler months.

The three boys were nice the first day, until I made a mistake.

"It's so hot I could take my shirt off," said the tall boy, pinching the Stussy logo on his shirt and pulling it away from his stomach.

"Please don't," I said, because I was nervous, and my mouth was so eager to impress them with my comedic timing that my brain couldn't stop it in time.

It was too late—I'd disrespected the tall boy, maybe even

pressed a tender wound. But I believe it was less what I'd said, and more that *I* had said it—a girl who was physically beneath them, even if she was Bianca's friend. The next day they began teaching me my place.

"Hey, Piper," yelled one boy from across the tennis court. I waved. "You look like a witch."

"I can see your pubic hair," another said by the pool.

They blocked the door to my room and tossed me between each other, grabbing at my chest. "Where are your tits? I can't find them!" At night, they would call the telephone in my room to tell me how they planned to rape me. They'd brought a gun to camp, I was warned.

I called my mother, as I always did, who called the head of the tennis camp, but encouraged me to stick it out.

"Be tough," she said. And this was when I discovered the knives in the butcher block behind my eyes. A whole selection of them to use on each boy in my mind. The gore was detailed, their cries of pain, delightfully scripted each night before I fell asleep. When I returned to New York, I told my mother I was tough. I was: I started cutting myself harder, deeper and closer to the vein, to prove that I was tougher than anyone thought. To cut them out of me. To protect myself.

To treat this situation, there was medication and the rubber band on the wrist, and a shame that came with being so seen, so classifiable. My story wasn't unique, nor were my various ever-shifting diagnoses—depression, anxiety and depression, borderline. The doctor said these kinds of impulses subside by the time you turn thirty. And eventually there was a tapering off—the need to cut overruled by the need to avoid broadcasting my issues each time I was naked with someone. But the actual impulse never completely went away.

Even now, when I think of those nights, hiding behind an armchair in my teenage bedroom—the pinch and swell of a dull kitchen knife, the sacredness of the ritual I'd invented—I almost wish I could feel it again.

old friends

I MEET SARAH IN A RESTAURANT with no prices on the menu. We are in Midtown, at a lunch spot that looks more like a ballroom for a charity benefit. Warhol portraits of Nureyev and the Shah of Iran stare down finance types in C-shaped booths. A glass chandelier, which looks like a wedding cake made from Krugerrands, dangles from the ceiling, sprinkling gold dust on our heads.

"You look so beautiful," I say when I get to our table because that is what you say to a woman you haven't seen in almost twenty years. But I mean it. She is still tall and lean-bodied, still elegant in the black wool tunic and tights she wore today, she says, because it reminded her of our old uniforms. Her eyes are narrower than I remember, harder to read.

I had posted a request on Facebook in search of Gary Wilensky's former campers. When a classmate suggested Sarah and tagged her name, I waited to hear from her. And when I didn't, I reached out.

She knew Gary Wilensky, too. She went to one of the camps where he coached. I had forgotten about this, like so many other things.

"You're not remembering correctly," Sarah says over a bowl of Amatriciana di tonno. She says we didn't go to clubs in ninth grade, but rather tenth grade. I look down at the coiled tubes in chunky pink sauce, an explosion of brain matter. So strange that the mechanism responsible for our own realities is a substance you could fit inside a bowl.

"Really? I thought we started going to clubs earlier," I say, trying to tone down my certainty out of respect. I've brought her here to share her memory. I need to honor it, and I should definitely pick up the check. That is the right thing to do, no matter how much it costs. I'll take home leftovers—I'll stretch it into two meals.

But Sarah suggested this restaurant, so maybe she picks up the check. What are the rules? Sarah comes here for lunch often enough that she knows the waiters. She usually sits in one of the booths, she tells me, but they didn't have any available today. A waiter comes over to say hello. *Ciao*, he says, or she says ciao. One of them says ciao, a greeting native to this restaurant-nation.

It almost feels inappropriate to take out my recording device—a cold proclamation of my outsider status, with respect to this setting and our once-close friendship. I most certainly will pick up the check now.

"Tell me about your memories of Gary at camp," I say, nudging the recorder between our plates.

"I used to receive birthday cards every year from him and I remember thinking, 'How did he remember my birthday?' because I never told him my birthday." She smirks as she says this. Her lips bunch together over her teeth, holding back a smile. I've missed her face.

"At camp, he was the hero," she continues. "He was why people went back there. They went for Gary Wilensky. They looked up to him."

She describes him as a Pee-wee Herman type. "He made tennis fun and unique and crazy and against the rules," she says. "That's why we liked it."

He broke the rules with no impunity—that's exactly it. Our early lives are spent learning the rules, and our adolescent years are spent questioning the validity of such rules. Even in tennis, there were so many rules with no explanations for them. And to see an adult, the person who's supposed to enforce the rules, breaking them was mind-bending.

"He would always come in the middle of your lesson and do something wacky and make the kids scream and get excited," says Sarah.

She leans in closer to the recorder and lowers her voice.

"I remember one summer, Gary had a breakdown," she recalls. "Something went wrong. He got in trouble."

"Do you know what it was about?" I ask.

"Hold on," she says. She is going to tell this story in the way she remembers.

"I'll never forget seeing him after we got the announcement that Gary wasn't going to be teaching tennis anymore and they sent him home in the middle of the summer.

"I'll never forget seeing Gary. He did a going-away sale of all his stuff. I remember clothing hanging around the courts. He was on roller skates maybe, or maybe he was in a tennis skirt. It looked like a flea market of Gary's stuff. It was a tournament and he gave away all his stuff—shirts and jackets with his face on it. Gary memorabilia. You'd win one if you hit the ball in the right way.

"I remember that as the downfall of Gary, that summer. I remember the announcement to everybody that Gary was leaving for the summer and he wouldn't be coming back. I don't know if he didn't come back or if he just got suspended for that summer."

"How old were you?" I ask.

"I had to be twelve, maybe," she says. "Then I remember seeing Gary before he left and he had these cats. He was petting the cat and I remember going up to him and saying, 'So sorry to hear you're leaving.'

"The way he was holding the cat and petting it—holding it so close. He wasn't his responsive self. He looked very depressed. Completely the opposite of that day on the courts. I knew something was wrong with him.

"After he left, through gossip we found out he had gotten obsessed with a girl at camp. I found that out on the bus ride home when one of the older girls told me. It was hush-hush."

I had reached out to the camp directors and not received a response. But shortly after Gary's death, they had spoken to the press about firing Gary, citing his favoritism and temper as reasons for letting him go. The camp directors told the *Times*, "His anger toward them and his attachments to favorite students became unacceptable." This is the first I've heard of the rumor, and perhaps that was all it was.

Rumors are slippery things, passing from girl to girl on the verbal condition of secrecy and the unspoken promise of betrayal. A story to be believed or discounted, but never forgotten.

Mothers share rumors, too. "I need to ask you something," my mom had said as I sat on the floor of my bedroom, a few years after my high school graduation. "Did you ever threaten Bianca with a knife?" She'd heard a rumor, which she'd kept to herself until enough time had passed that the truth would require no immediate ramification. The truth could just be the truth. "Of course not," I said, trying to hold her gaze. "I didn't, I swear." I have a problem with the truth—the more confident I am in it, the less I believe it. I understand how innocent people buckle under interrogation. Even if they never committed the actual crime, the accusation becomes a question of would you, rather than did you, and even if you wouldn't, you are forced to imagine the scenario in which you would. You are guilty of thinking it.

"You don't think I would do that, do you?" I asked.

"Well, you were pretty troubled back then," she said. My own memory of those days is imperfect, but I had no memory of this event. Still, the fact that my mother saw me as capable of it made me question my own certainty.

"Where did you hear this?" I asked.

"All I heard is that the reason you two stopped being friends is that you threatened her with a knife," she said.

"You know that's not true. You were there when I called them."

One year after Gary Wilensky died, I had broken up with Sarah and Bianca on a conference call. It was my decision, not theirs, though it was influenced by my sister. When she was home from college one summer, she had witnessed the three of us together, and how self-critical I'd become around them. "Your friends are supposed to make you feel better about yourself," my sister had said. "Not worse."

But it wasn't their fault. They never cut me down. I did it to myself. It was my approach to dealing with our increasing differences. I thought it best to be transparent, to call out what

I imagined they hated about me as much as I did—not just the physical disparities, but the mental ones.

Sarah and Bianca seemed to be growing in straighter directions, north toward adulthood. They'd found a new, more popular set of friends from another school. The friends all wore boots they called shitkickers and had boyfriends with facial hair. They listened to hip-hop, DJ'd at clubs, and spoke of relationships—not even sex, but relationships. They were flyer girls, and Bianca and Sarah were becoming such girls as well. It suited them, and whenever they'd bring me along, I felt like a relic of their past. A loose tooth clinging to a lone root. Something that needed to go, and soon.

There was also tennis camp and the three boys, which had left me so ashamed, I really didn't think I deserved a place in our threesome. I never told Bianca or Sarah what had happened while I was away, though I assumed they'd heard some version of the events. I assumed I'd let them down by not winning the boys over, and that my friendship was a stain on their reputations. Whatever these boys thought of me was the truth, and I didn't want my friends to be associated with it.

Pacing in my sister's room with the phone at my neck, I told Sarah and Bianca that I needed a break from our friendship. It was best for all three of us. We weren't good for each other. Friends are supposed to make you feel better about yourself, and other phrases I'd written down on an envelope to prompt me if I forgot the reasoning. I didn't mention tennis camp; I didn't mention Gary. I'd already buried him underneath the three boys.

I don't remember what they said, but I do remember their silence. "Hello?" I'd asked, and they were both still on the line.

When I hung up the phone, my sister said she was proud of me. My mother agreed. It was good what I did. We were best friends and then we weren't. I had peeled off the sticky tape that sealed the three of us together, and now I would be better. Fixed.

They were the problem, it was decided. But that wasn't entirely true. There is no accounting for the fear triggered in adults when three precocious teenage girls anoint themselves best friends, or how often that friendship is blamed for behavior by males in their orbit. The truth was, they weren't to blame for my self-loathing, and I knew that. I broke it off because I thought they were going to break up with me.

"You guys were so mature, and I was a such a little emotionally delayed weirdo," I tell Sarah over lunch.

"That's not true," says Sarah. "You were always so cool and creative." I can't tell if she means it or if that's another thing you're supposed to say.

I ask Sarah about Bianca. She's good. A mother now. They still talk and text, even if they don't live in the same city. This is how it's supposed to be—friends from high school keeping in touch, sharing memories as they grow, moving up the steps of adulthood in parallel.

Sarah's a shrewd businesswoman, as she always was, but now professionally. She's doing well, she says. She never was one to complain. "And you?" she asks.

I tell her about my last of a string of relationships that burned hot and then fizzled. And how I'm living alone in the city, working a lot, obsessively researching dead men.

"So I'm basically the exact same as when you last saw me."

She laughs.

"I think I'm stunted," I say. This time she doesn't laugh, because maybe it's sad. It's hard to know if I'm joking—it's been so long.

When we return to the topic of Gary, she says, "I always knew he was awkward, but I was the only one."

She speaks with an assuredness she's never not had—her humor, founded on the principle that the world is nuts and she isn't. I believe her. I believe I am part of the world. We are both right.

Sarah is the kind of person who knows things—a survivor, not with respect to being a victim of a specific trauma, but in the resilient, Darwinian way. She will be someone who lives long, I think, as if it were a fact written on a title card at the end of a movie, when the character is replaced by two sentences and a photo of the real person the character was portraying.

Sarah asks for the check and gets lost in her phone. I grab it, as I'd promised myself I would, but she insists we split it down the middle. I don't fight her on it. Maybe I should have. Maybe then she would stay with me a little longer. She reminds me of home—the one with all the rooms, the barricade of doormen, the water bubbling on the burner, the bird on its haunches in the oven, the shopping bags under the table, the father on the sofa, the mother with her desk drawer full of secrets I was too young to see, and the bedroom window I decided to close because more was coming. Impossibly more.

We hug outside the restaurant. "It was good to see you," she says, now that we've already seen each other and we're about to not see each other, because the past is the past and there's no going back to change it.

1993

man: costume

GARY WILENSKY IS READING A BOOK called *Notes on Love and Courage*, by the Christian self-help author Hugh Prather. It is a meditation on the notion of love and the link between loving another and loving one's self.

"We need other people, not in order to stay alive, but to be fully human," Prather writes. "Unless there is someone to whom I can give my gifts, in whose hands I can entrust my dreams, who will forgive me my deformities, my aberrations, to whom I can speak the unspeakable, then I am not human."

But it's another passage that strikes Gary. A section on what Prather calls oneness, the melding of oneself with the beloved. He warns that with such love comes a certain responsibility.

"There are people whose feelings and well-being are within our influence. We will never escape that fact . . ." Prather begins. ". . . when I choose peace for myself, I choose peace for her, but when I choose misery, that too becomes my shrouded gift."

Gary hits the caps lock on his word processor and hammers out his own version of the quote. "THERE ARE PEOPLE WHOSE FEELINGS AND WELL-BEING ARE WITHIN MY INFLUENCE. I WILL NEVER ESCAPE THAT FACT."

Return. Return. Return. Space bar.

There is more. He has questions for her.

WHO IS YOUR CURRENT COACH/TEACHER— HOW OFTEN—WHERE—SCHEDULE

WHAT IS YOUR WEEKLY TENNIS SCHEDULE—
AFTER SCHOOL—THURSDAY

Gary has tried to get this information, even going so far as
contacting the Mother without success. Now he has decided to
find out on his own.

The Daughter's school, a redbrick fortress with modern cas-
tle spires, covers the entire block. He watches from his parked
car, graph pad on his lap, and writes the days of the week in a
column down the left.

In the column marked MONDAY, he writes: BUS ARRIVES
AT MADISON, 8:40, W/TENNIS RACKET. A few hours
later, he adds to the column. OUT OF SCHOOL 11:30—
LUNCH. A little later, he jots down: BACK AT SCHOOL 1:00.

Each day for a week, he is there, marking down the time,
noting what she's brought with her.

TUES: BUS ARRIVES MAD 8:40 W/TENNIS RKT.

WED: BUS ARRIVES MAD 8:40—NO BOOKS, JUST
RKT.

THURS: BUS ARRIVES 8:40 LUNCH 11:30—1:00
BACK TO SCHOOL

FRI: BUS ARRIVES AT MADISON 7:40. NO RKT,
OUT OF SCHOOL 11:30.

At the end of the week, he knows her tennis schedule and the
times she leaves school, with or without company. He's learned
the mechanics of her days, ingesting the evidence of her life
without him, choking on questions he still needs to ask her.

DID YOU THROW AWAY EVERYTHING I EVER
GAVE YOU

WHY WERE YOU SO ANGRY WITH ME

DO YOU EVER BRING UP MY NAME IN CONVER-
SATION WITH YOUR PARENTS—IN WHAT WAY

WHAT IS YOUR ANSWER WHEN SOMEONE ASKS
ABOUT WHAT HAPPENED TO OUR COACHING
RELATIONSHIP—OR WHAT HAPPENED TO OUR
RELATIONSHIP

WHO WAS THE BEST TENNIS TEACHER YOU
EVER HAD

WHO WAS THE MOST IMPORTANT TEACHER TO
YOUR PROGRESS

WHEN WAS THE BEGINNING OF YOUR PROBLEM
WITH ME

His mind veers into memory.

LAST LESSON—NO BAGEL OR JUICE—HOT
WEATHER

BEADS

NO THANK YOU FOR ME

WHO WAS YOUR GREATEST SUPPORTER

I WAS ALWAYS HONEST

His final question is handwritten at the bottom of the page,
scrawled in capital letters as an afterthought, but a pressing one.
HOW FAR DID YOU GO WITH [illegible].

On April 14, there's a tournament in the Bronx. He pulls
up to the parking lot and hears the familiar symphony of balls
snapping against racket strings, balls bouncing on cement,
and words sharp as the point of a knife: "Out!" "Deuce!"
"Ace!"

For the occasion, Gary wears the costume of a 1970s TV
detective. A mustache has been pinned to his upper lip with

cheap glue and the press of an index finger. A puff of wig hair is pulled hastily over his hairline.

Parked in a lot overlooking the tennis courts, he pulls out his binoculars and scans the perimeter.

On the courts closer to Gary, high school girls swing their rackets, reenacting the movements another coach has modeled at another time. Beyond them, at a distant baseline, the Daughter is cocking her racket. He puts down his binoculars and picks up his telephoto camera. Its retractable lens juts out from his car window like the periscope of a submarine.

Despite what Gary thinks, there is nothing subtle about this mission, and it isn't long before he's spotted.

"Gary?"

Lowering his camera, Gary looks up and sees a young, strapping teacher who coaches a local high school tennis team. The man is crouched at his window, wrestling down a smile. On the nearest court, balls drop and heads turn. A smattering of girl-giggles.

The tennis coach wants to know what, exactly, Gary is doing, parked in his car with a comically large camera, dressed this way. "This disguise was so bad it was laughable," the coach will later tell a news reporter.

Gary, with his high-powered spy gear. Gary with his cheap wig and mustache. Gary the detective, the private eye, the movie villain. Gary the joke.

"It was a dare," Gary tells the tennis coach. The half-baked explanation tumbles out of his mouth. A knee-jerk excuse a child concocts when he's been caught. A last-ditch tactic to lessen the inevitable blow—a weak attempt to pass the blame, in the hopes that peer pressure will appeal to sympathies, though it never does.

Gary turns on the engine, grinds the car into drive, and screeches out of the parking lot, still in his stick-on mustache and wig, a disguise that failed him and only made him look more like the man he's trying to erase.

girl: play

THE UPPER SCHOOL PLAY THIS YEAR is called *A Voice of My Own*. It's an ensemble, which means everyone gets the same number of lines, which is boring. The play is about women writers throughout history. I play Jane Austen reciting a letter to her sister. "Pray remember me to everybody who does not inquire after me," and other lines like that. It is not the kind of role you can sink your teeth into.

There are other parts: Mary Shelley, Harriet Beecher Stowe, George Sand, Lillian Hellman, Sappho, Aphra Behn, Charlotte, Emily, and Anne Brontë. The girl who is playing Virginia Woolf is two years older than me and her earnestness and warm, almond eyes remind me of my sister. Before every rehearsal she says "unique New York" to herself over and over again, flapping her tongue and spreading her lips flat across her teeth. Then she makes enthusiastic oohs and ahhs with her mouth. "It loosens up your face," she says. I'm embarrassed for her.

She learned this from our drama teacher. She feeds her cats. *Careful*, I want to tell her.

My hair is blow-dried, curled into ringlets, and shellacked with hair spray. After Virginia Woolf puts the bonnet on my head with the loving maternity of a child dressing her favorite Cabbage Patch Kid, she cups my cheeks lightly in her hands and says I look just like Jane Austen. What did Jane Austen even look like? I must have seen a portrait of her before, but all I can picture is the folded, prim gaze of the Mona Lisa. What do I look like? I want to ask Virginia Woolf, but now is not the time.

George, Jane, Virginia, Sappho, Mary—the whole lot of us hold hands in a circle before the play starts and the drama teacher leads us in a nondenominational prayer to the goddess of school plays. We are wearing shawls and dresses with puffy sleeves, and blouses that button to the top of the neck and itch. The bonnet tie is too tight under my chin, but my hands are occupied by other sweaty hands. With heads bowed, I stare at George Sand's boots and the bottom of her pants cuff. I wish I were George Sand.

The lights go up on a group of girls frozen in midactivity. I wait for my lines. I say my lines. I stand up from the desk where I was once frozen and walk across the stage as I say my lines.

The drama teacher stands in the back of the room mouthing words. She wears her usually pinned-back hair down for the occasion. It billows around her face, all oily, black, and luscious. There is something obscene about it.

I return to the desk and say more lines before I freeze, holding a pen over an imaginary piece of paper as the spotlight goes from me to George Sand. When all of my lines are done, I want the play to be over. I can hear my dad breathing through his mouth in the front row. I look over at him, his eyelids heavy. Beside him, my mother sits with her arms folded over her purse. Her shiny black bob is motionless even when her head moves. She's knotted a scarf at her breastbone. I can smell the perfume she spritzed on it. She is looking at George Sand with the same fiercely warm intensity she shines on everyone she meets. I wonder how it doesn't exhaust her. I wonder if she feels me watching her. I wonder if she thinks I was good.

Last year I played Feste the fool in *Twelfth Night*—the biggest part of any eighth grader cast in the upper school production. One of the biggest parts in the whole play. I know because I counted my lines and then those of the other major characters.

You're supposed to want to play Viola, the play's heroine, or Olivia, the girl everyone is in love with. But I found that Feste suited me. I didn't mind being called a fool, because the fool opened and closed the show. He was never entwined in the actual drama, never pivoted the plot, but observed it all—the theatrics and the audience observing those theatrics. His purpose was to remind the audience and the actors that it was all a play, and with his ironic dirge about death, that none of it mattered anyway.

Feste gives meaning to all the nights I've spent waiting as Bianca and Sarah played out romantic entanglements, or listening from the bedroom doorway as my sister recapped an evening with a boyfriend. I have always believed my failure to be a main character, the heroine, the object of desire, makes me, by default, the villain. But Feste provides a third option. The fool is off to the side, but always onstage. He doesn't break the fourth wall, he is the wall—a fictional embodiment of the author, there to remind the audience that all this drama will eventually end.

He is the only character who doesn't covet a romantic partner. Maybe it's because he doesn't need one, I think. Then I try to imagine which character he'd date if he had to pick one. Who's left? The fumbling suitor. The drunk and his cohort. "And the fool shall look to the madman." Someone says that.

I wish I remembered who it was. I wish I was in that play right now and not this one.

I make out Bianca's outline in the second row of the audience. Sarah is beside her. When we catch each other's eyes, I remember I'm wearing a bonnet. She sucks in her lips to keep from laughing. Fair enough.

They must have seen my parents before the show and said hello in their polite talking-to-grown-ups voices. My dad probably mixed up their names, and my mother probably smiled that pursed way she does for pictures, examining Bianca's outfit to see if she's wearing anything I lent her.

I study my mother sitting in the front row. She is lit warmly by the soft edge of the spotlight. When she catches me staring, she sparkles in my direction and fans three fingers in a secret wave. I look away, poker-faced, relieved. I did good.

"Are you proud of me?" I asked my mother after *Twelfth Night* ended and she handed me a bouquet of flowers. She beamed in that beautiful way that she did when we left the bone doctor's office. "So proud," she said, because she was.

"I'm always proud of you" is what she says when there's nothing much to be proud of, like for example tonight's performance. Or in first grade, when I was selected to introduce an A. A. Milne poem our class recited during prayers, and I spoke the words into the shoulder of another classmate, because my nose was running and I didn't want to use my hands to wipe it.

At home, she showed me how I should have announced the poem—chin up high, legs and arms together like a soldier, but more radiant.

"A. A. MILNE," she said, her voice booming and directed

toward a picture high on the wall. It was one she had painted, of my sister and me, in matching star-spangled swimsuits on a beach somewhere. She copied the image from a photograph, though loosely. In the painting I'm looking up into the camera and not down at my shadow in the sand.

"This is just how I look," I say when she asks why I'm so *gloomy*, or when she pauses before taking a group picture to raise my chin with her hand. She wants me to be proud of myself or, barring that, to appear proud to others. But I am not a main character, I want to tell her. I'm the fool.

girl: man and girl

I AM SITTING SHOTGUN IN GARY'S sedan, the last of three girls to be dropped off at home after a lesson. It's April and winter-dark. There are still a few days before time rolls back an hour. Garfield, suctioned to the rearview window, watches a drop of drizzle inch down the glass with his two unblinking eyes.

Blinkers click like a stopwatch and illuminate Park Avenue in flashes. My tennis racket is squeezed between my legs, brick of a book bag at my feet.

Gary stares straight ahead as the streetlight turns from green to gold to red and then green again. I wait for him to say something like "All right, Piper-ooni, until next time," but he is quiet. I don't know what I'm supposed to do, so I grab a strap on my knapsack and reach for the door latch.

"Don't go just yet," he says. "Stay here with me for a minute."

My stomach forms its familiar wave, preparing for the worst. I did something wrong during practice. I was being lazy. My serves were inconsistent. I almost hit Emma with my racket when we were doing drills. She flinched, I apologized. Gary didn't say anything.

"Okay." I lean back in my seat.

Gary lowers the volume on the radio and looks out the windshield, two hands on the wheel.

"I'm depressed," he says and then is quiet again.

I am startled at first. These are words I have never heard a grown man speak, words I have spoken only to myself. There is something to the sound of it, the two-syllable arc that rises and falls, like a heaved sigh. The sound itself a perfect description for what I have and who I am, who Gary is, too. An explanation for us both.

I'm flooded with warmth for him, for his Garfield, for this soft, stippled velvety car seat. He wants my help; he sees I am someone who understands this kind of pain.

"Me, too," I say. Sometimes I imagine my skull is an eggshell with hairline fractures. A premature and pulpy creature taps its beak from inside. This is what it feels like to be breaking from within, waiting for the transparent coil of bones, sickly alive and mewing, to slip out. The kind of thing you'd step on to put it out of its misery. I want to explain this feeling to Gary, and tell him about dangling my feet outside my bedroom window seven floors up, how I have already written a note. But I don't dare disrupt this moment that belongs to him.

All afternoon, we shifted back and forth between the white lines stapled down to green clay. We aimed above the net, chased after small yellow balls, listened for the pop when one of them hit the sweet spot of our rackets. Now everything that matters is in this car with a man who has entrusted a girl with his secret.

"Why are *you* depressed, Gary?" I'm careful to emphasize the *you*, so he asks about me next.

"Because you're going to leave me," he says.

I don't expect this. It hadn't occurred to me that my own absence could trigger anyone else's sickness. Usually it's my presence that incurs the damage. I know how it feels to miss someone who's right in front of you. But I never thought I'd be the one who was missed. I want to hold Gary now and rock him, like my mother rocked me when I mourned her as a child, bleeding out all her imaginary deaths through my tear ducts. I want to show Gary how grateful I am to be the one who is mourned, and to prove to him that I'm worthy of it.

"Just for now, Gary," I say. "I'll be back Saturday, and you can always call me—"

"No, no, you don't understand, that's not what I mean."

He readjusts himself in his seat and slams a hand on the side of the wheel in frustration. This sudden violence startles me. Scary? Exhilarating. It's as if Gary has started the car inside the car, stirring away the stall of misunderstanding, so that we are swerving recklessly toward a new point. Gary stares out the windshield. The yellow traffic light glints on his face, like a tennis ball apparition.

"It's that everyone leaves me," he says, gripping the wheel with two hands.

"You all grow up and you go away and you leave me all alone." His voice is unusually flat, almost monotone. He sounds so removed, as if he's alone, looking at his reflection in the mirror, watching his own lips move. *You all*, he said, and it stung a little. Could it have been any one of us in the passenger seat?

I look over to see if he's crying. I wish he were crying. I listen for the gargled pooling of tears, but instead his voice grows softer.

"And after all we've been through," he coos.

A taxi speeds past and through another yellow light. The doorman clutches the door handle and squints to see inside the

car window. I am the shadowy outline of a girl inside a man's
car. A girl with her father, or somebody's father.

"What about kids?" I ask.

"What about them?" He turns to look at me. Even in the
darkness, I can see his thick caterpillar eyebrows inch closer
together.

"Maybe you could have your own?" I say, the words slipping
out before I can swallow them back.

"Maybe I should have," he says flatly, and turns again to the
windshield.

I'm afraid to say the next wrong thing. So I lean over to
hug him—a gesture I haven't made before. I've squeezed his
shoulder from the backseat, but never from the passenger seat
and never a full chest embrace. His windbreaker makes plastic
scratching noises as he presses against me. Neck to neck, he
smells like Big League Chew.

"I won't leave you," I say. "I promise." His arms gather loosely
around my back. They feel birdlike and bony through his rayon
sleeves.

"I love you, Gary," I say, because it's different from *We love
you, Gary*. It's not a consolation or a group decision, but a private
understanding. A snuggle between two Jews. A loose promise of
what—solidarity? A commitment. A casing that will preserve
what's been spoken between us, for us.

"I love you, too," he says.

And then I get out of his car like a girl who has just been
kissed.

2016

romantics

ON A TUESDAY NIGHT, I MEET the last man I loved. Genesee
and whiskey shots.

"Who you been fucking?" he asks.

"You first."

As he tells me, I count prime numbers in my head to distract
my brain from pairing images with his words.

"Careful," I say, trying to sound as casual as he does. "Fuck
too much and you'll end up a dad." Alex wants to live his life
alone in an A-frame house he's built with his own hands, or
a converted van. Whichever comes first. Alex—the name
crunches like a mouthful of crystals.

I fell for him when he was sitting at the end of a bar, showing
off the hole where his front tooth should be. Now both front
teeth are fakes, his beard is full, and his long hair is knotted at
his neck with a rubber band. Still, he is beautiful.

There is no "I miss you." Or there is, but it's garbled into the
hollows of green cans, and then crushed.

Alex was always trying to outmaneuver the magnetic field
between us—believing, fitfully, that no responsibility outweighed the chemistry we shared. His resistance only con-
vinced me otherwise. I wanted him, even if we had nothing to
talk about, even if we only mildly enjoyed each other's company when we finished having sex, even if we fought over back
scratches and who gets up from bed to get the water, even if we

couldn't agree on where to live together or were uninterested in each other's career pursuits or fed off one another's anxieties, differed on which addictions were worth the trouble, disagreed on politics but conceded to the other's worldview because it wasn't worth another fight. We tiptoed around each other and still set off bombs, because each of us had laid them inside the other when we thought we were just fucking.

The problem was that I didn't always respect him. The problem was that I thought he was exceptionally cool. There's a difference. Respect is vertical—an upward-looking aspirational reverence, reserved for someone who has reached a point, in age or wisdom, that you haven't yet, but might. Coolness is more nebulous and ageless, a force field that surrounds someone—an attribute you can't even bother striving to reach because it's not gained, it's gifted. Coolness is rule-resistant, untrustworthy in its nonlinear trajectory, cruel in its evasiveness, something we grow to dismiss as impermanent, contextual, unproven, immaturely experienced, and all because we know the more we try to attain it, the more unreachable it becomes. Coolness doesn't hinge on wisdom or kindness, financial success, talent, or intelligence. It was the currency established before any of those things mattered, when we were kids, when the data points were simpler, and we judged others by how they made us feel. Coolness could make you feel a variety of emotions—excited, relaxed, self-conscious, unsafe. The uncertainty it provoked was how you knew you were in the presence of someone who possessed it. Coolness excused all the qualities I was taught to fix. There was no fixing to be cool. You had it or you didn't.

Alex had it. He wore Vans because he thought they were

good shoes, black Levi's because they were resilient, and black T-shirts because his clothes got dirty when he worked his day job. He taught himself to play the drums and played in a semi-successful band, but not anymore. He wasn't on social media because fuck that shit. He lost his front tooth racing BMX bikes as a kid, and lost it again in a bar fight in Berlin. He could work a charcoal grill with precision. Crisp a whole chicken to perfection without ever watching the clock, choke me when prompted, throw me down, hold me tight, burp and have it be funny. He built his own bed frame, which faced his record collection, which bordered his drum kit, which he played naked once, black hair tossed about, muscles striating. But only for a few seconds, until he dropped the drumsticks and said, "Nah, I'm just messing around."

He was tall but not too tall, thin but muscular. His body was built from biking through Brooklyn and working a job that required heavy lifting. He'd never go to a gym or use hair products or admit that he was beautiful. But when he'd run his fingers through his black hair, walking down the street with a hand in his back pocket, he knew he was. Of course he did.

And when I was walking beside him, I felt beautiful by proxy. He was an outfit I wore, a full bodysuit that temporarily resolved the conflict between who I should be and who I was. I was Alex's girlfriend and Alex was a beautiful mess who tenuously approved that I was a mess, too. It was all I wanted to feel, that delirious infatuation fueled by sweat odor, the bodily urge to combine insides, that messy mixture of fluids, so molecularly matched that their dried-up stains seemed meaningful enough to wear on a T-shirt as a badge of honor. Animal love.

It didn't matter that he didn't want kids, or that he was considering moving into his van, or that he was always in the hole with money, or that he spent so much of it on beer and malt liquor. It didn't even matter that he shit in a bucket in his backyard and left it there for the winter. It mattered a little, but not as much as it should have.

I should have wanted more from a partner by my thirties—I have been told this plenty. But Alex was the boy I'd wanted as a teenager—the one I'd wanted to want me and sometimes just wanted to be. The adult me was powerless to resist the teenager's stubborn urges, or she claimed to be. I liked the powerlessness I felt in the relationship and its sideways-moving momentum. It was an addiction, and I like addictions. They make all the decisions for you, so you don't have to think too much about whether what you're doing is good for you. You will take it as long as it's given, because there is a built-in end date and you know you'll miss your poison when it's gone. Might as well enjoy.

At the bar, we talk about what I'm doing now, and I tell him I'm writing a book about Gary Wilensky.

"You were always interested in that shit," he says, not really interested in that shit.

But when he asks what I'm doing "after this," I believe he still loves me.

It's been a year since he broke up with me. Two since he left me at an abandoned bus stop in Maine to get drunk with his friends in a tent. Two since he said even if he wanted kids, he wouldn't want kids with me. Three since we made snowflakes out of white paper. Three since we holed up in my apartment for days making homemade dumplings and working through a thousand-piece puzzle. Four since I first saw his face across the bar, and I didn't care that he didn't support unions or whatever came out of his mouth, I just needed him, and we made out in a doorway holding cigarettes before cabbing to my apartment.

Four since he slept through our first official date, and our third. Two since he quit smoking and became disgusted by my habit. Two since he played me a song about a boy who drinks too much because his girlfriend doesn't understand him. Two since the point was taken, but not enough to shake me off. One since he called to tell me he was shaking me off.

We leave the bar to slow dance to a Linda Ronstadt record back at my apartment. He was always good at slow dancing, and at convincing me singer-songwriters I'd written off were underappreciated. Later in the night, when our skins lined up, eyeball to eyeball, I mouthed "I love you," twice in case he missed it the first time, which was one or two times too many because when I texted him the following day, asking, "What was that song we were dancing to again?" he texted back "Different Drum" and nothing else.

"You weren't his favorite," the criminal psychologist had said when I asked him why Gary Wilensky didn't drive off with me that one night in his car. Such a simple explanation for such a loaded question. It landed plunk in my lap and made me realize the question I meant to ask wasn't why I wasn't his victim, but why I wasn't his favorite.

This need, still so vital, to chase male rejection as if it were the answer to the riddle of me. A film negative of what I'm not rather than what I am, which can be used to see the perceived deficiencies clearly and adjust accordingly.

The notion of self-improvement is particular to girls and women. That perfection myth that begins with our bodies in adolescence continues to rear its head through adulthood, even when reframed as empowerment.

When my relationship with Alex failed, I was told not to question what I did wrong, but why I chose such unhealthy partners, why I didn't love myself enough to recognize the right ones. Not bad advice, but still, reinforcement of the issue that might have kicked off my poor choices long ago. Something was still wrong with me that needed to be fixed in order to be worthy of love.

The onus is on us to change, be better, be less like who we are. We're at fault for caving to our impulses and encouraged to steer ourselves toward more calculated decisions. Once we called this pursuit purity, now we call it evolving. But as much as women are expected to override their own urges, men are expected to cave in to them. If they do, we wonder if we are somehow to blame. If they don't, we wonder the same.

1993

girl: mean man

I HADN'T NOTICED GARY'S MOOD IN the car on the way to Long Island City. But now on the court, it's clear that something is very wrong.

It's been two weeks since we last played with him. Another instructor picked us up from school last week, because Gary was away or sick or something. And then Saturday was canceled, too. But he is back, and he is different.

What is different? His coloring is ashy gray. His stubble is growing out. It's disturbing, this visual reference to both his age and his biological masculinity. Gary Wilensky, half child, half gabby old woman, has turned out as a gruff man. It's not that I didn't think he could grow facial hair, I assumed he couldn't. The idea of him shaving at all never crossed my mind.

The gray coloring of his jaw makes his eyebrows seem thicker, darker, more intensely arched. Or maybe it's his mood. He is in no mood.

One clap and it's "All right, girls, practice."

He and I on one side, Emma and Tara on the other. He is at half court with a rolling basket of balls. Feeding them, feeding them.

Hit a forehand, hit a backhand. But there are no *goods* or *excellents* given out today. Instead it's commands. *Harder. Faster.* And when it's Emma's turn, he screams, gravely and frustrated, "Come on, you can do better than that."

But that's not all. Curses. Snarling. Spit talk in all directions. He keeps hitting balls in Emma's direction, making her dive for them, so that her knobby knees are singed with clay pebbles. But it's not good enough. Her return hits the net.

"Jesus Christ! What the fuck is wrong with you today?"

Then he drops the ball he was holding and walks over to her side of the court. I watch Gary's body blocking Emma and his flinching, jerky movements. He waves his racket as he lectures her or curses at her. *Fuck. Shit. Disgusted.* He marks the clay with the head of his racket to draw some sort of point-making line so she'll understand, but it's still unclear what it is she's doing wrong.

When he walks back to my side of the court, I study the green clay in front of my sneakers, so as not to call attention to myself. If I can't see him, he can't see me.

Emma is in tears. She runs past the benches and across my side of the court to the flap of the bubble that you have to unseal. The Velcro rips open and she is gone.

Gary resumes the lesson and doesn't look behind him, not at me nor at the opening through which Emma has disappeared.

I play carefully, with exaggerated effort, to avoid being his next target, but he ignores me. He seems satisfied now that he's torn Emma down.

Adults sometimes do this. You think you know their tolerance level, what sets them off, and exactly when it will. You know when to back off, or when, if you don't, you will get what's coming to you. And these unspoken boundaries, which vary from adult to adult, are comforting. They establish the *you* you are when you're with them. But sometimes, unpredictably, they snap. They target an unassuming student—not even the known troublemaker—and punish them viciously, publicly, scaring everyone else into silence.

Someone else's mother walks into a room at a normal hour on a normal day, glares at you, and screams, "You, out." A usually easygoing teacher slams the textbook closed when you mispronounce a verb and makes you stand in the hallway. It's so jarring you want to believe you've done something wrong. The alternative is much more frightening.

When child allies lose their temper, it's even worse. They've made unspoken promises to never pull rank unless safety was an issue, to never call out moderate disobedience that they've already approved, to never abuse their authority or snap like other adults, without providing some legitimate, apologetic explanation. We require these guidelines for child allies. Without them, they are neither allies nor adults, but large, physically dominant children whose dismissal of the rules is no longer liberating, but threatening.

Nobody wants to sit shotgun on the way home, so we all crowd into the backseat. Gary has papers on the passenger seat anyway. If we speak at all in the car, it is to each other in whispers—a short yes or no, questions and answers about homework. If Gary is driving fast, if he's jerking through turns or speeding through a yellow light, we hold our breaths. We check that our seat belts are fastened. We are good girls. We just want to go home.

girl: body

IN THE DRESSING ROOM OF BANANA Republic my mother sits on a stool holding hangers, buried under cashmere. "Just try this one on for me," she says. All three walls are mirrored. I look at me looking at me looking at me and so on. This is what I look like. This is the back of my head. This is one side of my face. This is all I am. "Come on, just try this last sweater on," she says. "Do it for me."

Turtleneck sweaters, all of them. One is taupe, another green, another royal blue. I pull one off, ball it up, and hand it to her. Next. She weighs in on each item, inspecting the stitching, the color against my skin, the way the fabric drapes over my body.

"That color isn't flattering on you."

"That one goes with your eyes."

"That one is meant for someone with a bigger bosom."

"This isn't my style," I say of everything she's picked out. "Well, what's your style?" Ribbed sweaters, spandex, baby tees with lace collars. I want to go to Urban Outfitters, but she won't go there because they make her check her purse and she doesn't trust strangers with her purse. She's not crazy, she says.

"There is another little store up the street that I want to take you to," she says. No more. I feel a tantrum coming on.

I once read that before you have a seizure, you taste almonds in your mouth. Not a bitter bilious taste that rises up when you're panicked or feverish, but something softer, almost a treat.

The salesclerk's heels appear under the dressing room door. My mother asks for a smaller-sized sweater and opens the door to hand over the larger version.

A mirrored ray of my pale, bird-boned body blasts through the opening.

It is followed by my mother's schoolgirl giggle. "Oops."

She runs her eyeballs up my body and smiles, pleased. When she catches herself in the mirror, hunched under sweaters and hangers, she straightens herself up.

"I worked in a store like this once," she says. "A boutique."

I know this story, but it's one I like. The store was called Apples, and when customers would come in, she'd help style them, finding a belt to match the dress they had selected, or choosing a blouse she thought might flatter their frame.

The idea of my mother working exists in a parallel universe. It's hard to imagine her as someone who stood behind a register in the service of strangers. She has never had a job in my lifetime. She gets her easel out sometimes and paints. She keeps busy. All day she picks lint off the floor, off my sweater, out of my father's hair. She tightens the sheets. She folds and sprays and scrubs and makes piles.

"I keep things in order," she says. She never says, "I don't care anymore." Never stays in bed and pretends to be sick.

She buys things and then returns them. She paces in the kitchen on the phone. She plans out dinner, vacations, every after-school activity, the expansion of our apartment, our world. "My job is you," she says.

I once read that manatee mothers are the most protective of their calves. The baby swims underneath its mother's flipper. If a predator comes between them, mother will offer herself up as prey to protect her baby.

I saw my first manatee on a pamphlet left on a chaise longue by the pool at my grandmother's Florida apartment complex. It was chopped up evenly into slices by the blades of an engine motor. "Save the manatees," the pamphlet read, and went on to detail all the brutal ways humans have treated them. In one instance, a mother manatee was skinned, and when her calf was spotted swimming over her carcass the following day, he was captured and skinned as well.

When I returned from the pool, crisp with a sunburn, I sat in my nightgown on the plush ivory rug in my grandmother's living room. My grandmother sat beside me in her armchair facing Perry Mason, as the horizon of Hallandale Beach turned violet. When I felt something drip in my underpants and down one leg, I ran into her bathroom and saw the thin stream of mucus with red hairline streaks between my legs.

"You're a woman now," my mother told me when I opened a balled-up tissue to show her. "Tell Grandma," she said. And when I did, Grandma laughed.

"Don't tell Dad," I asked my mother, though she already had. This is what people talk about when they talk about the anxiety of puberty: the conflict between disgust and elation. Something is changing inside you, which is healthy and messy and bloody. It's a secret everyone can see.

When male manatees experience puberty, tusks pierce through their skin.

"Get this one." My mother is holding up the royal blue turtleneck sweater in the dressing room. I hate it on me. It's saggy and loose and too preppy. I look like a middle-aged yuppie. But if I fight her on it, she'll want to continue shopping, and I can't look at myself in the mirror anymore. I can't see her looking at me in the mirror.

At home, shopping bags in hand, my mother makes me try on the blue sweater for my father, who is lying on the green couch in the library flipping channels. I am of the mind-set that my father doesn't care about fourteen-year-old fashion, while my mother insists the man should see what his hard work has paid for. So I pull the sweater over my head and present myself. When he sees me, his eyes fill up with blue. "What a beautiful sweater," he says. "Is that cashmere?" My father brushes my side with his fingers to feel the fabric. I pull away.

"A hundred percent," my mother says, yanking a tag from my neck.

girl: drugged

WHEN I'M IN TROUBLE, MY PUNISHMENT is that I'm not allowed to close my door. This makes me feel like I'm soaking wet without a towel. My mother and I are nothing alike. She says we have the same heart-shaped face. The same thin lips. I have her face but my father's nose. My father's hazel eyes. My father's legs. My mother's torso. My father's fair skin. My mother's thick, dark untamable hair. My mother's moods. My mother's sensitivity to the almondy aura of bad things coming.

"Where did you get that shirt? I didn't buy that for you." In her nightgown and slippers—ink-black, blow-dried bob, immaculate—she stands in the doorway of my room.

"It's Bianca's."

Kilt rolled at the waist, hair in a bun, frizz at my temples, homework half done and shoved in my book bag, I'm ready to go. I need to go. I can feel it.

"I hope you didn't trade that for something I bought you," she says.

"No, Mom, she knows I'm not allowed to lend my clothing."

"Isn't that shirt a little tight for school?" She hooks her finger in the V of the neck, it snaps back against my chest. She touches me with such entitlement, as if my body were her own.

"It's Lycra. That's what shirts are made of," I say, pulling away.

"Well, at least put a sweater on over it. And don't you need to wear a collar?"

She is a tornado this morning, vibrating with instant coffee, to-do lists, and unsettling premonitions.

"Is everything where it should be?" she asks, opening my cabinet, searching for a specific reason to feel as uneasy as she does this morning.

"Where is that royal blue sweater from Banana Republic?"

I sink. I thunk my bag back on the floor so she can hear how heavy she makes me feel.

We are nothing alike. I am incapable of holding on to my property and my mother is incapable of letting anything go. It's as much a product of her upbringing as it is a product of mine. There are times we try to reason with each other through insults.

"You're spoiled," she says.

"You're materialistic," I say.

No time for all of that today. "Mom, I'm late."

"Fine, but when you get home, I want to see that sweater."

She softens. "Give me a kiss."

I do.

We walk down the hallway to the front door, the dog following us, hoping we'll dangle her leash. Her tags chime and jangle, always the sound of my mother's moving shadow.

As the elevator door closes between us, my mother continues to talk, her voice rising to counteract the downward movement of the elevator. "Don't you need some break—"

By the time I reach the lobby, one of the doormen, a young blue-eyed man with a goatee, who is too pretty and close to my age to look directly in the eyes, hands me the house phone.

"It's your mother."

"You forgot breakfast," she says.

She says she's sending Billy down with toast. I wait in the lobby, inspecting the marble floor so I don't have to look at the pretty young man. Billy operates the back elevator, an old-fashioned hand-cranked affair, with nothing more than a fan to cool him off. He is the kind of man who pats his brow with a handkerchief. Watching him walk toward me, all three hundred pounds of him, a man who in another circumstance I would be calling *Mr.* followed by his surname, which I don't even know, hands me a square of tinfoil-wrapped rye toast.

"Sorry," I offer, and head for the bus across the street. The homeless man with the baritone voice is there. He sings low and quiet, shakes a cup, nods at me. I feel around in my knapsack for change and instead produce a little blue pill stamped with a V. It goes in my mouth. The last one I'll ever take from the bottle, I promised myself before I stole it.

The M86 stops at every avenue all the way to York, which is three blocks from the mayor's house in one direction, three blocks from school in the other, and one block from the river where Manhattan ends and the absence of anything concrete begins.

By the time I get to school, the Valium kicks in. I look around homeroom at my whole grade, sitting on red, knotty carpeting and in metal desk chairs waiting for class to start. Look at all the ponytails and topknots, the silver rings and jangling necklaces and bracelets. Sniff that fresh deodorant smell, hear the binders snap, feel the space between the back of the blue metal seat and the faux wood desktop where my body slips in. Look how it all bleeds together like a fresh painting doused in buckets of water.

Today is like every other day, except that it is different. There is no fear, no crossed fingers folded into fists hoping for a magically good grade, no looking over at the paper next to mine, no looking at Bianca's red tongue curling on her upper lip as she copies notes from a chalkboard. Just a blurry relaxation, a comfort within these walls, a familiar protection, a herd feeling, a oneness.

We are in the ninth grade. We are reading a poem. We are highlighting every word the teacher tells us is important and writing *symbolism* in the margins.

We are preparing for when we will dissect a frog by looking at a diagram of a frog on a piece of paper. We are conjugating Latin in the pluperfect. We are walking our trays into a steamy silver room. It is taco day. We ask for one shell, no meat, and we ladle the soupy salsa into a paper cup; we tong lettuce onto our plates. We break off little pieces of shell and dip them in the red sauce sparingly. We talk about the history test, the boy who got stabbed, when he's going back to school, how lucky he is. And then we place our trays on the tray cart and walk downstairs to the student lounge, where we buy Diet Cokes from the vending machine and sink into the worn-out plaid couch—the most comfortable couch we've ever sat on because it's ours.

We change for gym class in the locker room, we see skin, nipple yolks balancing on egg whites, their gelatinous jiggle. We run ten laps around the gymnasium. We are called "GIRLS!" We ball our fists together and pump a volleyball into the air, passing it back and forth, diving, calling out "Got it!" slamming it with an open hand over the net.

We make our math teacher cry because we won't stop asking

her personal questions: "How old is your daughter? What kind of work does your husband do?" We make her a card out of spiral notebook paper that reads *We Love You.*

And then the bell rings again and we walk through the science corridor, the walls lined with the seventh-grade drug project. There's COCAINE in red block letters and a Ziploc bag of baking soda stapled in the center of the poster. There's LSD and PCP and so many glued on pebbles of Advil and Tylenol.

Now we've entered the middle school wing. There is carpeting on the floor and the whole hallway smells of art-teacher perfume—a mixture of sandalwood and clay. We want, when we enter this wing, to go back to the way things were, but instead we keep walking down another carpeted hallway past the arts-and-crafts room, where the kiln is baking fresh ashtrays, and into the room at the very end of the hall where our French teacher is waiting for us.

"Bonjour."

"Bonjour, madame."

"Comment allez-vous, aujourd'hui?"

"Bien, merci."

There is a TV/VCR setup, and we are grateful. We watch *The Rules of the Game*, and pass a game of Hangman back and forth, along with some Saltines from the soup section of the cafeteria. This is a room filled with light. Windows form the back wall and face the front of East End Avenue. Four floors below, chauffeured cars are already starting to pull up outside the school. Nannies gather in front of the main entrance.

The sun hangs low. Three of its rays are in our French class, pointing at the mass of bodies lying on one another on the floor.

We are reading subtitles; we have forgotten this movie is even in French.

"I want to disappear down a hole," says one character in the movie to another.

"Why's that?"

"So I no longer have to figure out what's right and what's wrong."

man: revenge

THIS IS IT. AN OVERCAST THURSDAY. April 22. A high of 54 degrees with light rain showers expected. A baseball star has died. A labor leader has died. The ashes of a cult compound settle and snuff out.

Gary Wilensky is transferring items from one bag into another, filling a black duffel with the bulky essentials: night vision goggles, guns, ammo, stacks of money he'd withdrawn yesterday. A fellow pro who had spotted Gary at the bank, looking gaunt in his tennis shorts, later describes his mood as "distressed."

Papers, papers, papers. In a briefcase and a duffel, he packs his notes, poems, questions, the lease to the cabin, and the audiotapes of the letters he'd written.

Drizzle shakes across windshields; wipers bat them away. They swing from side to side like legs sashaying between two white lines, an exercise to prepare for the match. Suicides, they're called.

All along the New York State Thruway, broken limbs dangle from trees, snapped by the storm five weeks ago. Gary is driving a new car, a white Lincoln he'd rented from a New Jersey dealership the week before. A luxury car for the rule-abiding middle class. Not a Mercedes, but also not a clunker like his regular ride. The kind of car an old man drives through the retirement towers of South Florida. A clean white American cruiser. A new set of bleached teeth to match.

He'd made this drive the week before: almost three hours

from Manhattan to Colonie in Albany County, noting the nearby Kmart where he'd pick up supplies, the three area tennis courts, and the strip of motels down Wolf Road.

All of it, a rest stop on the way to his final destination, farther north.

He arrives at the Sheraton Airport Inn around four P.M. and leaves his car packed while he checks in. At the front desk, he pulls out a roll of bills and licks his thumb as he separates hundred-dollar bills from fifties.

"Is there a tennis court here?" he asks the desk clerk, who hands him the key to room 164.

There isn't. It's an airport-style hotel on the outskirts of downtown Albany, not a resort. The Sheraton is located on a strip of Wolf Road alongside several other hotels and motels. It is a part of town designed to accommodate tourists visiting the capital for work or pleasure, but mostly work. A strip lit up by fluorescence in the night—clean, standard, and all business.

"There is an indoor pool straight ahead and to your right."

The ETA-K-Swiss Junior Grand Prix Tennis Tournament is happening in town throughout the weekend—and the teenage players will soon be swarming the Sheraton's lobby, double racket bags dangling from their shoulders, hands clutching Gatorade bottles, eyeballs darting around for competition, doing the math on other players with numerical rankings higher or lower than their own.

Back in his car, Gary drives to the courts and finds the tournament's information desk.

"Can I get a draw?" he asks. He's looking for the tournament pairings so he can find out who the Daughter is competing against and where.

"Sorry," the tournament organizer says. They don't give the pairings out early, as a rule. "Try tomorrow. Do you have a daughter playing this weekend?"

"No," he tells the organizer, "but I wish that I had a daughter."

Big old Gary grin. Whitened.

In the hotel he pulls out his tracking device, which provides the location of another car, not his own. He'd managed to slip the small chip on her family's vehicle before he left New York.

On Friday, he calls the tournament organizer, again asking about pairings. They're available now that it's the first day of matches.

Gary keeps a low profile in the stands during the Daughter's game and goes unnoticed.

At around 4:30 P.M., he is in the parking lot behind the Sheraton, scratching about in the trunk of his car.

A woman pulls up and parks nearby. In town for a wedding, she is returning to the hotel after a day touring downtown Albany, and she sees Gary in his oversize trench coat, gray curls poking out the sides of a knit wool cap. "I noticed him because he appeared to be homeless by the way he was dressed," the woman will state in a police report several hours later. She'll assist a sketch artist in drawing his likeness, recalling his "dark and gray" eyebrows, his "intense-looking eyes."

Wolf Road is a flat ruler with home goods stores, family-style restaurants, and midrange hotels as units of measurement. Gary drives slowly, three or four units past his hotel, and pulls into the parking lot of the Lexington Grill, a family-style restaurant. Burgers, fries, Cokes in foggy yellow plastic pierced with partially undressed straws. Through the green tint of his night vision goggles, he watches from his car as the Daughter and the Mother eat dinner behind glass.

Soon he is driving his white Lincoln down the signage-lit Wolf Road, like a unicorn streaking through an electrified forest. Pulling into the Sheraton parking lot again, headlights directing him toward the rear of the hotel, he slides the car between two yellow lines. It is ten P.M. and the lot is quiet when he turns off the ignition and walks to the trunk of his car. Inside is a folded wheelchair. The one item on his master list he'd written down twice, the device he envisioned when he imagined this plan, another wheeled prop in Gary's act. He unfolds the contraption, unlocks the wheels, reattaches the footrests, which snap into place, and then walks his toy to the passenger side of the car, preparing to load its seat with another toy he's brought along.

Headlights. A car eases into the rear parking lot where Gary is standing. The driver is a woman, the same woman who spotted him earlier in the day.

She turns off the ignition, opens the car door, walks to the curb to the hotel's back entrance, and disappears inside.

Gary stays in the parking lot with his wheelchair, setting up his gear, waiting for the minutes to pass.

In the rear of the Sheraton parking lot, Wolf Road is invisible. There is only the darkness, and the flash of high beams from the highway behind the brambles.

As the clock nears eleven, Gary lurks by his parked car, gripping the handles of the wheelchair. Headlights—two wide, blinding eyes—approach the rear lot and pull into a spot. He sees them.

For so long, he's watched from a distance, observing his targets through binoculars and cameras, glass screens that separated him from the movie he was observing. Now he will soon walk into the scene. The weeks of planning, the shopping trips, the visions of a future that lived only in his mind—all are about to converge here.

Gary Wilensky, the villain, the hunter, the man in disguise, with his oversize trench coat pulled up at the collar. His hair covered by a sailor's cap, a wool hat pulled down to his eyes, or a gray wig—accounts will differ. His face is concealed by the shadow of his collar, and a charcoal stubble—that may, in fact, be charcoal-colored makeup. He looks homeless, older, ragged, dangerous. He looks nothing like himself as he approaches the Mother and the Daughter, grinding the wheelchair's wheels over black cement. On its seat, underneath a blanket, is a shotgun. In his hand is an electric cattle prod.

They don't notice him, and when they do, they don't recognize him. He is a man raising a weapon and slamming it down on a seventeen-year-old girl.

There is the sound of a hammering alarm from a human throat. Two throats. The throats of women. Words. Directions. *Go. Help. Please.* A question: "What do you want from us?"

The Daughter—she is on the ground, out of his reach. There is a weight on top of his back, another person. The Mother—Gary has turned his attention to her, tamping down all the sounds with his cattle prod, until there is a new sound.

"Okay, pal, the police are on their way." Gary Wilensky peeks out from behind a parked car. Beneath him, the Mother is bleeding on the ground, trying to stand. A minute before, the Daughter had run into the lobby. "Help! My mother is being attacked!" she screamed to the desk clerk. Now the desk clerk stands above the scene and sees Gary Wilensky in a large dark coat, a scarf wrapped around his neck, walking toward an empty wheelchair and pulling a rifle out from underneath a blanket on the seat. Gary points it at the desk clerk and cocks it.

Back up, back up, back up. Gary raises and lowers the tip of the gun as if it were his own chin, approaching the clerk with his rifle pointed.

"Okay, pal, I'm moving," says the clerk, arms above his head. "Where do you want me to go?"

Gary changes his tack. He returns to his white Lincoln, sliding in the driver-side door and turning on the ignition.

The trunk is still open when he backs out. He leaves the wheelchair in the parking lot with the desk clerk, the Mother, and the Daughter.

The gun, he keeps.

girl: revenge

THE BLUE PILL HAS WORN OFF by the time I'm walking home along Eighty-Sixth Street, back in the realm of the hissing, the eyes on my kilt, the hooks my fingers could make, should I need them to. And the fear, the inner shakes, return when I open the door to the apartment and hear the clacking of her heels on hardwood. Louder, closer.

"I couldn't find it," she says, her voice low and unsettlingly calm.

The cabinet doors in my bedroom are open and there are sweaters strewn on the floor.

"The blue Banana Republic sweater," she says. "Where is it?"

Hands on hips, she presses her lips tightly together, holding back something alive inside her mouth. She knows where it is, even if I'm not 100 percent certain. I want to believe it's at the bottom of my closet, in a trunk in my sister's room, in the laundry basket, even in a ball in a backpack that went to Bianca's and returned without ever being removed.

"You call her up right now and tell her to bring that sweater back," she says. "And God help you if she doesn't have it."

She leaves the room and slams the door, and then returns to leave it ajar. In the kitchen, she opens cabinets and slams them closed, muttering *bullshit* and thwacking the tile with her feet. I rummage through the closet, toss shirts out of the armoire, take armfuls of wool from the trunk and dump them on my bed.

Please, God, let that sweater be here. Let me find that sweater and dangle it in front of her face so she can apologize that she ever doubted me, that she ever saw me as spoiled and reckless. Let her be wrong about me, even if I did give it to Bianca because it was ugly and not my style; it was her style and I'm not her and she can't fix me. There's no punishment in the world, no doctor who will ever hammer away what is mine. Hideously mine.

I could smash things, start a fire, go out the window.

But she is back in the doorway, surveying the explosion of fabric.

"Does she have it?" She's had time to think a little more about how much she buys me and how I treat these things. How I treat her.

"I'm not calling her."

"Excuse me?"

Our faces are now inches apart. One a product of the other. I'm afraid she's going to hit me. Then I want her to.

"Fuck you," I say, because it is the worst thing you can say to your mother, and because I'm daring her. Because when I ran away as a child, she hit me, and when I tried to hit her back, she held down my arms, and because I'm bigger now, my cavity of rage is endless, my pain threshold has been tested by knives, my muscles are shaped from swinging a racket hard enough to crack a girl's face, and I feel nothing.

She slaps me across the cheek. It is a good burning. I'm hot now and ready to go.

"You want to hit me again? Go ahead. Hit me again."

"Don't make me."

I throw my arms on her shoulders and burrow my fingernails into her skin. Her eyes dart up my forehead to my hair, the wild bun uncoiling from a rubber band's stranglehold. She yanks at it, that familiar tangle I imagine she hates. It burns for a second, a good burning. I press down harder on her shoulders.

I want to corkscrew her into the blue-knit carpeting, into the floor beneath ours, and when she is low enough, finish her off with a stamp of my foot to her head so she drops into the neighbor's bedroom, mortified. *Missus Weiss*. She is Missus Weiss to the contractors, to the doormen, to the cleaning lady, to my friends, to whoever is at the other end of the line as she paces the kitchen tiles in her boot heels roped by a phone cord. But not to me. I see her clenched teeth, the slight overlap of the bottom row. I see her fingernails opaque with the glue where her tips fell off. I smell her parched animal mouth. She tries to muscle my arms off her by forcefully twisting her shoulders, but I won't let go.

"You little—" she shouts, her voice doubling, as if someone else inside her had studio-recorded the words first in order to thicken the sound of her voice now.

We twist in a circle, spinning into the bathroom, pulling down the shower curtain with the force of our bodies, all hands reaching for and missing an anchor. We will ache later, but there will be no marks left behind, only the overheated flush of a steady workout.

I have pinned her to the mirrored wall. *Look who's little now*. I am as tall as she is. Stronger than either of us anticipated. One of my hands is holding down her arm, soft wonton skin wrapped around spunky little meat. My other hand is at her throat. Her skin is soft there, too. I squeeze a little, then a little more. I feel each cord in her neck, those delicate wires of a homemade bomb. Her eyes bulge at me. I feel electrified. In the unlit bathroom mirror, the shadow of one wild-haired creature looms over another. *Is that me?*

I have to tell my hands to drop, to let her go. Her eyes still bulge. My heart laps for air. I have the rapidly fading feeling I've just won something.

man: gun

GARY WILENSKY'S WHITE LINCOLN SCREECHES TOWARD the
exit of the Sheraton parking lot. On Wolf Road, he can turn left
or right.

Soon the police will be alerted about a perp in a white Lincoln; an ambulance will race to assist two victims attacked in the
Sheraton parking lot. In the meantime, a heap of shopping bags,
gifts he might have planned to give her, wait in his Sheraton
hotel room. His name is posted in the reservation book. More
bags, stuffed with items he'd checked off his lists, fill his car.

GLASSES

SCISSORS

NIGHT MASK

SEXY NIGHTWEAR

He was there and so was she, and then she wasn't. She is
behind him in the parking lot and he is moving away from her.
But in which direction? South toward Manhattan, where the
TV he left on casts his studio in the gray-blue light of midnight
programming, or north toward the cabin, where the relics of a
botched plan are all still about?

PULLEY

CHAIN

EXTENSION CORDS

Left or right. Right or wrong. Are there only two options in
the end, and which is more right or less wrong? Which way is

home? Straight ahead, across both lanes of Wolf Road, a sign
for the Turf Hotel calls to him. He can cross the street in his
white Lincoln and start over.

Around midnight, the lobby of the Turf is quiet. A lone night
attendant greets Gary under a sleepy haze of artificial light.
News travels slowly along Wolf Road, and the frenzy that took
place across the street moments ago might as well have happened in another dimension.

"Joseph Jeffery," he tells the desk clerk who asks for his name.
The bills, still wadded in his pocket, peel away.

A new hotel room, a new bed draped by a new patterned
blanket. He takes the phone off the hook. He riffles through
his duffel bag—a clown sack of costumes and surprises he'd
collected for this night.

Outside in the ragged, dried-out bushes behind the hotel
parking lot, he shakes out another bag of belongings, leaving a
trail of his intentions to be discovered in a matter of hours by a
man walking his dog.

CLOTHING

BAG FOR HEAD

KINKY

Back in his car, he turns the key and the engine hums alive.
His eyes are open, but he can't see. The order of things—the
carved-out parking lot path that leads to the main road—grows
fainter.

His wheels thump over a grassy curb toward the entrance to
Wolf Road. He is almost there when the alarm goes off again—
the spurt of a wild, angry siren. Red and blue lights heat the
interior of his car.

Behind him, a traffic inspector has spotted a white Lincoln with its headlights off, bowling over the curb. The car matches the description of an alert sent over the radio earlier in the evening. It is nearing one in the morning when the traffic inspector turns on his siren and follows the car down Wolf Road.

Gary drives a few hundred feet and turns right at the sign for Calico Corners, pulling into the parking lot, which curves around the back of the unlit fabric store and comes to a dead end. The police car stops behind him.

He is overlooking a marshy swampland. There is nothing ahead of him but the reflection of an odd-shaped moon, just a skin-peel away from being complete. Inside his car, there are no more bags. The wheelchair sits in the Sheraton parking lot. The rest is scattered in brambles and inside two hotel rooms. Even that Smith & Wesson is behind the parking lot of the Turf Hotel. Only the rifle is with him.

The car parked behind him shines a spotlight on the last scene: a desperate, wild, hand-waving debate between Gary Wilensky and Gary Wilensky and Gary Wilensky. The brake pedal is stamped down with the anxiety of group indecision.

Next, a small cannon boom is swallowed whole.

"He shot himself!" the officer screams, slamming a car door, releasing a barking dog who runs toward the white Lincoln. "He shot himself!"

Gary Wilensky is dead, but another Gary Wilensky—Gary the escape artist, Gary the practical joker, Teflon Gary, one of them or all—releases the brake pedal. The white Lincoln screeches forward and skates a hundred feet over the side of the parking lot toward the scalped moon.

Fragments of Gary Wilensky are shaken loose as the wheels hit the mud and sink into the marsh. Two officers, a dog, and a cameraman charge through the marshland and open the door. Inside, Gary's knob knees are splayed apart, a gun between them, and his mangled head leans on the headrest, turned in the direction of the empty passenger seat.

girl: dead man

IN THE KITCHEN, AS MY MOTHER steams broccoli, we watch Gary die. *A Current Affair, Hard Copy, Inside Edition.* One of those. The segment had already started when I walked into the room. I missed the part where they explain what happened. My mother looks around for a blank VHS tape, but it's already too late. *What we are about to show may be disturbing for some viewers.*

It is night, somewhere without buildings or streetlamps. A spotlight is fixed on a white sedan and a man in the driver's seat. He waves his hands above his head frantically, as if he's in the throes of an argument and not being heard, not getting his point across. The car then lurches forward, screeching as it hurtles away and comes to a full stop. A dog barks, gruff and throaty, running alongside other men to the stopped car. The door is yanked open and there is the familiar jaw of a man I know. It is tilted up, turned away from the camera, but unmistakable: Gary Wilensky, all dressed up in khakis and a collared blue shirt, fast asleep. His legs loose and open. One hand is relaxed on his thigh, a gun resting against it. The dog is still barking at the car. The dog is in the kitchen barking at the TV. "It's okay," my mother tells her. "It's okay."

But all of that comes later. First there is a phone call.

I am in the library, on the sofa with my dad, who is flipping through channels for something to watch. The phone rings on my line.

It's Emma. She has to tell me something. Listening to her breathe through the phone pinholes reminds me of pressing my ear to a conch shell. You're supposed to believe you're hearing the ocean and not the sound of two canals pressed together with air whirling between their folds.

"Gary killed himself," she says quietly, solemnly, the way you're supposed to, if there is such a way. The way someone tells someone else in a movie, before the scene cuts to the funeral. The mind works fast, writing the scene that came before this one, of the act itself. Gary, gray and alone in his studio apartment, with a telephone coil wrapped around his neck, stepping off a stool, so that all you see are two feet gently swinging.

The mind works fast. It favors a flashback montage with all the signs pointing to the inevitable. The last lesson, with his temper, and before that, the secret we shared inside the car. "I'm depressed," he had said. "Me, too." We were both talking about the same thing; we were both saying we think about it, and we might do it. But I was too chicken, still clinging to the belief that maybe I could change and it would be better. Gary was old, and he was ready. There is a logic to it, which I can't explain to Emma, but I understand.

"He was depressed," I tell her. I imagine him, so alone in his apartment, convulsing in tears, wondering whether he should bother calling for help, not wanting to be a burden. *Gary is dead.* I hold on to this fact, as if I were holding his hand as he dangled out the window. *He committed suicide.* It keeps slipping from my grip. *Gary Wilensky was depressed, so he killed himself and now he's dead.*

"How did he do it?" I ask Emma, but she won't say. She has

to get off the phone; she can't talk about it right now. She just wanted to let me know before someone else did.

"Who else would tell me?" I ask.

"Piper," she says, and then she's quiet for a second. "There's more." She doesn't have all the facts, but it's going to come out. "Turn on the news," she says, or "You'll find out." Something like that. It's hard to pay attention. I'm still at that part of the movie where he's alive but almost not, opening the wooden box with the pistol inside, or opening the window and climbing out, the way you'd climb over a fence.

"I have to go," she says, suddenly so rushed, it sounds like someone is coming for her. So we hang up.

What happens next? I tell my father, who's already sitting up, alert on the couch, concerned after overhearing my half of the phone call. I tell my mother, who's standing in her nightgown in the doorway. I remember to tell them to turn on the news, but it's too early, it's too late. There is no news. The only information is what I know from Emma—he killed himself. And what I know from Gary: He was trying to warn me. He was depressed, and I tried to make him feel better. I promised him I would be there. He should have called me; I would have understood.

I should cry when my mother comes over to hug me, but I don't. That's not the feeling. The feeling is more like a geometry problem, not an impossible one, but the kind where you have to take a shape and turn it around, and apply logic, arithmetic, and the laws—what are they? They are written on chalkboards and copied in notepads, to be used when such a problem presents itself. Somewhere I have it written down.

In bed I think only of Gary, of how he might have done it and how he must have felt when he was ready. The risk of failing outweighed by the prospect of another living moment. Hanging. It must have been hanging. His two Nike sneakers dangling above a hardwood floor. That is how I imagine the scene ends.

A reporter on the morning news speaks of a bizarre stalking incident that ended in suicide. *A popular Manhattan tennis coach. His seventeen-year-old student. Upstate New York. This past weekend.* Eat toast. Drink milk. Take the elevator down, counting backward. The newspaper kiosks are all empty. The homeless man sings low and shakes a coffee cup.

Before classes start, someone whispers, "Did you know her?" I didn't. He'd mentioned her once. She was older, at another school, ranked. We know better than to speak too loudly, or to act like we know what's going on outside, or to talk about how it feels. Some things are just not discussed in school.

A block away, at Brearley, where Gary coached the tennis team, a cluster of reporters wait. Two wait outside my school as well. Maybe they're confused, or maybe they're visiting all the private schools, or maybe they know I was his student. I walk past and they don't notice me. On the way home I pass a newsstand.

The *Daily News* headline reads "Fatal Obsession," and has a photograph of a detective squatting in front of a mess of wires and handcuffs. *Newsday*'s cover reads "House of Terror," and has a closeup of the handcuffs and chains on the floor, and beside them a wig and a white mask.

At home, the *New York Post* is open on the coffee table to a page with the headline "Coach Kills Self After Kidnap Plot Fails."

Kidnap. The word itself makes me think of milk cartons and missing children. I skim the columns for his name and the name of the girl.

". . . rushed to a local hospital, where the mother took 70 stitches."

I am looking for my own name or a photograph of the inside of his car—something familiar—but the only picture is on the bottom half of the page: Woody Allen and Soon-Yi walking down the street, with a caption about where they were spotted yesterday. My mother is in the kitchen on the phone with a school administrator or another mother of another student.

From behind the swinging door, in the dog's hallway outside the kitchen, the conversation sounds like this:

"Seems . . . so far . . . talk to her?" [Heel on tile, heel on tile] ". . . Planning to say . . . I know . . . Frightening . . . Never known . . . She's . . ."

What? What am I? I push open the door to the kitchen and she looks at me.

". . . fine, good. She just got home, so I'm going to run, but we'll catch up in a little . . . Sure. And you, too."

She rests the receiver in its cradle and turns to me with an expression I've missed. It's how she would look at me when I'd just fallen off my bike or bumped my head—her own body reeling from the pain, but restraining herself from showing it. It's a look I will crave from her for the rest of my life, one that is followed by arms wrapped around me and my face in her chest, smelling, underneath the perfume, her sweat—the scent of slightly sour chicken broth.

But there is another layer to her expression today, which is new: a tilt of her head that suggests a certain hesitancy to touch me, as if for the first time, she doesn't trust herself enough to know what I need.

"Tea? Cookie?" she asks, pointing to the Entenmann's box on the counter.

We sit at the kitchen island, bouncing tea bags in mugs.

She's spoken with Tara's and Emma's parents and made a few calls, and there's a doctor available to speak with anyone who took lessons with Gary.

"Do you want to talk to someone?" she asks, meaning someone other than her.

"What would we talk about?" I think back to the doctor with the boring toys, the beads on bended wire, who asked me questions and took notes. *What makes you frightened? What scares you?*

"I don't know. You could talk about how you feel, if you have questions about what happened."

"There were reporters outside of school today," I say.

"I'm not surprised," she says. "You know you don't have to talk to them if you don't want to."

What I know is that you're not supposed to. When we're walking out of school, it's not unusual to see an occasional adult holding a flashbulb camera. There are a few students whose parents are so famous, I don't need to be told why the cameraman is there. And others who I learn about only when I'm flipping through a magazine and see their last name, or when my parents are watching the news and say, "Don't you know their daughter?" and I do. But it's hard to understand why the world cares so much. It's all about divorces, mostly, and affairs.

A court case involving some company or other. Adult outrage is so hard to understand. But I know their rule, the one we learn early on, after *Don't talk to strangers*, but long before *Never make the first move*. It's this: *Don't talk to the press*.

The *private* in private school means just that. It is a class distinction. Ours is the world others want to expose, and it must be closely guarded. Unless it's a magazine interview—a feature in a certain caliber of glossy print—it's tacky to reveal yourself as eager for attention. More than that, it's a betrayal. A secret tattled. That is what I've gathered, over the years: Privilege is based on secrecy. Our parents know what others want to know, and so do we. They have the code of entry, and we know what really happens once we are inside. Privilege comes with a certain trust that if broken results in the loss of such privilege. The codes are changed, the gates are locked, and the traitor is left outside without protection.

My mother explains that she spoke with the school, as they were aware that Gary was my coach. His name was written on some form she had filled out granting him the right to pick me up after school. They prepared her to expect media requests, she says. They advised against it.

The next day on the cover of the *New York Post* is a picture of Gary in roller skates playing tennis. He is younger than when I knew him, and his legs are muscular. Beneath his picture is a photograph of his victim. She is also playing tennis. She is older than me and has straight brown hair in a ponytail. She stands in profile, her face partially covered by the arched rim of a hat. Above her, the headline reads: "The Teen He Stalked."

This is not my Gary. Not the one I knew, who wore wind-breakers that filled with air around his bones, whose body was a clumsy cartoon with gag limbs. That night in the car with the engine off and the lights cycling through their colors. The night he hugged me, and I smelled his candy body. I was the one he would have tried to take, but he didn't. I am safe, I am lucky, but I have a secret: I wish I was his favorite.

I wanted it so much when he was alive, but even more now that he is dead. I know I'm not supposed to think this. I know he did a bad thing. There was a cabin with chains inside it. They belonged to him. I saw a pile of them on the cover of a newspaper, and I knew they had to do with sex or violence or both. Something was wrong with him. He said he was depressed, like me, and now he is dead. I saw him die. I've never seen anyone die before. And now I see the reporters huddled around the entrance to his favorite student's school. *The teen he stalked.* I don't know what exactly happened to her or what he tried to do, but I know she matters. He picked her and now she matters. Everyone wants to know what she has to say and how she feels because he chose her. She matters and I do not.

My mom wants to know how I feel. "Fine," I say. I feel nothing I can share. All the feelings are drowned out anyway by the clamoring adults—those who want to know the secrets and those who want to keep them. The ones who want to sell us our fears, and the ones who want to believe such fears don't exist. All of them making up the rules. None of them listening to us. I feel like I want to scream, but I'm not supposed to. If I must, I can whisper to a therapist, a keeper of secrets who will deposit my feelings in a vault with the others, because the side I'm on is the side that's been chosen for me.

Something awful happened—to us, not them. And I can see right through their rules, set up for their own protection, to keep us in line like good little girls. I'm sick of being a good girl. I'm sick of what's appropriate: skirts six inches or less above the knee, collars on shirts, closed-toe shoes, straight hair, perfect teeth, small noses, the Bible verses in unison, eating too much, not eating enough, the Pythagorean theorem, the golden rule, faith in the school, faith in our friendships, faith that the people we love will never leave us, faith that this whole system works if we don't question it.

I feel angry. I feel like breaking the fucking rules.

A woman in an overcoat holding a reporter's pad stands at the metal fence outside Asphalt Green, an outdoor athletic space where we have our gym classes in the springtime. I am running around the big rubber track when I spot her. I jog in place.

"Were you one of Gary Wilensky's students?" Her face is divided by a fence of octagons. Her hair is shiny and brown; her features are pointy. She is young for an adult. She wears a trench coat and holds a pad, as I imagine all reporters do; only she's fragile, with the kind of skin that could tear if a vein in her forehead pulsed.

"We're not supposed to speak to you," I say. "We'll get in trouble." Now more girls are gathering around and talking all at once.

"I'm the one," I say, gripping the wire on the fence. "I knew him."

Someone else says something about going to his camp a few years ago, and it's become a competition. This time it's about who knew him best, but it was me. I am the winner.

"Girls!" The word is thrown from across the track and intended to hit us in the head. Everyone is back to jogging again, but I stay at the fence with the reporter. I have something to say. What is it? What do I know?

"He was a great coach. The best. I loved him."

Then I run away, as fast as I can, but it's too late. The gym teacher calls out my name. She is power walking toward me in her turtleneck and Keds.

"What did that woman want?" Her face is so aggressively close to mine. I can see the white foam she has in the corners of her mouth is not in fact toothpaste but an assortment of saliva bubbles that taken together appear white.

"I don't know."

"Did you say anything to her?" She eyes me in a way that lets me know what my answer should be.

"Of course not."

She holds my gaze a little longer, cop style, and then waves for me to keep jogging. So I start again, jogging along the track that parallels the street the reporter fled. "Other way," the teacher yells, because we're all supposed to run in the same direction.

"I want to talk to someone," I tell my mother when I'm home. "Not a shrink, a reporter." Screw the school.

I'm ready for a fight. I'm ready to test her loyalty to me, to make her undermine the social code, the oath I imagine she took when she, a Jewish girl from Queens, enrolled her two daughters into a legacy we didn't inherit and will not carry on.

She looks at me. I am still dressed for gym class in green school shorts and a black T-shirt emblazoned with the rubbery imprint of Jim Morrison's face. A crown of frizz fills out the bony, wild-eyed creature she and my father once made.

"Okay, let me think about it."

There is something stuck to my lip. Pen ink, maybe, from anxiously chewing the tops of pens. She takes her thumb and rubs my bottom lip. It won't come off. She licks her thumb and returns it wet to my lip. She rubs and rubs, spreading my lip with her thumb. "I got some of it," she says. "The rest you'll have to get off yourself."

When the reporter calls on my parents' line, my mother speaks first, setting the ground rules. No names in print. No mention of my school. No questions that might be upsetting.

The reporter's voice is direct but respectful. No baby-talking bullshit. Mom waits on the other side of the kitchen's swinging door. I don't know what I'm saying. I'm saying how I felt about him, how I think I still feel. I'm saying this is what he said to me in the car, this is what he told me, and this is how he was during our last lesson. My face is on fire; my ear feels like it's having a fever. I am talking to someone about Gary Wilensky and he is listening to me.

She is listening, too. My mother stands on the other side of the door, a finger to her lips. It is her index finger, soft and pink, shorter than usual—the French manicured tip has come unglued and now sits in a small bowl on the kitchen counter. I press the swinging door open so I can see her again. That unvarnished index finger still on her lips. It's a gesture she doesn't know she makes, but I know. It's what she does when she's unsure, conflicted about whether she's made the right decision. In this case, it's whether she was right to defy the school in favor of her daughter's insistent desire to be heard. She is shushing her mind, the rattle of her own insecurity, so she can hear only me.

"Thank you," I tell the reporter before hanging up, but the words are meant for my mother, and my mother alone.

2016

mothers and daughters

AT FIRST I THOUGHT MY MOTHER had kept the folder of Gary Wilensky out of some maternal guilt—a scrapbook of her own oversight, a reminder of what could have been. She has always been an involved, concerned parent—the organizer of teen programs, the supervisor of field trips, the point person for other mothers deciding on their own daughters' curfews or allowances. This one oversight, I thought, might have haunted her as it has haunted me. That would make this story somewhat neater.

"No," she says, "how could I have known? Everyone went to him. He taught at the other girls' school. Our friends from Fire Island had him over for the Jewish holidays!"

She is a woman who worries whether she made the right decision to install track lighting in the renovated kitchen, even though, she says, track lighting is considered dated. But she does not often question her own parenting decisions. She did what she thought was right at the time, and I admire her for this as much as I disagree with some of her decisions. I am the opposite. I put my own instincts on trial.

"Did you predict I would ask about him years later? Is that why you kept the folder?"

"No, I kept the folder because I keep everything that has to do with you girls. He was an important figure in your life at the time, and it was all over the news," she says. "I keep our history. That is my job."

"That's true," I say. "You are the family archivist."

"You know, my mother was the opposite," she says. "She didn't save anything that had to do with me. She preferred to ignore me. My whole life as a kid—it was like I wasn't there. I remember asking her a question in the backseat of the car and she acted as if I hadn't said anything. She never even bought me a birthday present. Can you imagine that? It's not like I hate her for it, but this stuff, it stays with you."

This is why she was so involved with me, she explains. Why she retained every report card, every note I ever wrote, everything that ever happened or didn't happen to me. This is why she kept the folder on Gary Wilensky. This is why she always wanted to fix me.

"You were always so sad," she says. "I didn't know how to help you."

"Mom?" I ask her during another one of our late-night phone sessions. "Why am I still fixated on Gary?"

She is endlessly patient, endlessly cooperative and sensitive to this particular obsession. She still wants to help.

"Well, you were always interested in the macabre," she says, but I reject this explanation as oversimplistic. There must be a more psychologically illuminating reason behind it all.

She is thinking now, as if she had been me at fourteen, imagining what it was about him that impacted me so hard when he was still alive, before we knew what we knew.

"He came at a time in your life when you needed him," she explains. "He praised your talents. He was good for your ego. He explained to you who you were on another level. He saw you as something different from other people. He saw a side of you that was quite strong and special and gifted. The girls in your class didn't see this side of you."

She pauses for a moment.

"With Gary you were the chosen," she continues.

"But I wasn't," I say, though she doesn't hear me.

"Playing with him represented change, growth, and you wanted change." She pauses again, slipping further back in her memory. "I used to lie awake in bed at night as a teenage girl just thinking——" She grows quiet.

"Thinking about what?"

"Oh, about what else was out there, outside of my house in Queens. I could feel there was so much more I was missing, and I wanted to know what it was. A fourteen-year-old has a very limited exposure. School is the same every day. It was for me, and more so for you, in the same school for all those years with the same girls."

She moves so easily between the two of us, overlapping our two girlhoods to thread us together.

"But you had something separate from those girls," she says. "You had Gary."

"But, Mom——"

She is still talking, still polishing the silver of one memory or another. "It's funny, because you never acted like you needed anybody," she says. "You always used to slam your door shut and say, 'Leave me alone, Mommy,' and I never knew what I did to make you so upset."

"I thought you thought I was a monster."

"Never," she says. "I never, ever thought of you that way. That's how you thought of yourself."

There is such a thing as an inherited self-image. You can see it not in the mirror that faces you, but in the one behind you, with its infinite reflection. The way I saw myself at fourteen was a warped reflection of my mother's self-perception as a child, which was a dented reflection of her mother's childhood reflection, and so on—each burden passed down from mother to daughter. And in the era of your life, when your identity as an individual is struggling to break through the surface, it's this history that holds it down.

My mother's mother was a great beauty. There are stories of how she stopped traffic when she crossed the street, how strangers would propose to her, how wherever she went, she was always the most beautiful woman in the room.

Before these stories were passed down to me, they were passed to my mother, who slept with her hair wrapped around soup cans and starved herself until she looked longer than her five-foot frame.

My grandmother didn't understand why my mother's hair didn't fall smoothly over her face, like her own, or why, as a teenager, my mother begged to have her nose refined to mirror her mother's delicate features.

"My mother never once helped me look pretty," my mother said once as she dug a bobby pin into my scalp to fasten a curler. "I had to do it all myself."

My mother was a substitute for her dead brother, who was found cold and blue in his crib at age two. When she was born, she was supposed to make it all better.

Still, my grandmother blamed herself for her child's death, for allowing the doctor to use forceps to deliver him, for not checking on him in his crib sooner. To cope, she avoided painful reminders of her lost child—my mother being the most vivid of all. My mother skipped kindergarten because my grandmother didn't care to walk her to the bus stop. She bought her own birthday presents because my grandmother didn't shop for her. And each summer at camp, she'd be disappointed when my grandmother failed to show up on parents' weekend.

There are few pictures of my mother as a child, and none of her as a young teenager.

"She was trouble," my grandmother would say, lounging on the crack between two twin-sized beds pushed together, the lone photo of my mother, sullen at age seven, hanging on the wall beside her.

My grandmother was twelve when she came to America from Poland. On a ship bound for New York, she slept on the bottom bunk with her little brother, who died of an illness during their voyage. Her mother slept on top with someone who wasn't her father, but that was a secret. She watched the sagging shape of two bodies on a mattress above her, and listened for their moans. At eighty-three, my grandmother told my mother this story for the first time. "Eighty-three," said my mother, a second time.

Beauty came easily to my grandmother, but survival was a struggle. She saw in my mother a spoiled child who didn't appreciate her relatively easy suburban upbringing. My mother saw in her own reflection a girl who didn't engender her mother's love. So she taught herself to appropriate her mother's beauty, and vowed to herself that she'd be different with her children. To her, rolling hot curlers in my hair was an act of love. To me, it was a punishment.

When I was fifteen, my mother took me to a plastic surgeon who shaved the bone of my nose while I slept. For a week, my eyes were rimmed in blue bruises and my nose leaked stale blood. When we removed the cast, I studied myself in the mirror. I was a new person I didn't recognize, smoother than the old one, full of a newly discovered shame. A new secret to keep. Even now, when I look in the mirror, I'm surprised by my own face. I try to memorize it, but when I walk away, the memory always fades.

"I don't know what I look like," I tell my mother when we argue about this part of our past. "I was only trying to help you," she said. "I thought I was helping."

When my mother was defiant, my grandmother would put a curse on her.

"I wish daughters on you," she would say, and now my mother understands what she meant.

In Florida, I lay on my grandmother's bed and listened to the voices in the kitchen.

"Nonsense," said my grandmother, dressed in the yellow housecoat my mother gave her. "I loved you and your brother just the same."

My mother told me to pack, and we moved to a hotel. When we came back the next season, my mother brought my grandmother a new housecoat. When we came back again, my grandmother was in the same housecoat in a new apartment in a bed with protective rails. My mother rubbed Vaseline on her lips. "I love you," my grandmother mouthed. "I know," said my mother.

This is the line of women that has led to me. Each one with

her own struggles and resentment, which she tried to correct with the next generation. Each time creating new struggles and resentment.

"I love you," says my mother before we hang up the phone, which means *be careful* and *good night* and *I'm sorry*.

"I love you, too," I say, which means *I know*.

ghosts

COLONIE'S WOLF ROAD IS ONE LONG supermarket aisle of familiar brands: Arby's, Chili's, Cheesecake Factory, all aglow with fogged plastic signs lit by a hundred fizzing bulbs. It's the kind of strip-mall road so familiarly American, so boxy and uniform, that it fits like a thin, flat Lego piece over the memory of similar roads. When you're on it, you know exactly where you are, and after you've left, you forget you were ever there. Convenience, you might call it.

Once upon a time Wolf Road bisected a rural residential community on the outskirts of downtown Albany, comprised of family-owned farms and blue spruce driveways. But in the midsixties developers began to descend, staking billboards in sand dune lots and replacing the once stately country club with an indoor shopping center.

By the eighties and nineties, the weeds of mall culture extended along Wolf Road. A Stop & Shop, a Chinese restaurant, and a family-style grill bled into new franchises—Red Lobster, Outback Steakhouse.

In 1993, the area was Albany's rest stop—an assortment of cheap hotels, family-style restaurants, and shopping outlets. A collection of commercial cul-de-sacs and parking lots. Twenty-three years later, the drive-through dazzle is brighter, the signs have changed, but the architecture remains largely intact.

The Lexington Grill where Gary spied on the Mother and

the Daughter is now a jewelry store. The Sheraton where Gary pushed a wheelchair toward his victims on a Friday night is now a Best Western. The Turf, where Gary checked in after his failed abduction attempt, is now a Radisson. And the Calico Corners, where Gary shot himself, is now a day spa called Complexions.

The map of his last hours—dodging from one parking lot to the next across the lanes of Wolf Road—is still a perfect parallelogram.

Even the floor plan of the Best Western, where I book a room, is the same as it was in 1993, when it was called a Sheraton. It is motel style with a front desk and lounge area, a dining room where the complimentary breakfast is served. The two-story track of modest rooms are built around an indoor pool, the color of a Midori sour and the odor of stale cookies.

In room 164, overlooking the pool, police found a portion of Gary's belongings.

Property Report 1: *A Wilson Quick Fire tennis racket, a roll of brown tapes, a child seat locking clip, 7 Tic Tacs, a T-shirt marked "Gary's Girls," blue Prince jogging pants, a blue-and-green Prince bag containing toiletries, 2 empty Kmart bags, Macy's bags, CVS bag, Victoria's Secret bag with wrapping, a blue-green Swatch watch, 3 wigs, a beard and a mustache, 1 large garbage bag, two handwritten notes, 1 large garbage bag, a cassette tape marked "Favorites."*

The old Sheraton's white, shale-like walls are still the same, as are the two exit doors that lead to the back of the motel and the parking lot, where Gary's attack took place.

The back lot is lit only by the flickers of headlights on a nearby highway. To reach the front desk, you have to cross rows of parking spaces and a broad, dark corner of Dumpsters, before the entryway pillars are even visible.

The Mother had wrestled Gary Wilensky away from the Daughter and lifted her body up and off to the side, freeing the Daughter to run to the front of the hotel and scream for the desk clerk's help.

After the desk clerk arrived in the parking lot and Gary fled, the Mother and the Daughter were taken to a local hospital and treated for head wounds. Nineteen stitches for the Daughter. seventy-one for the Mother. It was there, when asked about possible suspects, that Gary Wilensky's name was first mentioned. By then Gary was already frantically shaking out his belongings in the parking lot across the street from the Sheraton. Less than forty-eight hours later, they were discovered by a local resident walking his dog.

Property Report 2: 1 pair of clear glass lenses. 1 Smith & Wesson blue steel model .38 caliber loaded with 5 rounds, 1 pair of black scissors, 1 black piece of plastic, 1 black blindfold, green and white sweatbands, 1 black strap-on penis, 44 photographs (marked to be turned over to the victims), letters, notes, audiotapes of letters, papers, correspondence, 3 paperback books.

I take a hard right outside the old Turf Hotel onto Wolf Road, and then another right into the parking lot of the day spa that was once Calico Corners. The parking area is short and dead-ends at the border of an overgrown lot—a land swamp at night, empty enough that the eye passes over it, scanning for something more concrete. There is a red neon sign for a local newspaper sizzling with the words *Times Union*, and then beyond that, a space in the sky where the moon should be.

Twenty-three years ago, Gary Wilensky parked right in this spot, propped the base of a rifle on his khaki pants, and leaned into the barrel.

Behind him in another vehicle, Ric Easton, a local news cameraman on a police ride-along, had pulled out his camera to capture what happened next. A screech as the white Lincoln careened off the lot into the marsh. Easton followed the police to the car, capturing the moment they opened the driver-side door and shining his camera light on the body they found slumped inside. The ammunition still perched on Gary's lap, next to his open palm, which was coated in a dark orange fluid.

"Let's roll the tape," said Maury Povich two weeks later. His soft gray suit, padded at the shoulders, matched his gray swoosh of hair, which matched the gray, fog-lit night Ric Easton shot his footage. *Inside Edition*, *A Current Affair*, and *Hard Copy* vied for the video, while one upstate newspaper decried the bidding war between networks for pictures of the gore.

But before all that, before Gary was buried in a small service in Long Island, before his gadgets were auctioned off, before the footage of his death was released, officers removed a room key registered to the name Joseph Jeffery, from Gary Wilensky's soiled denim jacket. When they opened the door to room 161 of the Turf Inn, they found a phone off the hook and a duffel bag with more supplies.

Property Report 3: Two firearms, handcuffs, night vision equipment, disguises, paperwork involving a lease of property on Cemetery Road.

At five in the morning, when the highway is still dark, I drive farther north toward the cabin. By the time I reach Warrensburg, the sun has already gone through its early purple phase and is starting to seem familiar again. Straight along one numbered route, left at another, through towns and the absence of towns. Then down into North Creek, where river rushes over rocks and the trees form a cave around you.

As the car climbs up Cemetery Road, the narrow gravestones look like the willy-nilly guffawing of old teeth. A gang of wild turkeys fan out on the road. One turns to me with a fierce eye. The only address I have to follow is from a copy of the lease Gary signed. It reads "off Cemetery Road." All that is off Cemetery Road is a gravel path crackling with ice and broken branches, shaded by trees.

I look at the picture of the house from the ripped page of the old *New York* magazine and then I look at the house in front of me. They are close, though this one appears slightly bigger, slightly greener in color. Perhaps an addition was added, or the wood was replaced.

Even now, there is something cruel about this house. A ruthless industrial quality that evokes images of canisters of syrupy gasoline, axe blades, preparations for an ending.

Was that even the right house? I'll wonder later.

Back in Colonie, Steven Heider meets me at the entrance of the police station. He is heartier, taller than I imagined him to be.

"Good to see you, Chief," says the officer at the front desk. Everyone still calls Heider chief, even though he's recently retired. He is dressed like my father in dungarees and a blazer, with the same brush-needle mustache. It's the costume of a man who doesn't wear costumes, a man who earns the admiration of other men without working for it.

That was never Gary Wilensky's strong suit. I try to imagine a meeting between the two of them. Gary hunched forward, twirling in his seat, while Heider leans in with the alpha body language. Gary the delinquent.

"Patty," Heider says when we walk into an office with a large round table and a woman seated at a desk behind it. "This is Piper Weiss, who I talked to about a year ago. She's doing a story on Gary Wilensky. You remember Gary Wilensky."

"Oh, yeah, I remember well," she says. She looks to be in her fifties, with blond, neatly trimmed hair, and a sturdy smile.

"So can we interrupt?"

"Of course, you're still the chief." There is a practiced ease to their rapport. It almost feels staged on my behalf.

Heider is all meat and muscle, straight-backed. He carries himself with the casual pride of a man who's seen enough in his life to know which seat he belongs in. He sits facing Patty, so I sit facing him, with my back toward her.

"I got an eight-pound Yorkshire terrier at home with a small bladder," Heider says, to let me know our interview has a time limit. And then he tells me about his recent vacation, in which he witnessed some kind of explosion. "I'm an interesting guy," he says. "Bad things follow me."

He tells a good story. Restraint is required to land enough unanswered questions that the retelling is more interesting than the actual event. His calloused hands are planted on the table, inches from a slide carousel situated hors d'oeuvre style between us. Now it's down to business.

"I know specifically the town attorney said no videos, no pictures. So that's why you got what you got," he explains.

"What's in there?" I nod to the carousel.

Heider cups it with his cigar-sized fingers. "Pictures," he says.

Here lies the additional evidence—photographs of the cabin when it was discovered by police. A few were released in 1993, but many more were not. The attorneys who approved my FOIA had concluded that these visual components should remain private out of respect for the victims. I'll have to file new forms and appeal that decision, Heider explains, if I want to see the photos inside the carousel.

It feels like a psychological study, where a researcher places a cookie in front of a child and says someone else might suffer if she eats it. The stacking of personal satisfaction against moral consequences to be used in arguments over whether humans are essentially good or evil. Which one is it?

"No, I don't need to see it," I say, and I wish saying the words would make it true. I'm a sniffing dog, hungry for scraps. I would leap on the table and eat off the dinner plate if I wasn't so tamed by the consequence of shame. And I already feel the shame, the fact that the victims must be protected—no longer from Gary but from me.

"Can you tell me what it looked like when you found the cabin?" I ask.

"Shackles on the beams," says Heider. "All the windows were boarded shut. Video cameras in all the windows, video cameras in the woods—in case somebody drove down the driveway, he'd be able to see him. He had wires strung a hundred yards in the trees. The windows—some had wood or heavy blinds with cameras pointed out. And then he had six TVs, six little screens to watch the footage from the security cameras."

All of it, spoils from his SpyWorld $10,000 shopping spree.

In a clearing down a narrow gravel path, a half mile off Cemetery Road, detectives found a small one-story cabin, the stain of driftwood, iced with vertical window frames and a sloped gray roof. A tangle of wild-haired birch and spruce trees guarded the property, reaching over the roof, needle to needle, creating a top layer of protection from anyone who might be looking down at the area from above.

Ice patches, the last remnants of a brutal winter, soaked into the yellowed dirt. Their deterioration observed with vigilance by camcorders stacked on tripods inside the house. The three-legged cyclopes were placed at each window, peering through partially boarded-up glass when the officers arrived on April 24, 1993, to dismantle them.

There were other cameras, some affixed to the trees, more surveying the cabin's interior. A trail of wires snaked through the rooms and united at a collection of monitors flickering with real-time footage of the driveway, the living room, the bedroom, and the four-poster bed, neatly made with brown-striped sheets and matching shams. There was a long, thick silver chain that ran across the headboard, tightened around two wooden pillars, and another horizontal chain tied to the ends of the footboard. They were presumably intended to be clamped to handcuffs on a human being.

A pulley system had been installed on the ceiling, one that could be linked to shackles found inside the house and allow for a hostage's limited range of movement.

Inside the fridge were wine coolers. Elsewhere were ammunition, a carving knife, an assortment of shackles and handcuffs, pornography on VHS, a flashlight, scissors, wigs. One was red and loopy, another straight and black, another gray with tight little bobby-pin curls. There was a white mask with uncanny features—pursed lips, a sharp nose with nostrils, delicately indented smile lines, painted-on eyebrows, and two black holes to look through.

When an officer opened an overhead storage space, he thought he'd discovered a hostage, but when he felt her skin and pulled her from her hiding space, she flopped down like a crumpled shower curtain and looked at him with blue acrylic eyes, not understanding. *A rubber sex doll found in the cabin.*

"In my memory, he had cameras arranged so he could film the bed and what was happening," says Patty, from the desk behind me. "He was checking angles with himself in the bed making sure the angles were right."

Heider jumps in: "Obviously he'd been up there for days, putting it all together and then following her around when she drove upstate. We know the father of the victim found some surveillance equipment on his car at one point."

He leans in, with a slightly raised eyebrow. "But what was he going to do after he got her?"

"What was he going to do if he failed?" adds Patty.

"Gary had no plan B," Heider says. "He didn't even try to leave the area. He drove back across the street and into the middle of a police dragnet. My guys were stunned at the time. There was that white Continental."

"If Wilensky had jumped back in his car and driven to Manhattan, we wouldn't have known about the place in North Creek," he continues. "It wasn't until the victims were at the hospital that they mentioned his name, but still, we'd have had to track him all the way back to New York City and prove he was up here. This was before the days of GPS, before the days of E-ZPass, before there was digital evidence tracking someone's whereabouts. So all he had to do was say 'I wasn't there.'"

Instead he scattered his letters and photographs around the area as if they were his own ashes.

"I always found it interesting his throwing all that stuff around. Sooner or later somebody would find it," says Patty. "Why are you doing it? Because you want someone to know?"

The initial burst of coverage began with newspapers—the Associated Press, followed by the *New York Post*, the New York *Daily News*, *Newsday*, and the *New York Times*. The headlines were blunt at first. "Coach Kills Self After Kidnap Fails," "Tennis Pro's Dark Secret." But soon, they resembled R-rated psychological thrillers. "Fatal Obsession," "Little Cabin of Horrors," "House of Pain."

The Daughter, by then exposed in the press, was photographed in a baseball cap, flash-eyed, outside her school, while her father begged one reporter camped outside their apartment building for privacy. More reporters parked outside Manhattan private schools bombarding other students with questions, while whisperings of a made-for-TV movie landed in print.

"Word spread when we started making inquiries with the NYPD in our investigation," says Heider. "The fact it involved New York City people—I think once we brought up the Brearley school—from there it went like a rocket."

The crime had followed Gary from Colonie back to Manhattan, and soon Manhattan reporters were following Gary's crime up to Colonie.

"It had to be a slow news week because we had camera trucks and trailer trucks here right out front until Friday," says Heider, who landed on the cover of the New York *Daily News*, standing among a pool of chain links, electronic devices, and a white expressionless mask laid on the cabin floor.

"They called me Hollywood Heider," he says. "I was on *Hard Copy* three nights in a row. My sister was on a trip in Puerto Vallarta. She wakes up and there I am on the news. At one point, this thing was on fifty-seven news channels around the world. It was just huge. Nobody had anything else to talk about."

While Manhattan reporters hunted for Gary's colleagues, friends, and family members, a local Colonie reporter learned that the part-time Sheraton desk clerk who helped ward off Wilensky's attack had been fired from his second hotel job. He had overslept after fielding several interviews the night before, and missed his shift.

By Friday, a week after the incident, Heider put a cap on the media's feeding frenzy with one last supper. Seventy reporters gathered at the station to hear Gary's audio recordings, which he'd left behind the Turf. On them, he dictated the letters he'd written to the Mother months before his death.

"Dead silence," says Heider. "The tape went off. End of story. They all walked out the door and I never heard from them again."

Back in Manhattan, reporters asked psychiatric experts to elaborate on the term now associated with Gary Wilensky: stalker.

The concept was relatively new by mainstream standards,

having surfaced in the media the prior year, when a sitcom actress was murdered by an obsessed fan. But by 1993, after David Letterman's stalker and Amy Fisher's act of violence, the term was trending.

Stalking behavior generally describes an individual acting on his obsessive fixations with another person, but because the motivations and features of stalkers vary widely, there is an ever-growing number of subtypes. For example, love obsessional stalkers harass victims they've never met. Simple obsessional stalkers are motivated by a severed relationship with someone in their lives, and more likely to become violent. Erotomaniacs are delusional stalkers who believe their (often famous) victim is in love with them. An expert suggested this as a possible diagnosis for Gary in a 1993 article, though I believe Gary falls on a spectrum between erotomania and simple obsessional.

Dr. Eric Hickey, a psychologist and criminal profiler, has described Gary's condition as relational paraphilic attachment, in which a person's unusual fantasies attach themselves to the concept of relationship that isn't really there. His fantasy of a consensual relationship with the victim becomes his own reality, but when it begins to unravel—for example, when Gary was fired by the Mother—he becomes desperate to fix what he believes to be a legitimate romantic relationship. In this way, Gary was delusional but not sociopathic. Sociopaths don't have attachments to their victims. Based on Gary's letters professing his devotion to the Daughter, he did.

After his death, the Colonie Police Department reached out to Gary's psychiatrist, but because of privacy issues, she was hesitant to divulge much.

"She basically said, 'Yeah, he had his issues,'" says Heider.

"He was in a time warp of age fourteen or fifteen. Wouldn't you say, Patty?"

"Yeah. I think he was overly obsessed with her," says Patty. "Usually those kinds of people, as they go into this kind of obsession, they tend to escalate. People who are off like that have ups and downs and they spiral. They start to become worse. He was really decomposing at that point."

The story took another turn when, days after the incident, the *Daily News* reported that this wasn't Gary's first illegal act. In 1988, he was arrested for stalking two young boys and a little girl over a period of a month. The mother of one of the victims claimed she alerted the private schools about Wilensky, but said her warnings went unheeded. ("I feel like I'm going to be sick," she told the *News* after Gary's death.) Later, the two boys, teenagers in 1993, sat on a stage with their mothers and described their 1988 encounters with Wilensky on an episode of *Geraldo*.

The first boy says he spotted a man in a mask filming at his bus stop, and recalls how he'd follow them in his car to their next stop and continue to shoot them. The second boy had first believed Gary to be just a "New York neighborhood guy," but looking back is "horrified that I let it last for so long."

After Gary's arrest and the retrieval of his stalking tapes, the victims provided depositions and their families hoped to press charges, but the district attorney had other plans. A representative from Robert Morgenthau's office did confirm to the media that the case was dropped, but didn't elaborate.

As I understand it, since stalking wasn't a felony in the late eighties, Gary's record of community service and his willingness to seek court-appointed treatment made for a quick conclusion to a comparatively small case in a city reeling from a crack epidemic and rising homicide rates. When I spoke with Gary's then lawyer, he didn't immediately recall the case or his former client.

But in 1993, news of Gary Wilensky's stalking past—which coincided with him coaching children—made him in death a sudden poster child for more stringent antistalking laws. Only a year earlier, California had instituted the first in the country, and several states, including New York, followed suit, but there was now a public call for tighter protections and nationwide mandates.

In the fall of 1994, Congress passed the Violence Against Women Act, which criminalized crossing a state line "with the intent to injure, harass, or intimidate that person's spouse or intimate partner." The act was expanded two years later to include all victims of perpetrators. While stalking a child in New York became a misdemeanor in 1992, it wasn't until 1999 that the state upgraded the charge to a class E felony, punishable by imprisonment.

"One of your questions was about other victims," says Heider. "We know he was stalking a bunch of people, whether or not they were at his school or on his tennis team, or strangers in Manhattan we don't know. I mean the two boys he stalked in 1988, they didn't know him at all. But we found a lot of pictures on Manhattan streets."

In order to determine if there were other victims, the NYPD briefly made the photographs available to the public, so that those who recognized themselves could come forward. Nobody did.

"Are those pictures still available?" I ask. These are the images I want to see, the images Gary took of other girls he was stalking, an image of me.

"I don't think so . . ."

I dig a nail into my skin to distract my facial muscles from revealing an emotional response, but it's a failed tactic.

"Look," says Heider. "He obviously had an infatuation toward a number of people. This was the only one, we determined, this was the only one he acted on."

Heider explains that child predators like Gary use their authority to create a pipeline of potential victims so that even if his interest is centered on one child, there are others he's grooming as backup. "They make it so they never feel like they're alone," says Heider. "I'm sure there was a favorite in every one of his lesson classes. And his version of crossing the line wasn't necessarily sexual—more psychologically controlling. He became in control of their parents. He dictated when their kids came to practice. He dictated how long they stayed. The parents were on the outside. But the victims weren't having it. They finally told him off, and that's what started the whole process. I take that back: the Daughter was the first one who went to her parents to say he was getting a little crazy. Other girls had not done that."

He might have been most infatuated with the Daughter before he was fired, but losing her triggered his exclusive fixation and desire, as Hickey had suggested, to rectify the fantasy relationship he believed they shared.

In the end, his abduction plan was as deranged as the strategy with which he executed it.

"Why use a cattle prod to attack them when he had a gun under the blanket of his wheelchair? Why not use that?"

"I don't think he wanted to kill anybody," Heider says.

But another predator might have wielded the gun swiftly to force his victim into his car. Gary, whose thoughts were so disorganized at the time of the attack, and his impulsiveness so unrestrained, lost sight of his own plans, and unleashed a violence less calculated than any he might have fantasized about or strategized around.

"He was smart enough to effect a ruse that worked," says Heider. "And if it wasn't for them fighting him off, Lord knows what would have happened."

He pauses and leans in closer, palms flat on the table. "He just never figured on the Mother fighting back."

The Mother. It was her sheer presence in that parking lot that might have thrown Gary off. And she was the one who physically thwarted his attack on her daughter.

In a 1994 *McCall's* article, the Mother penned her own account of the man in the trench coat and hat who approached them in the Sheraton parking lot and suddenly began beating her daughter.

She describes instinctively jumping on her attacker, tearing buttons off his coat in a desperate attempt to free her child. Then she recalls lifting her daughter's crouched body, flinging her out of the line of attack, and screaming for her to run. As the attacker turned his rage on the Mother, her daughter ran for help. "I'll kill you if you hurt my daughter," the Mother screamed, even though she had become the focus of his violent assault.

"At the second I knew my child was in danger, I had no fear for my life," the Mother wrote. This act of maternal heroism, which she humbly attributed to science and the production of adrenaline, ultimately saved both their lives and the lives of other potential victims.

Four years after her mother's essay, the Daughter shared her own experience in her college newspaper. Her focus was not on the attack, but the scars that remained in the aftermath.

She feared he was still lurking—underneath her bed or behind the shower curtain. She felt unsafe closing her eyes to sleep. To help, her family made "rounds," checking beneath the bed and in the shower every night so she could rest. "Sometimes," she wrote, "I still like to check."

To process their experience, her family shared their fears about what had happened, as well as what could have happened.

Back in 1993, news reports speculated that Gary could have taken her life with his own.

In a way, Gary's fatalistic vision of romance feels very teenage. It's a perversion of a pubescent fantasy—that pang of longing for the unattainable and the mistaken belief that if one's feelings are requited, all will be resolved. A love hologram. I know it well. My bedroom shrines of books, posters, and carved candles, willing Jim Morrison into my own existence as a way out of the life I was living. My obsession was also conflated with another escape fantasy: death. Jim's appeal was inextricably linked to his early demise, and I wondered if a shared ending could bring us together. "Love-death as the ultimate high," Joan Didion wrote of Jim Morrison's mystique in an essay in *The White Album*. Perhaps Gary was chasing that high.

But love is not obsession. Love is survival. It is the Mother and the Daughter fighting to save each other's lives.

I came to Colonie in search of evidence—a photograph Gary took of me walking to school, a found letter referencing our conversation in his car. A reciprocation for this tedious, one-directional obsession I seem to favor. A confirmation of my place in his story, a love note from the afterlife. Instead, I've found nothing. That love means nothing.

"How are you doing?" Patty's voice is soft on my back. Turning around, I see a sun shard cut through the window, breaking over her blond hair, turning it white.

I don't know how to answer her question, or what exactly she's asking. "I'm fine. I guess, for some reason, I just want to understand why he did what he did."

Heider shakes his head. "You'll never figure it out, because if you figure it out, you're one of them."

Patty nods.

"There's a reason why you've probably put it aside for a number of years. Until you're old enough to really handle it," she says.

"He was a person of power, of trust," says Heider.

"A person your mom or dad would let you be with because he's a teacher, and let's face it, that's part of your mother's feelings, too, because she let you go with him," adds Patty.

"He knew what to say to them, he knew everybody wanted their kids to be the new Chris Evert and he made them feel you could be the new Chris Evert," says Heider. "The money didn't matter to him. That's why he wasn't charging your mother for those additional lessons. He would have done it for free just to have access to you."

I am standing, gathering the paper where Heider drew a rough map of Gary's last hours on Wolf Road, and shoving it into my bag. I am ashamed to hear them validate Gary's interest in me, because I shouldn't need it.

"One thing to keep in mind, as you go through this journey and you're writing this book, is that it's going to bring up a lot for you," Patty says when I walk over to her desk to get her business card.

Beneath the Colonie Police Department logo, imprinted in gold, is her name and title: Patrice Lockart, *Victims Services Specialist*.

It occurs to me that Heider may have brought me into her room for a reason. Did I lead them to believe I was a victim? I'm not. I'm something else, but what?

"Remember," says Patty, still seated at her desk, neatly covered with relics of a paper-clip era. "You were fourteen when it happened and that fourteen-year-old is still in there."

Facing her, I can see the slight brushstrokes of her age, the slits at the corners of her eye sockets, the blueprints for two pillars between her brows.

"What happened—whatever confusion you had then—it's still there," she says. "And it will carry with you."

epilogue

WHEN YOU GROW UP, YOU'RE SUPPOSED to stop believing in monsters, but there is one inside my desk drawer, buried under a stack of police reports. She is folded at the limbs and flattened onto a torn-out magazine page. Yellow face, lips parted in mock surprise, one eyelid drearily half open.

She is a child's doll whose eyes close when she's tilted, cross-bred with a man's violent, red-lipped fantasy. A love object, a receptacle for loneliness, anything you want her to be and nothing at all. *A sex doll found in the cabin.*

When I first saw her in the magazine, beside old photos of Gary Wilensky, she seemed like another version of him. What he looked like from the inside out.

Stalker, hebephile, erotomaniac, psychotic.

Of all the diagnoses used to explain Gary's mind-set, she might provide the most visceral indication of what gripped him in his final days: his disconnect from real relationships, the conflicts of his desire, and his delusional belief that a young woman was an object he could fold up and store away.

The problem with diagnoses is that they're mistaken for

answers. We are either our diseases or the diseases we've overcome.

Separation anxiety, panic attacks, self-harming behavior, borderline, depression and anxiety, suicidal ideation, mixed bipolar.

I take an assortment of prescriptions to sleep, to stay awake, to stay medium. What I had then is what I have now, only there is a different language surrounding it and there are somewhat unreliable tools to blunt it. Sometimes, what you believed you'd grow out of, you end up growing into.

At thirty-eight, I am single and childless, not by choice, but by instinct. The fourteen-year-old in me would consider this condition a point of shame and frantically try to root it out. I am not who I thought I would be, but that is what happens when you look ahead. All you see are the possibilities for change.

When you look back, you see what you've held on to, what was stronger than outside influence, what you carried with you all these years.

Maybe it's something you need.

I have always been drawn to the company of my own obsessions—dissecting the reasons behind them, following the trails they leave behind. Not all obsessions are destructive. Some force you to confront your privilege. They project your fears through a clearer lens and reveal patterns you hadn't noticed before. Some even come alive in your mind, so that neither of you are ever really alone.

Remember the night in the car when the bargain was made. The blinkers flashing gasps of light down Park Avenue. The candy-coated smell of the upholstery. The windows coated in something, too. Sometimes it's light snow; other times it's rain.

Always it's night—black with headlight circles. The door locks are sunken, the heater breathes. I am looking at Gary and he is looking at the street. The traffic light cycles back to yellow. Always he says: *You all grow up and leave me.* Always I promise I won't.

acknowledgments

THIS BOOK WOULD NOT HAVE BEEN possible without three women: Nicole Tourtelot, Jessica Williams, and Margaux Weisman. I'm eternally grateful for their faith in my work, patience, guidance, support, and constant wisdom. Every writer should be so lucky.

There will never be a sufficient way to thank my family— Monroe, Sasha, Phoenix, and, particularly, Marilyn. They are my inspiration, my backbone, and the greatest loves of my life.

My deepest thanks to the dear friends/readers/mentors who guided me through this process: Jessica Dimmock, Jennifer Romolini, Sarah Weir, Sarah McColl, Michael Dumanis, Michele Filgate, Beth Greenfield, Lauren Elmer, Konstantin Steshenko, Amy DiLuna, Ricardo Castaneda, Brooke Posch, Colleen Kluttz, Meredith Blake, Ryan Green, Margot Nason, Margaret Eby, Maggie, Hildy, Chris.

My endless gratitude goes out to those who provided personal and professional insight: Steven Heider, Patrice Lockhart, Erica Goodstone, Michael Stone, Fredo Weiland, Neal Pilson, Kate Zuckerman, Dr. Eric Hickey, "Sarah," "Tara," "Emma," cohorts of VCCA, the Bryant Library, Sackett Street Writers' Workshop, and countless others who helped me piece this story together.

Thank you to "Sarah" and "Bianca" for your friendship all those years ago.

I also wish to thank the victims and their parents who shared their stories in 1993.

My humblest appreciation is reserved for the Mother and the Daughter, who endured trauma and acted with tremendous bravery. Because of their actions, other potential victims were protected from harm. They are the heroes of this story.

about the author

PIPER WEISS is a writer based in Brooklyn, New York. She was a features editor at the New York *Daily News* and Yahoo and the editorial director of HelloGiggles. Her writing has appeared in Hazlitt, Elle.com, and other publications. Her first book, *My Mom, Style Icon*, was published in 2011.